*H*aiti's *B*ad *P*ress

*H*aiti's *B*ad *P*ress

Robert Lawless

Schenkman Books, Inc.
Rochester, Vermont

Copyright © 1992

Schenkman Books, Inc.
118 Main Street
Rochester, Vermont 05767

Printed in the United States of America

ISBN: 0–87047–060–4 cloth
ISBN: 0–87047–061–2 paper

Library of Congress Cataloging in Publication Data

Lawless, Robert.

Haiti's bad press : origins, development, and consequences by
Robert Lawless.
p. cm.

Includes bibliographical references and index.
ISBN 0–87047–060–4 : $24.95 — ISBN 0–87047–061–2 (pbk.) : $14.95

1. Haiti—Civilization—Public opinion. 2. Prejudices. 3. Public
opinion—United States. 4. Public opinion—France. I. Title.
F1916.L39 1992
972.94—dc20   92–7130
CIP

Contents

*F*oreword

The author of *Haiti's Bad Press* notes the inability of the press to register the actual characteristics of Haitian society and analyzes the relationship between the social sciences, the media, and the public. At the same time, he challenges the reader to think about the relations between the media and political structures, or, more precisely, to think about the reciprocal influence between the world political order and the message conveyed to the public about that order.

Interest and curiosity in a given society are not directed toward resources readily available or totally unaccessible. The public scrutinizes mainly such issues opposing the implementation of its societal goals. A community cannot include in its world view information that may challenge it ideology unless its values and plans for the future are being questioned.

This is why the knowledge produced by anthropologists seldom affects the power structure—it is useless for a given establishment. Conversely, journalistic cliches are evidences of the establishment's value orientation, and inasmuch as anthropology tends to correct such cliches, it is unlikely to enrich any institutionalized practice. In these circumstances, social criticism becomes the prime political goal of anthropological discoveries.

Many of the findings of anthropologists about the behavior of Haitians show that the values that underlie their history are the end result of a sustained resistance at attempts to destroy, dehumanize, and deculturize their society. Nonetheless, this resistance has not influenced the setup and functioning of political structures. Haitians have sidestepped these structures in order to shield themselves against the State, as the main source of exploitation and imposition. Their pacific resistance has ignored the source of politics, leading them to flee away from the seat of current power.

In consequence, the Haitians have been suffering a curious blindness, perceiving from their normative perspective only one half of

vii

the world. They formulated a societal project with an incomplete set of variables and hence were doomed to certain failure. Thus, from one point of view, the Haitians contributed to their own bad press. Fleeing away from State power was the social cost to pay for their survival as a nation. Robert Lawless writes:

> Despite the isolation and ill will of the surrounding white world, Haitians have continued to maintain their independence.... Haitians themselves thought of their country as a center of freedom in a world of oppression.

Nowadays, having exhausted the limits of flight, the Haitian people find themselves obliged to meet face to face with the "culturally" invisible source of their exploitation, the structure of the state, as the genuine author of their bad press.

An encounter between the societal projects built into the international power structures and the solitary and independent path chosen by the nation was inevitable. The elections of December 16, 1990 marked a turning point in the history of the country. Using the accepted mechanisms for achieving formal political power, Haiti moved away from the dead end where its tradition of isolation was cornering it.

By so doing, the Haitian people endowed themselves with contemporary political instruments suitable for implementing their societal goals. By the same token, they exposed the archaism of their power elite, incapable of satisfying the least aspiration of the people, and forced this elite to resort to a coup d'etat. Much embarrassment for the managers of the international power structure resulted from this action.

The inability of the Haitians to counter the responses of their traditional elite becomes more and more evident from the end of the Second World War onward. Hundreds of thousands of them flew in successive waves towards the accessible shrines of modern life— New York, Miami, Boston. And with the last coup, all of a sudden, the Haitian issue emerged near the center of local political maneuvering in the last of the superpowers. This discovery by the Haitians of the international power elite is bound to correct the built-in myopia of their cultural patterns.

Presently, since the press cannot ignore the challenge posed by the unexpected presence of the Haitians to the basic values of the American dream and project of society, the anthropologists and the knowledge they accumulated becomes relevant to international public opinion and to the dominant power structure.

By putting anthropology and the press on the same plane of thought, Robert Lawless's book comes as a presage. It brings to mind the cartographer's criticisms about the incongruities of navigation before 1492. Many travelers had reached America's coasts before Christopher Columbus, but the international community had to wait for this opportune voyage to modify its perception of world geography.

Similarly, the recent discovery of the Haitian nation by the international press reminds one that of the island of San Salvador. A whole universe of thoughts lies beyond this "new" nation.

A number of anthropologists have touched upon Haitian culture. Today, the press is compelled to use those findings to understand the behaviors deriving from this culture and to question the folk models it normally uses to address Haitian issues. Have we reached our 1492, the eve of a new conception of humankind?

On the one hand the international power elite to satisfy it own vested interests, has to solve an embarrassing equation: The distinctiveness of the Haitian people, the pertinence of their project of society in the light of a new international order, and the inadequacy of the international power structure to accommodate this pertinent project.

On the other hand, these transplanted people are ironically becoming a testimony of the favorite subject matter of anthropological studies, i.e., a testimony of the treatment given to America's native cultures. *Haiti's Bad Press* will be succeeded by the bad press of Peru, Suriname, Guyana, Bolivia, Ecuador...wherever the cleavages between newcomers and natives grow blurred during their resistance to the structures of the State, the press must eventually shed its cliches and turn to the findings of scientific thought.

Robert Lawless diagnoses the uneasiness of contemporary civilization when confronted with *Haiti's Bad Press,* when confronted with the bad press of all of the indigenous people of America, Asia, Africa, and ... Europe. The indigenous people that the dominant cultures conceived of as irrelevant and ignorant constitute a fascinating universe, haunting international relations.

The discovery of this lost paradise, so close and inaccessible, will help correct the myopia of the dominant culture, making the people of the West little by little more human, more capable of assuming their limitations, and more inclined to overcome these limitations using the only faculty exclusive to human beings: the possibility to engage in peaceful dialogue and discussion.

In the process, the indigenous people of this world will in turn discover the dominant culture in its contribution to humankind and be relieved from all forms of political violence. The special violence of the indigenous people will be cured, since it will become useless to their mental health.

Then, ties of solidarity will gradually become woven between the different nations of the world. Thanks to the media, all nations will learn to know and to help each other and altogether to better manage the structures of the State. A new international political order is emerging, the limits of which we cannot yet foresee.

Jean Casimir
June 1992

Acknowledgments

In Port-au-Prince, Max Paul, director of the Bureau d'Ethnologie, facilitated my research. Others who helped me include Rudy Auguste, Gladys Baril, Jean-Claude Baril, Michaëlle Dérose, Joël Delaroche, Paul Larquet, John V. D. Lewis, Albert Mangonès, Glenn Smucker, Edmond Ulrick, and Danielle Wahab.

In Cap-Haitien, I was a visiting fellow associate professor at the Université Roi Henri Christophe, and I wish to acknowledge the encouragement and support of that university's president, Louis J. Noisin. Others who helped me include Andy, Jean M. Bruno, Margarette J. Brown, Denise, Michel Descouens, Jean-Jacques Estimé, Barthelem Exhalus, Tony Marcelli, Joseph Monpemien, Louis Pierre, Reynold Pierre, Roger Pinkcombe, Auguste E. Robinson, Harry Sanchez, Utlande Séraphin, Clifford Torres, Toussaint Toussaint, Roger Valdez, Henri Valkou, Jean-Pierre Valkou, Jean Robert Vastey, and Michel Vita.

In the United States, many Haitians and Haitianists helped me, including Gabrielle Antoine, Donald Assali, Daniel Baril, Reginald Baril, Patrick Bellegarde-Smith, Paul Farmer, David Geggus, Pantéléon Guilbaud, Jean-Marie Guillaume, Michel Laguerre, Léon-François Hoffman, Linda Jackson, François B. Laroche, Maurice Lubin, Martin Murphy, Gerald Murray, Florence Sergil, and Alex Stepick. Many thanks are due to Thea de Wet for helping me with the mysteries of the computer.

Finally, I would also like to thank the people at Schenkman Books that brought my words into print: Joe Schenkman, for his foresight; John Matthews, my editor; Kathryn Miles, for her production and typesetting skills; and Susan Kashanski, for her proofreading and indexing abilities. I would also like to particularly thank Robin Lloyd, whose whole-hearted enthusiasm and practical advice gave the book more strength, and Ambassador Jean Casimir, for his suggestions and support.

*I*ntroduction

Few people would disagree with the statement that favorable reports about Haiti are as rare as positive declarations on the nutritional value of cannibalism or the healing power of black magic. In the 1960s the eminent anthropological scholar of the Caribbean, Sidney Mintz, remarked, "Few countries in modern times have received as bad a press at the hands of foreign observers as Haiti." [1] In the 1970s another anthropologist, who specializes in studying Haiti, complained, "Haiti still has a uniquely poor press as New World societies go." [2] In the 1980s still another anthropologist, who conducted a detailed survey of magazines in the United States, came to the same conclusion. [3] And this situation continues into the present.

In fact, most of the works on Haiti that the public reads are based on myths, most of which are, at best, uninformed and plagiaristic and, at worst, mean-spirited and narrow-minded. These myths are intimately connected with broader forms of racism against blacks by whites. Since the late 1960s, however, most Americans have increasingly recognized the immorality, perversity, and vacuousness of racist perspectives. The press has responded by muting its more blatant racism. Although the press's lack of explicit racism does not excuse the writings of contemporary journalists from their ethnocentric assumptions, it does make it more difficult to spot their more unconscious prejudices.

This book will examine these prejudices through the writings of journalists, historians, travelers, writers of adventure stories, and even some social scientists. I will trace these writings about Haiti through their historical development and perpetuation. I will also demonstrate the reasons that Haiti has been targeted by these writers.

Although most of the social and behavioral scientists separate their perspectives from those of the lay public, anthropologists are the most precise in distinguishing their explanations of a peoples'

beliefs and behaviors from the explanations of the people themselves. No doubt anthropologists are more aware of and sensitive to
indigenous explanations because anthropologists are generally from
a cultural tradition alien to the one they are studying. Social and
behavioral investigators with no cross-cultural experience might
well accept without question their informants' notion that, for
example, it is natural for parents to have the final word on their
child's discipline because that is the natural order of the family.
Anthropologists would never accept such a notion as anything more
than an indigenous justification for a culture-specific custom because anthropologists are all aware of cultures in which the "natural"
order of the family is for the mother's brother to control the child's
discipline.

It is, indeed, perfectly acceptable to most of us that most of our
actions most of the time seem to be perfectly natural. If this were not
the case, we would be psychically immobilized. Not only does
whatever we do usually seem to be the most natural thing to be doing
but we also believe that we are dealing with a very real world that we
perceive very correctly. In other words, in our day-to-day life we
receive the subjective impression that we are experiencing reality
directly. Science tells us, however, that reality is filtered through our
many biochemical mediators, beginning, of course, with our physical senses. These senses are influenced by our expectations as well
as by our biology. The anthropological importance of such a realiza-
tion lies in the fact that expectations of reality vary from society to
society and from culture to culture. What we accept as "real," then,
is at least partially determined by what society we live in and what
cultural beliefs and behaviors we learn as we grow up.

One of the basic philosophical assumptions of science concerns
the unknowability of reality, or at least the unknowability of raw
reality and pristine order. In the sciences no conclusions are final and
absolute; immutable and unquestionable knowledge belongs to the
realm of religion. Although all forms of human knowledge involve
some sort of basic beliefs or assumptions, anthropology and other
sciences always leave everything open to discussion. Anything can
be investigated. Anthropologists do not accept the notion that

society works in mysterious ways. Everything is potentially understandable.

To reach a sort of workable understanding, anthropologists in their investigations and scientists in their experiments, like all people, employ a manageable simplification of the world around them. Most scientists and philosophers call these simplifications *models*. Models are used to help people make systematic interpretations from the mass of information that their senses give them about their surroundings. These models substitute for the reality that we cannot know with certainty.

The models that we use daily as guides to mundane concerns are termed *folk models*.[4] These everyday representations of reality allow us to remain reasonably sane in the face of an overwhelming and largely undifferentiated mass of stimuli that continually impinges on our senses. Folk models let us make decisions easily by eliminating most alternatives. Different societies have different folk models that supply different alternatives and expectations. For example, as an American male, I have little difficulty deciding what to put on over my legs when I get dressed in the morning; I generally decide between a pair of faded jeans and a pair of not-so-faded jeans. I don't have to decide whether to wear a sarong or a dress. When I lived with the Kalingas, a tribe of headhunters in the mountains of northern Luzon, I had a choice between a faded g-string and a not-so-faded g-string. We may think that we make lots of decisions about what we wear, when actually we are quite limited in a transcultural perspective to a small portion of the clothing spectrum of the world's societies.

An interesting characteristic of folk models is that they make us feel as though we want to choose what we must choose. A major function of folk models, then, is to limit our thinking. Conversely, one of the major goals of science is to achieve unlimited thinking. To do this, scientists must always fight their folk models. Much of the struggle for anthropological understanding comes from unlearning what the folk models have taught as unquestionable.

A folk model also seems to explain behaviors and beliefs, but actually it only "explains" them as normative. A folk model identifies and justifies as correct and proper whatever behaviors and beliefs exist in its own culture. And evaluations of other societies by the standards of one's own society—that is, through the perspective of one's own folk model—simply label those other behaviors and beliefs as wrong, crazy, irrational, or stupid. These labels are the essence of ethnocentrism and a major barrier to the unlearning of folk models. Unfortunately, most popular materials on Haiti consist of similar limiting labels.

One reason for the difficulty in unlearning folk models is that we don't have much influence over them. They were developed for us before we were born. We learned our folk models as very small and impressionable children searching for order in a chaotic world. As we grew older, we may have questioned some of the tenets of the folk model, but it is doubtful that we questioned basic components such as numbering systems, kinship categories, concepts of good and evil, the necessity of incarcerating criminals, the advantages of advanced technology, the existence of nation-states, and so forth. We may not have liked some things around us, and we may have, for example, developed some cynicism about big corporations. But, by and large, we accept the life we lead as the proper life to be led.

One way in which *analytic models* differ from folk models is that we can control analytic models. In fact, we can make up analytic models; analytic models are representations of reality developed by scholars. Ideally, these analytic models are created and based on criteria originating outside the phenomena they are trying to represent and explain. In anthropology we try to get outside the folk models of our own society. Only by going beyond or loosening the bonds of our folk models will we be able to develop scientific explanations of human beliefs and behaviors.

Good analytic models are inclusive, universal, logical, simple, flexible, and open. One model is more useful than another when it can inclusively explain greater amounts of phenomena and larger quantities of data. Models that admit few or no exceptions are more useful than models full of holes. Good analytic models are internally consistent and rational, and they follow their leads to their expected ends. Simple models with a few basic premises are easier to work with than are complicated models. Inflexible models will be short-lived in the fast-changing world of science.

Since we can never know about phenomena that may exist outside our experience and current instruments of measurement, all analytic models are open. Even if the world were a closed, determined system, we have no hope at present of achieving ultimate, complete explanations of all things under one model. Anthropologists can, however, hope to break out of their own folk models.

Traditionally, anthropologists try to transcend their own learned reality by living in other cultures for long periods of time, an often excruciating experience called fieldwork. For a year or more, anthropologists live with and partially accept the beliefs and behaviors of peoples with radically different customs. It is a basic belief of anthropologists that only through living with people, speaking to them in their own language, engaging in their activities, and seeing things from their viewpoint, can culture be truly appreciated as a system of interrelated patterns. Good fieldwork, moreover, is based on the anthropologist's ability to empathize with others and to participate in and observe without judgment alien customs. In addition, fieldwork requires the anthropologist to have the ability to see patterns, relationships, and meanings that may not be consciously understood by a person in that culture. In other words, anthropologists must go beyond the folk models of the people being studied and start developing analytic models even while they are in the field. Anthropological fieldwork, then, often differs considerably from the experiences of tourists, journalists, and travelogue writers.

From these experiences anthropologists usually develop a sincere empathy for another way of life and may find it nearly impossible to take seriously the dictates of their home folk model. Anthropologists then begin to develop their transcultural analytic models. I will depend on the reports on Haiti by anthropologists as some of the most reliable guides to an analytic model that will counter the many folk models of Haiti.

It should be understood that anthropologists not only have different standards by which they evaluate beliefs and behaviors, but also that their publications generally are not widely available to the public. As I have pointed out elsewhere,

> If journalists cannot persuade a publisher to print their work, they are no longer journalists; and the publisher will not print the journalists' work unless it is salable to a wide audience. But anthropologists can keep their job with no wider audience than the few students captured in their classroom and the still fewer colleagues that read their articles in the subsidized journals. Anthropologists need satisfy only themselves and the colleagues they respect; journalists must satisfy their audience (though not necessarily please them).[5]

And before the late 1960s North American publishers were quite willing to publish highly insulting and inaccurate information about Haiti.

Although "the essence of *both* journalism and anthropology lies in getting people to talk about what they know best and then reporting to others what was found out,"[6] their different perspectives on how to deal with folk models have striking consequences. James Lett, who has a Ph.D. in anthropology partially based on fieldwork in the Caribbean and who has also worked as a broadcast journalist, pointed out, "Unlike anthropology, journalism lacks a systematic foundation of explicit theory and method."[7] Lett explained that instead of developing an analytic model, indeed, instead of even operating within the framework of an acceptable analytic model borrowed from any of the social or behavioral sciences, "journalism reaffirms and reinforces the general public's world view, while anthropology questions and challenges that world view"[8]— the reigning folk model.

We have few examples of good analytic works on Haiti. As a Haitian scholar complained, "Haiti has generally failed to elicit much scholarly interest abroad, save for a titillating exoticism which led to the image of the country as being an isolated, unique, or extreme case."[9] Perhaps this work will help to lead to a greater interest in writing more accurately and analytically about a country that is more fascinating than exotic and more instructive than extreme.

An Overview of Haiti

The second oldest independent nation in the Western Hemisphere, the Republic of Haiti occupies the western third of the Caribbean island of Hispaniola, which it shares with the Dominican Republic. Containing about 10,714 square miles, it is roughly the same size as the state of Maryland and lies 56 miles southeast of Cuba, 116 miles northeast of Jamaica, and about 621 miles from Florida. Most of the countryside is mountainous with the highest point being La Selle Peak at 8,793 feet. Haiti does have some flat, semiarid valleys. The average temperature falls somewhere between 24° and 27° Celsius.

Although demographic information is scarce and unreliable, the total population is estimated to be about six and a half million, with most of this population located in rural areas. Port-au-Prince, the capital and largest city, has about 1.25 million people, and the second largest city, Cap-Haitien, has about seventy thousand. The regional cities, such as Les Cayes, Gonaives, Port-de-Paix, Jacmel, Jeremie, St. Marc, and Hinche, have populations of only about ten to fifty thousand. According to various studies, the birth rate from 1980 through 1985 was 35.6 per 100,000; the annual growth rate was 1.8; the mortality per 1,000 was 13; the infant mortality per 1,000 was 117.7; and life expectancy at birth throughout these same years was 54.5 years.

All Haitians speak Haitian Creole, but for most of modern history the official language of government, business, and education has been French. Due to the lack of educational facilities, however, only 10 percent or so of the population speaks French with some degree of competence. Traditionally the elite have used the requirement of French to exclude the Creole-speaking masses from competing for positions in government and business. Currently, the prestige of French is rapidly declining in Haiti, and Creole is becoming recognized as the appropriate national language. Due to the recent flood of Haitian immigrants to Florida and the economic and cultural trends in the Caribbean, the future will see an expansion in the use of English by Haitians.

Although the island of Hispaniola had a pre-Columbian population of Amerindians, they were rapidly killed off by European diseases and slavery. The modern history of this island began when the Europeans started looking toward Africa for the labor they needed to work their sugarcane plantations. The sugarcane system destroyed the forests of Haiti and enslaved the people of Africa but made the French landowners among the richest people in the world at the time.

The extraordinary brutality and exploitative extreme of the French colony of Saint Domingue on the western part of the island of Hispaniola resulted in many slave uprisings until, in August 1791, the slaves in Saint Domingue managed a major war that the plantation owners could not contain. By 1796 white supremacy was at an end, and black rule was established under the leadership of Toussaint Louverture, a charismatic ex-slave. In 1800, however, Napoleon sent twenty thousand troops to retake the colony and reenslave the blacks. By late 1803 the Haitians had defeated the French troops, and on January 1, 1804, Jean-Jacques Dessalines, Toussaint's successor, proclaimed the independence of Haiti. Dessalines changed the name from Saint Domingue to Haiti, signifiying the end of colonization and slavery.

Haiti has remained self-consciously independent except for the military occupation of the island by the United States from 1915 to 1934. Among the consequences of this occupation were the rising black consciousness of the elite, the suppression of peasant movements, the training of the army, and the concentration of sociopolitical power in Port-au-Prince.

The twenty-three-year period between the occupation and the election of François Duvalier as president was extremely important in terms of the consolidation of nationalism along the lines of pride in African heritage, the increasing interaction with other Caribbean nations, the development of peasant economic cooperation, the introduction of a progressive income tax, and, especially, the rise of the new black middle class. In 1957 Duvalier won the presidency with a decisive margin as the proclaimed heir to these new developments.

After a few years of Duvalier rule, Haiti saw a heightened campaign of oppression against opponents and increased isolation from the international community. The 1971 transition from Duvalier to his nineteen-year-old son Jean-Claude brought Haiti into close economic tutelage by the United States government, a relationship featuring private investments from the United States that would be wooed by such incentives as no custom taxes, a low minimum wage, the suppression of labor unions, and the right of U.S. companies to repatriate their profits from their off-shore plants.

In addition to the economic exploitation by the United States, Haiti suffered greatly from the oil crises of 1973 and 1974, and 1980. Within the past fifteen years, hurricanes have devastated the coffee trees and ruined the production of coffee, one of Haiti's most significant exports. Then, in late November 1985, street protests began in towns throughout Haiti, and the violent police responses led to further protests. Finally, on February 7, 1986, Jean-Claude Duvalier fled to France, and the Duvalier era ended.

With the army supplying what little government existed, Haiti attempted to have elections in November 1986 and in January 1988. The first election was aborted, and the second was widely regarded as illegitimate.

After a series of military coups, a legitimate election was held in December 1990, and Jean-Bertrand Aristide was declared president of Haiti. He was installed in office on February 7, 1991, five years to the day after the end of the Duvalier dictatorship. On September 31, 1991, Aristide was ousted by the military. The Organization of American States has declared the new government to be illegitimate, and in November 1991 the United States imposed an embargo on Haiti demanding that the army allow a democratically elected government to take its place.

The arguments that recurrently lead to instability occur among a small group of people. Aside from a very small but somewhat influential group of Middle Eastern merchants, Haiti is exceptionally homogeneous culturally and linguistically. The only real divisions—and they are important—are the ones that concern socioeconomic class and rural-urban differences, with most Haitians living in a rural setting.

With about 65 percent of the labor force in agriculture and only about 7 percent in manufacturing (with 1 percent in construction and 27 percent in other sectors), Haiti is, indeed, one of the most peasant of all countries. Its agriculture is precarious, however, since the countryside is 95 percent deforested and 25 percent of the soil is undergoing rapid erosion. Most of the people, nevertheless, can be found living in villages made up of scattered huts of wattle and daub, villages that are loosely tied together by well-traveled trade routes. These rural farmers organize their lives around their extended family, usually a cluster of joint households composed of loosely related residents serving a particular Voodoo spirit under the guidance of the oldest male family member.

The true character of Haiti resides in the rural areas, and to understand the peasant character of Haiti, one must know something about the history of this peasantry. The two crucial problems facing Haiti immediately after independence concerned access to the land previously owned by the French and maintaining that land's agricultural production. Initially, the Haitian government attempted to reinstate the plantation system of colonial Saint Domingue. When these attempts failed because of the association of plantations with the hated slave system, land was, for the most part, simply distributed among the ex-slaves. As a result, from 60 to 80 percent of the farmers currently own their own land, though the plots are fragmented and small. The urban-based government has rarely shown a sustained interest in agriculture, and although the state owns land, nobody seems to pay much attention to it, and peasants occupy most of it rent-free.

Haiti's primary products of coffee, sugar, rice, and cocoa have traditionally come from the rural sector. Light manufacturing in Haiti has consisted of shoes, soap, flour, cement, and domestic oils. The off-shore industries manufacture items almost exclusively for the American market, and most of these products have consisted of garments, toys, baseballs, and electronic goods. This small-scale industrialization has, however, always been a minor part of the Haitian economic scene and has not added much to the national economy since the purpose of it is to supply cheap labor that American corporations can exploit. In addition, the instability of the government since 1986 has resulted in a number of these off-shore industries leaving Haiti. Those that had not left by November 1991 did leave during the imposition of the U.S. embargo during that month.

Many Haitians also engage in part-time craft work, particularly in the manufacture of wooden utensils, tools, and furniture. Haiti was, in fact, well known for its fine mahogany carvings, and most of the artistic products were aimed at tourists. The tourist trade, however, declined drastically in the early 1980s due to the AIDS scare and has further declined to almost nothing with the sociopolitical instability following the 1986 ouster of Duvalier.

The rural sector continues, of course, to trade in the traditional manner with most of the commercial exchange carried out in open-air markets. In contrast, Haiti's international trade is very closely tied to the United States, with most of its imports and exports connected to North America. The urban economy, indeed, depends on governmental and nongovernmental aid from the United States.

The history of Haiti is especially important for understanding why Haiti is so different from the rest of the Caribbean and from Latin America. The plantation system and the institution of slavery throughout the eighteenth and nineteenth centuries had a profound influence on all aspects of Haitian life, including the domestic sphere. For example, the plantation system did not encourage slaves to develop a legally recognized family institution. And most of the laws of the early republic reinforced the tendency of the rural population to avoid legal and church marriages.

Instead, Haitian mating, parenting, and householding are performed within a wide variety of types of marriages. In addition to conventional church weddings, long-term monogamous unions, and neolocal nuclear family households, there are also unions without formal sanction, couples who do not co-reside, fathers who do not participate actively in rearing their children, and households without a nuclear family at their core. And, for example, the same man may simultaneously marry, maintain a consensual union in a second household of which he is the titular head, and conduct one or more relatively stable extraresidential affairs in which the women head the household. Women also may legitimately enter several different kinds of union in succession, either with the same mate, or a number of different partners. In their turn, children may be born to a married couple, to a married man with another woman, to a couple in a consensual union, to a mother not in union with any man, and so forth.

The complexity of such domestic units means that inheritance can become a great problem. The general rule in Haiti is that all children from all the varieties of conjugal union have equal rights of inheritance. In practice, however, residence, contacts, and personal feelings play important roles, and the inheritances may end up with people that an outsider could not have predicted.

Despite the fact that most of the political and social questions are decided by custom and consensus, Haiti does, of course, have a government that interacts with its citizens and that represents the country on the international scene. This government is currently in a state of transition—some may say in a state of chaos. After brief flirtations with democracy at various times in its history, the country seems to inevitably turn to strong-man rule, with the strong man often coming from the upper ranks of the army. The tension between the military, the urban-based elite, and the peasantry was often expressed in a division between mulattoes and blacks.

One result of the distribution of the land in the early eighteen hundreds to the largely black rural people was the retreat of the largely mulatto elite to the cities. With no land of their own, this elite made its living from taxing peasant markets and the nation's imports and exports. The nation became traditionally divided, then, into a very small European-oriented, mulatto elite located in several coastal urban centers, and a large rural, scattered, interior black peasant population. The peasants, then and now, regard the government as having little relevance to their lives.

Politically Haiti is traditionally divided into several regions called *départements,* each of which is further divided into several *arrondissements,* each with an administrative center. Each arrondissement consists of several *communes* that usually coincide with church parishes. Finally, each commune is divided into several *sections rurales,* each of which is headed by an appointed *chef de section,* who reports to the *commandant* of the commune, who reports to the *préfet* of the arrondissement. The little contact that rural Haitians have with the government is generally with the chef de section. Much of this traditional organization is overlaid with military entities, and all of this political organization is now being reconsidered as various Haitian governing bodies attempt to regain control over the countryside.

Governments in Haiti have been run primarily by members of the elite, and despite the early and heroic independence of Haiti from France—and from slavery—the attitude of the elite classes of Haiti has traditionally been a colonial one. Although nativism, negritude, and the increasing use of Creole as the appropriate language of Haiti have made all Haitians more aware of their Haitianness, tension continues to exist between the urban elites and the rural peasants and urban poor.

A cementing element of Haitianness is religion. Although some of the population is nominally Roman Catholic, and although Protestant missionaries have made considerable headway in the poorer rural areas of Haiti, the religion of Haiti is still Voodo. Voodoo is an ancient, positive, and legitimate religion that focuses on contacting and appeasing immediate relatives, such as dead parents and grandparents, and ancestral spirits which include distant, stereotyped ancestors. Many Voodoo rituals can also be seen as healing rites, making up a folk medical system that attributes illness to angry ancestors.

Western medicine has been available to the urban elites for some time now, but in the rural areas most of the healing is handled by Voodoo healers, along with herbal medicine, bone setters, injectionists, and a rich body of folk knowledge. The poorer masses, nevertheless, suffer many health problems of malnutrition and disease. Only about 25 percent of the population has potable water;

measles, diarrhea, and tetanus kill many of the children. The daily per capita food consumption is estimated at sixteen hundred calories. Tuberculosis is the most devastating disease, followed closely by malaria, influenza, dysentery, tetanus, whooping cough, and measles. Eye problems are endemic in Haiti with the chief causes of blindness being cataracts, pterygium, scarring of the cornea, and glaucoma.

Despite these difficulties Haiti is internationally famous for its art and literature. In the 1940s Haiti burst into the consciousness of the art world with an astonishing display of paintings, and its artists justly deserved the worldwide attention they received for their so-called primitive or naive art. Haiti is also renowned for its literature, much of which initially centered on concepts of negritude foreshadowing the black power and anticolonial post-World War II movements. Voodoo has also been a major theme in Haitian art. The most famous novel in Haitian Creole, for example, Frankétiene's *Dézafi*, is about the revolt of a colony of zombies. This highly literate production is even more amazing in light of the high rate of illiteracy, probably around 85 percent. Fewer than half of the rural children attend school, and only about 20 percent of those complete the primary grades.

Haitians have traditionally emigrated as one of the solutions to land scarcity. Large numbers of Haitians live in the Dominican Republic where they are involved in the harvesting of sugarcane and in the construction industry. Haitians also live on other Caribbean islands, in the countries of Central America, northern South America, and in North America. After Port-au-Prince, the second largest Haitian community is in New York City.

Despite their emigration, however, Haitians continue to be one of the most nationalistic peoples in the world and to have one of the most culturally homogeneous populations of any nation-state. Haitians will also no doubt continue to be plagued by economic and ecological problems that seem insolvable by the current sociopolitical arrangements. The genius of the Haitian people has been not only their survival in the midst of niggardly environment but also their astonishingly good-natured production of cultural brilliance in art, music, and the letters. When this genius to put to solving the political and economic problems of Haiti, the world will witness an event that parallels the victories of ex-slaves against the armies of Napoleon.

1 Ships at a wharf in Port-au-Prince used for transporting goods to coastal communities in Haiti and for smuggling people into Florida.

Current Biases

It is said, usually with more sadness than amusement, that the western media covers the Third World only in cases of coups, calamities, and communism. Historical accuracy will suffer slightly by saying that the press covers Haiti only in cases of coups, calamities, communism, and cannibalism. Some of the first western media coverage of Haiti in the nineteenth century emphasized an imagined innate cannibalism, and the coverage in the 1960s emphasized an imagined communist threat. An excessive media interest in the *tonton-makout* (officially the *Volontaires de la Sécurité Nationale* or Volunteers for National Security) and zombies has now replaced the fanciful notions of widespread cannibalism and communism, but the press on Haiti continues to be, in a word, bad. By saying that Haiti has a bad press, I mean both that Haiti is presented in a bad light and that the quality of the media is inferior to its coverage of many other subjects.

When attempting to summarize the bad press of Haitian refugees in the United States, two scholars complained,

> The Haitian peasant has long been portrayed as a savage cannibal; the folk religion, vodoun, has received a Hollywood reputation far out of proportion to reality; the name Papa Doc is better known than those of more influential despots; and more recently, Haitians were quick to be branded as the carriers of acquired immune deficiency syndrome.[1]

The press certainly has given an inordinate amount of publicity to Haitians in terms of their being a "boat people" and carrying AIDS— and has consistently misinterpreted the quantity, characteristics, causes, and consequences of Haitian refugees and diseases. The other area of misplaced and misunderstood emphasis has been on the religion of Haitians, commonly known as Voodoo.

1

The Voodoo focus has traditionally been on cannibals and zombies. The press is not entirely to blame for disseminating incorrect information on Voodoo since the press, particularly the North American press, generally reflects the folk model of a readership whose interest in Haiti rarely extends to serious matters. As a Spanish-language publication noted, "All Americans who disembark in Port-au-Prince have only one thing on their minds: Voodoo, and just one desire: that of witnessing these ceremonies that they imagine to be cruel and orgiastic."[2]

It is also a fact that the press is not alone in giving Haiti a bad name. Recent travel books actually contain the largest amount of contemporary misinformation and racism about Haiti. Also, some contemporary writing that has pretensions to scholarship seems to build more on offensive folk models than on analytic perspectives. About a decade ago a major book—if one may judge by size—written by a U.S. military historian who had spent considerable time in Haiti in an official capacity in the Haitian government (and coauthored with his wife) concluded, "Are the Haitian people, living endlessly in a perverse continuum, oblivious of their past, doomed always to repeat a history that has been written in blood?"[3] This image of blood is, of course, easily connected in the minds of naive readers with the notion of Voodoo sacrifices. The history of Haiti is, in fact, surprisingly void of "blood" by any objective measurement of casualties per capita in the coups, elections, and various other changes in government; the fact is that most of these switches are among a small elite of interrelated families who are not wont to kill each other.

Packed with valuable information but essentially misdirected, the book does exemplify the newest and most subtle form of insult to the Haitian people. Most of this writing avoids the nineteenth and early twentieth century racist interpretations of Haiti's problems; instead, the problems are defined in terms of savage rulers who are either buffoons or madmen—or both—and a weak, easily controlled mass of ignorant peasants. Such writing started in the mid-1960s when straightforward racism first became unfashionable in North America. The journalistic equivalent is the 1969 book about the Haitian dictator François Duvalier, *Papa Doc*.[4] The cover of the paperback edition is illustrated with a black hand holding up a burning skull impaled on a wooden stake. The cover blurb reads "Atrocities in the Realm of a Madman." The fictional equivalent is Graham Greene's 1966 novel *The Comedians*, which was made into a popular 1967 movie starring Richard Burton and Elizabeth Taylor and which furthered the image of Haiti as a bizarre land of madman rulers manipulating a Voodoo-infested interior of superstitious savages.

Even in the 1970s in writing with an analytic perspective, authors evidently felt obliged to point out, in the words of a Ph.D. dissertation, that Haiti "suffers the morbid distinction of having a population that is one of the most disease ridden, poverty stricken, malnourished, rural, and illiterate in the Western Hemisphere."[5] The description is probably true, and there are good reasons for such a condition. The point is that it is much rarer that such works gave to the Haitians of only a few generations ago credit for having carried out a historic and uniquely successful revolution against slavery. It is rarer yet that contemporary Haitians were given any credit for the relative success of their economic and social systems in the light of the oppression of the surrounding white world from the destruction of their environment by the colonial sugarcane plantations to the exploitation of their population as cheap labor for American off-shore assembly plants.

For the most part, journalistic writing on Haiti has been simply an elaboration of the denigrating folk model of evil and darkness, the negative of the clean, white, modern western world. Even in the late 1980s in respected newspapers such as the *Wall Street Journal,* writers continued to speak of Haiti in terms of "spirits" and "strangeness" where "things seem weird," "anarchy isn't far off," and "Western notions of progress and development fade in the smoke of a voodoo priest's flaming magic stones."[6]

Although analytic models of Haiti had been developed before 1980—indeed, a superb anthropological account was published before 1940[7]—the relative burst of scholarly accounts and sophisticated perspectives since 1980 has provided information of unprecedented accuracy and reliability.[8] These works have come about partially as a consequence of the fairly significant amount of public-

ity that Haitians received in the 1980s, beginning with the boat
people in southern Florida in the late 1970s and continuing through
the fall of the Duvalier dynasty in February 1986. This interest has
been accompanied by a sharp increase in the number of scholarly
books in English on Haiti since 1985[9] and even some good journalistic accounts.[10] Pioneering research on Haitian-Americans also
emerged in the 1980s.[11]

Some specialized areas have become well covered. Besides the
rather misguided research about Haitians and AIDS, which I will
discuss later in this chapter, there has been a considerable amount of
scholarly research into health in Haiti in the last five years.[12]

The availability of these works also means that journalists and
others who write for the general public no longer have any excuse for
maintaining allegiance to a discredited folk model. In fact, anyone
who is at all interested in writing accurately about Haiti can easily
find all the pertinent literature with the help of three current bibliog-
raphies.[13]

The Boat People

Traditionally, Haitians have been ignored in North America. For
example, at the beginning of the 1980s, the participants in a sympo-
sium on the fastest growing immigrant groups in New York City
failed to mention Haitians at all and concentrated only on Hispanic
and Asian groups, stating, "Orientals, who numbered at most 60,000
in 1965, have reached an estimated strength of 200,000 in 1980."[14]
By 1980, however, New York City contained well over three
hundred thousand Haitians,[15] and most of this rapidly growing
population had arrived there after 1957. Almost twenty years later a
journalist, nevertheless, stated that Haitians "are probably the most
isolated immigrant group in [New York City]."[16] A review of the
literature on migration and Haitians pointed out that at the beginning
of the 1980s "scholarly studies and textbooks on ethnicity and
immigrant groups ignored the Haitians entirely or mentioned them
only in passing."[17]

In my many discussions with students at the University of Florida, I came across several who had never heard of Haiti—or who confused it with Tahiti. Most of the other students routinely displayed the prejudices and repeated the misinformation about Haiti that composes the folk model I will explore in the rest of this book. In my talks before both academic and civic groups in north central Florida I have heard every silly question asked about Haiti that anyone could possibly imagine. Most of the questions pointed out a great ignorance about Haiti and Haitians, but, more importantly, many of the questions also indicated an increasing interest in a nation that is, after all, a close neighbor of the United States.

The traditional invisibility of Haiti began changing as early as 1977 when Haitian immigrants, the "boat people," started arriving in southern Florida in significant numbers. The first Haitians to reach Florida by boat and request political asylum actually came in 1963. Perhaps as a deliberate signal of things to come, American authorities denied political asylum to all twenty-five passengers.

Arrivals in Florida by boat were rather rare after that until the now legendary 1972 crossing, which was recounted by Jake Miller, a professor of political science at Bethune-Cookman College in Daytona Beach, Florida,

> In November 1972, 65 passengers set out for Florida in a leaking sailboat. The captain of the vessel identified his passengers as 12 political prisoners with their families and friends. According to his account, the release of the prisoners was made possible by a bribe to a prison guard. The Haitians first came ashore in Cuba, but because of their refusal to embrace communism, they were denied political asylum. . . . When they arrived in Bimini they were given food and water by the Bahamians, who wished them well. Upon their arrival in Pompano Beach, Florida, local residents displayed their hospitality by setting up an improvised beachfront kitchen and feeding them.[18]

Many other voyages in small leaky boats followed this first one, and many of them ended tragically with unknown numbers of people drowning off the shores of North America. In 1981 one of these

tragedies received national television coverage when thirty-three
Haitians drowned after their twenty-five foot homemade boat cap-
sized within fifty yards of the shores of the affluent Florida community
of Hillsboro Beach. Subsequent crossings also received considerable notice in the American and international media, even showing
up in a novel on the harrowing experiences of a Haitian mother.[19]
This widespread publicity quite literally put the Haitians on the map;
the July 1985 issue of *Time* magazine featuring immigrants included
a schematic representation of New York City showing the location
of Haitian-American neighborhoods,[20] and the new Haitian immigrants in Miami were mentioned throughout the issue.

In addition to the dangerous passage on the open sea, the boat
people who survived this ordeal faced "the invariably discriminatory
and often brutal treatment of . . . the U.S. Immigration and Naturalization Service (INS)."[21] I will discuss the activities of the INS in
chapter 5.

Several factors contributed to the sharp increase in the number of
Haitian immigrants to the United States after 1977.

> The usual immigration targets [for Haitians] of the Bahamas and the
> Dominican Republic became increasingly difficult to enter and, in
> fact, began expelling Haitians; in the early 1970s the United States
> raised the labor certification requirements and in 1977 introduced a
> quota for Western hemisphere countries; later the United States and
> Canada sharply curtailed the granting of temporary visas, internal
> political repression in Haiti increased, two major droughts in 1975 and
> 1977 led to out-migration from rural areas, and several mining and
> manufacturing firms in Haiti closed down.[22]

These events resulted in the migration of Haitians with rather
different socioeconomic characteristics than the pre-1977 migrants.
The earlier immigrants usually traveled legally on temporary visas
and arrived by airplane. They had access to funds and came from
urban families. More than half of them were women, and they were
usually able to obtain work in garment districts or as domestics.
Their major target was New York City, and they often overstayed
their legal time limit.[23]

In contrast to this earlier group, the predominately male boat people headed for southern Florida. They were poorer, more rural, and, of course, arrived without any legal documents. They were not, however, as rural or as poor and certainly not as unskilled as most Americans believe, though most of what people in the United States think they know about Haitians comes from their folk models of these boat people. Most Americans think that these boat people come to the United States only for economic reasons. The fact is that the extremely difficult economic situation of Haiti has resulted from the deleterious political decisions of Haitian governments and the governments of the surrounding nations.

Fortunately, some serious studies have been carried out on the Haitian boat people so that we do have accurate information gathered by legitimate scholars. In particular, the work of Alex Stepick, an anthropologist at Florida International University in Miami who has focused his research on Haitians in southern Florida since 1981,[24] provides an informed antidote to the sensationalist and inaccurate accounts of journalists.

Based on both intensive fieldwork and a questionnaire survey administered in mid-1983 to 150 Haitians released from INS detention camps, one study by Stepick clearly demonstrated that these Haitian boat people are not the "penniless, illiterate, unskilled" human wrecks described in the American press.[25] A deleterious by-product of this image is that the INS eagerly embraces the notion of the boat people as coming to Florida purely for economic and not political reasons—the better to deport them.

Certainly by Haitian standards the boat people are far from poor. Furthermore, Stepick said, "They are highly motivated and anxious to improve themselves through education and hard work."[26] Also, few of the boat people come from Haiti's most impoverished regions. In fact, these Haitians are, on the average, better educated than those remaining in Haiti. Most of their education is vocational, and many were engaged in semi-skilled trades in Haiti. According to Stepick, "Most characteristic were such trades as tailoring, carpentry, and auto mechanics."[27] He believes "This educational background provides the best hope for the Haitians' future in the U.S."[28]

After the initial sympathy they received at some of the affluent Florida beach communities, the Haitian boat people soon fell prey to the usual discriminatory treatment reserved for blacks and the poor in the United States. In addition, these Haitians, as Stepick has pointed out,

> came uninvited . . . unlike most other immigrant groups. . . . There were no jobs awaiting them. They had not been recruited into Florida's agricultural fields as Mexicans have been into California's. In Florida these jobs were already filled by black Americans, undocumented Mexican workers, and in sugar cane, by legal temporary foreign workers from Jamaica and other Caribbean islands. There is little industry in Miami such as existed in the late 19th and early 20th centuries for the millions of immigrants from Europe to the Northeastern U.S. Miami's restaurant and hotel labor force was primarily American black or Hispanic. The garment industry has been dominated by Cuban workers.[29]

This has meant that the boat people released into Florida have had a choice of either going on welfare or struggling to find their own ways of making a living. Again, contrary to public opinion, Haitian refugees typically do not accept food stamps or go on welfare.[30] Most of the boat people have, instead, gone into the type of temporary and part-time work highly necessary in North American communities and have usefully applied their skills throughout southern Florida at auto repair, barbering, carpentry, cooking, and tailoring.

In addition, many Haitian women engage in small-scale commercial activities with capital investments of often less than fifty dollars.

> Many of these women go to the local flea markets to rent stalls. . . . Others operate from small makeshift stands on corners or in empty lots. Some...also go door-to-door to sell items such as tailored and ready-made clothing, various decorative and gift items, and Haitian snack foods.[31]

Many of the activities of Haitian men in southern Florida focus on remodeling and new construction.

Informal transportation is also important in sprawling urban areas, especially in those that are lacking adequate public transportation systems. Some Haitian men drive vans and old school buses between various places of work such as the vegetable fields, shopping areas, and residential neighborhoods. Many Haitians have bought used cars since they have been in the United States. These cars often need repair and maintenance, which has created a demand for the flourishing, informal auto repair industry that operates in the streets and empty lots of Haitian neighborhoods.[32]

Stepick also found, "Many have become a part of the nation's. . . stream of permanent migrant laborers."[33] Karen Richman, an anthropologist who did research among Haitian farm workers, reported that Haitians are heavily exploited as stoop labor in North America because they do not complain, cannot argue in English, and they work hard.[34] Although most of the new Haitian immigrants had unrealistic expectations of their life in Florida,

> few suspected that they would find themselves fettered to a brutal system of migrant agricultural labor, destined to travel from state to state to pick fruit and vegetables, performing the type of lowly task reserved in rural Haiti for the most desperate, landless peasants.[35]

The new Haitians in America find such work very degrading. In Haiti itself, "young men who have no other option will travel to distant villages...rather than suffer the humiliation of laboring for wages in a neighbor's garden."[36]

It is evident that the analytic model of Haitian immigrants differs considerably from the common folk model, which, in particular, denigrates their education, training, and motivation. Adherents to this misleading folk model will, at best, consistently underestimate the potential of Haitians to make positive contributions to American society, and, at worst, will display an attitude of contempt toward these newest immigrants leading to their further exploitation. It is worth noting that Miss America 1991, Marjorie Judith Vincent, is the daughter of Haitian immigrants who fled from poverty there in 1964.

The AIDS Connection

During the 1970s an unfounded rumor circulated in Miami that Haitians were spreading tuberculosis, which caused many to be fired from their jobs. However, the bad press of the Haitians reached its modern-day zenith in 1982 with the alleged connection between Haitians and the acquired immune deficiency syndrome (AIDS), which is an incurable disorder of the body's mechanisms for fighting infections. The information about AIDS and Haitians came from official U.S. sources and had the backing of scientific research. The North American media collaborated uncritically in publicizing the allegations about Haitians and AIDS.

By the mid-1980s Americans who knew nothing else about Haiti did "know" that Haitians transmitted AIDS. According to the Haitian physician Guy Durand, these erroneous reports soon resulted in "Haitianophobia."[37] In 1984 one Haitian wrote, "Over the past three years...Haitians have been subjected to devastating and inescapable publicity....AIDS has become a scarlet letter pinned on all of them—young and old, male and female, long-time residents and recent arrivals."[38] Roger Biamby, director of the Haitian American Community Association of Dade County, Florida, was quoted as flatly stating, "Haitians are considered disease carriers."[39]

The consequences showed up in a number of ways. "A pregnant mother in labor was placed in isolation at a Chicago hospital—a measure normally reserved for carriers of infectious diseases—presumably because being Haitian was synonymous with having AIDS."[40] Some people refused to get into a cab in New York City upon learning that the driver was Haitian.[41] Still another writer flatly stated, "To be a Haitian and living in New York City meant that you were perceived as an AIDS 'carrier.'"[42] Claude Souffrant, a Haitian Jesuit with the Haitian Catholic Center in Chicago, said, "People are now scared of Haitians because of the AIDS question."[43] Even after Haitians were officially "cleared" of somehow being especially susceptible to AIDS, the coordinator of the Haitian Coalition on AIDS in Miami pointed out, "The stigma persists....Police are afraid of Haitians, ambulance workers are afraid of Haitians, health workers are afraid of Haitians."[44] And even in the sophisticated atmosphere of a large university, when I mention to colleagues that I spent time in Haiti they often respond, "Oh, did you catch AIDS?"—and laugh nervously.

In the minds of racists, the association of AIDS with Haitians has carried over to all blacks. In January 1987 on CNN, the white supremacist J. B. Stoner declared, "When niggers come in, they bring dope and AIDS."

The AIDS scare has, indeed, been well publicized in the United States. Just a few months before Haitians were removed from the list of high risk groups, the Associated Press quoted James Curran, head of the AIDS research group at the Centers for Disease Control in Atlanta (CDC), as saying that as many as three hundred thousand people may have already been infected by the virus believed to cause AIDS and about thirty thousand of them are likely to develop the disease in the next five years. The story stated that "The Centers for Disease Control reported...AIDS...had struck 8,057 people and claimed 3,863 lives in the United States since June 1, 1981."[45] The story continued, "More than 90 percent of AIDS cases continue to occur in the groups previously identified as being at high risk: homosexuals, abusers of intravenous drugs, hemophiliacs and Haitians, according to a report by Curran."[46]

In 1981 the CDC in Atlanta began weekly reports of AIDS statistics, and included Haitians among groups that were at high risk of contracting AIDS until the Haitian category was dropped in April 1985. Up until that very month the American media broadcast that Haitians were somehow connected with AIDS. The wire services, for example, carried statements such as, "AIDS is most likely to strike homosexuals, Haitians, abusers of injectable drugs and hemophiliacs. It is apparently spread by sexual contact, contaminated needles and blood transfusions."[47] The journalists apparently never questioned just why Haitians should have more difficulty than other nationalities with sex, needles, and transfusions. Stories in national news magazines such as *Newsweek* also characterized AIDS as a disease occurring "among homosexuals, intravenous drug users, Haitians and hemophiliacs."[48]

Some of the more sensationalist segments of the American press passed off bizarre speculations as news, such as a story in the *Boston Globe* that cited a Harvard School of Public Health report as conjecturing that AIDS "may have originated with one Haitian homosexual who ate infected pork."[49] This account apparently grew out of some journalist's confusion about the outbreak of African swine fever in Haiti in 1979. The Harvard School of Public Health later denied any such research. "The New York *Daily News* cited one American researcher, Dr. Jeffrey Vieira of Downstate Medical Center in Brooklyn, as drawing a potential voodoo-AIDS link. Dr. Vieira sent a letter to the *Daily News* denying he had ever made such a suggestion; only one month later did the *Daily News* see fit to print his refutation."[50]

Despite the curiousness of the connection between Haitians and AIDS, the CDC continued to include Haitians among those groups at high risk of contracting AIDS for four years until the Haitian category was finally eliminated on April 8, 1985. On that day Walter Dowdle, director of the CDC's Center for Infectious Diseases, was quoted in an Associated Press story as saying, "The Haitians were...the only group identified because of who they were rather than what they did. It has always caused problems for us. . . . It became less and less justifiable to include the Haitians as a pear among all the apples."[51] According to the story, "Dowdle said the change was 'something we've been wanting to do for more than one and a half years.'"[52] CDC spokesperson Charles Faller was quoted as saying, "It was unfair to do. They [the Haitians] were just like anyone else."[53] Even then, "Dowdle said Haitians will remain on the Public Health Service list of groups who should not be allowed to donate blood because of the danger of transmitting the AIDS virus."[54]

Although the North American mass media quickly stopped naming Haitians as a risk group for AIDS—for example, the cover story of the July 1985 issue of *Life* was on AIDS and did not mention Haitians at all[55]—the removal of Haitians from the various CDC listings was not nearly as widely publicized as had been their placement on the listings. In a letter published in the September 15, 1985 issue of *Newsweek* the Haitian ambassador to the United States complained that *Newsweek* "dismissed the CDC action in a foot-note" and continued to describe AIDS "as 'common' and 'prevalent' in Haiti."[56] The editor's response admitted, "AIDS is not 'common' in Haiti." There were, however, no explanations or journalistic investigations of why the category of "Haitians" got on the lists in the first place.

The source of the notion that Haitians were susceptible to the virus that results in AIDS illustrates that many Americans are ready to believe the worst about Haitians. The few studies that made the specious connection between AIDS and Haitians as an ethnic group exhibited extraordinary sociocultural naivety.[57] These studies expected, for example, that Haitian men would respond reliably to point-blank questions about their homosexual practices. These medical researchers obviously had no special knowledge of Haitian culture.

> Homosexuality in Haitian society is a strong cultural taboo. Known homosexuals are shunned regardless of their wealth or position…, and it is not a topic Haitians would openly discuss, least of all with non-Creole-speaking American researchers jotting notes on clipboards.[58]

In fact, it is well documented in the social science literature since at least 1937 that "the most prevalent Haitian attitude toward homosexuality in either sex…is one of derision."[59]

The researchers also never made clear whether their conclusions applied to Haitians as an ethnic group or as a nationality. Were Haitian citizens who are somatically white, for example, those of Middle Eastern descent, also at risk? Or was the notion simply based on the concept that all Haitians are black, and probably racist in its orgination?

Nevertheless, after a brief examination of ten Haitian men with AIDS at Kings County Hospital–Downstate Medical Center in Brooklyn, the physicians concluded, "This outbreak is unique in that it occurred within a single ethnic group of previously healthy men without histories of homosexuality or drug abuse."[60] And, again, after a cursory examination of eight Haitian men with AIDS in

Montreal, the physicians wrote, "All denied homosexuality, bisexuality, intravenous drug abuse, any history of sexually transmitted disease, promiscuity or a significant medical history."[61] An often cited article from Jackson Memorial Hospital in Miami stated, "This is the first report of an outbreak of an acquired cellular immunodeficiency syndrome among heterosexual patients who are not intravenous drug abusers. The fact that it has occurred in a specific subpopulation is of epidemiologic significance."[62] The article reported, "All 11 Haitian patients studied...stated that they were heterosexual and denied any genital-anal or oral-anal contact."[63]

In discussing this research Durand declared,

> It is doubtful...that ever before in the history of modern medicine has a condition brought along with its discovery and description such a maze of confusion and irrationality, both in the professional and lay press. . . . Never before in modern medicine has a pathological condition been linked to a nationality.[64]

He concluded that the faulty reporting of the alleged AIDS-Haitian connection "is in stark contradiction with the basic principles of scientific methods"[65] and that the risk group classification "resembles far more a caste systematization than groups arranged in function of their susceptibility to the condition."[66]

Despite the work of Haitian physicians and researchers into AIDS, and despite the fact that enormously significant and negative publicity was directed at Haitians, "the Haitian medical professionals have never been invited to participate in the ongoing researches."[67] And, according to Dr. Jean-Claude Desgranges of the Downstate Medical Center in Brooklyn, "The *New York Times* has never sought out Haitians for their point of view. They only want to talk to American doctors, it seems."[68] The one piece of reliable research that includes Haitian physicians is rarely cited.[69]

The notion that AIDS is restricted to homosexual men is now known to be false. "Although homosexuals still account for 73 percent of all AIDS cases in the United States, and intravenous-drug abusers account for another 17 percent,"[70] the virus had already spread among heterosexuals in central Africa by mid-1985.[71] The reason the virus showed up first in homosexual populations is probably due to the fact that it is largely passed by the exchange of blood and that the act of anal intercourse practiced by many male homosexuals results in numerous small abrasions in the anal tract. In addition, research has discovered a significant presence of the virus in semen. Small abrasions in the reproductive tract resulting from vaginal heterosexual intercourse apparently also facilitate the spread of the virus. And, of course, it is possible that the virus is mutating and can spread in ways now that it could not have several years ago.

Once AIDS was introduced into Haiti, however, it could have spread rapidly through means other than sexual transmission. Among the traditional Haitian folk healers are numerous so-called injectionists, who generally have had some experience with hypodermic injections, often as paramedics. Haitians commonly use these injections for a variety of ailments, and the equipment is rarely sterilized due to a lack of facilities.

At any rate, the speculation that AIDS is somehow peculiar to Haitians as an ethnic group, or that AIDS originated in Haiti, or that Haitians were the first nonhomosexual population to contract it, remains an erroneous component of the western folk model. The strongest case for the origin of AIDS in Haiti or in Africa, with the disease subsequently transmitted to New York City through Haiti,[72] is not only weak, but makes the unsubstantiated assertion that "many voodoo priests are homosexual men."[73]

If there is anything that AIDS is related to in Haiti, however, it is poverty and the consequent exploitation of this poverty by North Americans through their encouragement of prostitution in Haiti. For several years Haiti has been a major vacation area for New York City homosexuals. "Numerous charter flights from New York, and at least one per year from Chicago, regularly took vacationing gays to Haiti. . . . American money apparently was irresistible; prostitution and gay resorts flourished despite societal injunction."[74] One travel guide from an agency in New York City specializing in gay clients claimed, "Haitians are cheerful, honest and have a very easygoing attitude towards sex in general. Much of the population is bisexual and age is irrelevant."[75]

Most researchers are unable to say conclusively whether AIDS appeared first in New York City or in Haiti. The virus could well have been in New York City and then spread to Haiti. One medical researcher flatly stated, "AIDS in the United States antedated that in Haiti, and the disease was probably introduced into the Haitian population by American homosexuals."[76] One careful review of the literature by a medical anthropologist concluded, "AIDS in Haiti is a tale of ties to the United States."[77] Research does, indeed, show that indications of AIDS first appeared in the United States in early 1977. AIDS was first detected in Haiti only later in 1978[78] or perhaps in mid-1979.[79] Most of the early cases of AIDS in Haiti were found in Carrefour,[80] a Port-au-Prince suburb with numerous night clubs, prostitutes, and a reputation for catering to the every sexual whim of the tourist. Recognizing the potential dangers, the Haitian government closed many gay establishments in Carrefour in 1983, which is much earlier than any similar action by the government in the United States.

If AIDS did originate in Haiti it should also be in rural areas; however, "AIDS in Haiti seemed to be largely an urban disease.... The Albert Schweitzer Hospital, situated in a rural area of Haiti, had not recognized any cases at all."[81] The whole argument is moot since the discovery of a case of AIDS in St. Louis, Missouri, that apparently occurred in 1969.[82]

In August 1986 the CDC once again revised its reporting to shift Haitian AIDS cases into a heterosexual transmission category. The CDC apparently still considered Haiti to have an AIDS problem. And two years after the elimination of the Haitian category by the CDC, supposedly informed persons still speak of Haitians as being one of the high risk populations, such as the reported remark of a member of the AIDS committee at the University of Florida in February 1987 concerning "high risk populations such as homosexuals, Haitians or intravenous drug users."[83] In February 1990 the U.S. Food and Drug Administration (FDA) instituted a policy recommending that blood collection agencies refuse blood from people born in or that might have emigrated from Haiti (as well as from any of the thirty-eight sub-Saharan African nations)—much to the dismay of health officials in southern Florida. As Dr. Charles Rouault, president of the Broward Community Blood Center, said in an interview on March 2, 1990, "This could be devastating to us. We've had a good experience with Haitians and have had several hundred as blood donors for the last several years." On April 20, 1990, a crowd in New York City, estimated by the police to exceed fifty thousand, demonstrated against this policy, and the FDA promised a review.[84] The FDA finally scrapped its policy on December 5, 1990.

In the case of AIDS, the split between folk and analytic models is not as sharply drawn as the differences between the public's and anthropological notions of Haitian refugees in southern Florida. The origin of AIDS is still wrapped in controversy and may never be known with certainty. In addition, the first knowledge about Haitians and AIDS came from medical personnel, who are generally assumed by the public to have access to privileged knowledge. The analytic model of these physicians was, however, seriously contaminated by their folk notions of Haitians and the lifestyles of Haitians. Consequently, the public developed a folk model of Haitians and AIDS that not only reinforced previous prejudices but that was also supported by an misguided analytic model.

I have demonstrated that the recognition of biases from the folk model must be identified and considered in any proper construction of a useful analytic model. In fact, analytic explanations that too easily flow from folk expectations should be immediately suspect. The approach of anthropology should be particularly helpful in this respect because the discipline, with its emphasis on the inherent dignity and functional appropriateness of other cultures, is in the position of being able, ideologically and methodologically, to describe and incorporate folk components into its own analytic models. I am speaking about the folk elements of health in general and AIDS in particular in both the western biomedical model and in the Haitian model.

As a demonstration of the possibilities that anthropology offers, I will briefly discuss some of the work of the anthropologist Paul Farmer, who has had many years of research experience in Haiti and who has developed an ethnography of AIDS in a small rural village in a central plateau of Haiti.[85] Farmer demonstrates that the Haitian folk explanation of AIDS is "embedded [in] understandings of blood, tuberculosis, and microbes [that] have been worked into a 'master paradigm' that links sickness to moral concerns and social relations."[86]

According to Farmer, "Two major causal schemes, magic and germ theory, are elaborately intertwined" in the Haitian folk model.[87] In its broadest sense, AIDS is linked to "such diverse associations as the endless suffering of the Haitian people, divine punishment, the corruption of the ruling class, and the ills of North American imperialism."[88] As caused by local sorcery, AIDS has a peculiar class characteristic; it is "an illness visited on one poor person by another, even poorer person."[89]

These cultural meanings that Haitians give to AIDS have no less of an influence on their perception of the illness than do the prejudices of the white world and the reflected prejudices of the western media. An understanding of these folk models will give us information on how to prevent the further spread of AIDS as well as letting us empathize with the victims. Indeed, anthropology's major strength and greatest contribution to knowledge about AIDS should be the transcultural, holistic, evolutionary, and empathetic perspectives on how different peoples experience their different worlds.

Cannibals and Zombies

A Haitian intellectual has complained, "Voodoo is certainly the most publicized, the most misunderstood, and the most misinterpreted aspect of [Caribbean] cultures. Too many people equate Voodoo with superstitions and all degrees of witchcraft and sorcery."[90] And there is no doubt about the accuracy of the statement by the journalist who reported in the *New York Times Magazine*, "Voodoo has always suffered from a bad press."[91] He then quoted the community affairs police officer of a Haitian neighborhood in Brooklyn as stating, "In my 26 years here, I have never come across any crime actually linked to Voodoo."[92]

The contrast of this report with the popular presentation of Voodoo is striking. Current portrayals of Voodoo have concentrated on the extraordinarily rare occurrence of zombies, as the notion of the living dead is commonly called. An article in *Time* magazine on zombies labeled Haiti "a land where the line between myth and reality is faintly drawn."[93] And fictional accounts of Voodoo usually connect the religion with criminal activity. On September 22, 1985, for example, the popular television show "Miami Vice" showed Haitians involved in the drug trade and high-powered crime and showed a weird version of zombiism.

Less than a year after the "Miami Vice" story, one of the worst portrayals of Voodoo ever seen on American television was featured on Jacques Cousteau's public television series on the evening of May 23, 1986. Jacques Cousteau and his crew concentrated for the most part on their specialty, the sea world and its dynamics. Part of the presentation, however, purported to educate the viewing public about the culture of Haiti, and, of course, about Voodoo. For its brief portrayal of the pilgrimages associated with Voodoo, the camera primarily focused on the buttocks of topless women gyrating in the mud—an activity that Haitians view as a sacred dance performed in the cleansing waters of a mud spring where spirits dwell, but which was presented only for its entertainment value.

On November 27, 1987, the television show "Beauty and the Beast" had an episode featuring a muddled notion of Voodoo. Some might argue that the fictional presentations are only entertainment and should not be criticized for their inaccuracies. It is obvious, however, that these iniquitous fictions reflect a widely accepted folk model and give support to the misinformation contained in this model.

Furthermore, the "Beauty and the Beast" plot—and many others like it—had various "experts" on Voodoo to explain the practices and beliefs to the main characters. Even if the lay public dismisses the bizarre plot, it probably accepts the "expert" testimony, erroneously assuming that the story writers have actually done research. In the plot for "Beauty and the Beast," for example, one of the experts claimed that the rulers of Haiti have always used Voodoo to try to stay in power. Actually, all of the urban-based, elite-controlled governments of Haiti have either studiously ignored Voodoo or have actively attempted to suppress this dangerously democratic religion. Even François Duvalier eventually accommodated the Roman Catholic church and implicitly disavowed Voodoo—though the foreign press was often taken in by stories about his connections with Voodoo and rumors of strange activities in the palace.

On December 12 and 13, 1988, the daytime drama "The Judge" carried a episode on zombies containing pejorative references to Haiti and to Haitians. The story itself featured a black Haitian who had supposedly turned a white sixteen-year-old girl into a zombie and was using her as a prostitute.

The television show "Inside Edition" on February 20, 1991, began with anchor Bill O'Reilly intoning,

> Voodoo and zombies. Kid's stuff, right? Grade-B movies. Well, that's wrong. Just one hour plane ride from Miami is the Caribbean country of Haiti, and this country is literally being held hostage by Voodoo priests who can and do turn people into zombies. The motive: money.

Much of the show revolved around ethnocentric comments on Voodoo ceremonies, such as labeling animal sacrifices as "disturbing," and erroneous notions about Voodoo, saying that Voodoo priests "can order anyone to be possessed." The program focused on how exploitative the Voodoo priests are—referring, incidentally, only to male priests and thereby ignoring the gender egalitarianism of Voodoo. Of course, the broadcast emphasized the Voodoo priests' alleged power to create zombies.

A peculiar connection was made between Voodoo and poverty, with O'Reilly saying, "Some believe Voodoo is used to keep these people in economic slavery." O'Reilly continued this theme by saying, "Some unscrupulous people have used Voodoo to keep the population poor and under control. While the average peasant makes just $150 a year, millions have been made by criminals who threaten these poor people with the hellish vengeance of Voodoo." O'Reilly then claimed that the most notorious Voodoo priest was François "Papa Doc" Duvalier, apparently using as his authority the well-known Baptist missionary Wallace Turnbull. Turnbull stated, "So, Papa Doc Duvalier said he was a black magic practicer [*sic*], and people were afraid of him because of that. Well, he was definitely, ah, ah, [a] practicing Voodooist from many years before he became president." Actually, before he became president, Duvalier was a physician by training and a published ethnographer and had served as Ministers of Public Health and of Labor in previous administrations, though he did court the support of Voodoo priests during his 1957 campaign for president and for sometime thereafter.

The rest of the show concentrated on zombification and the depravity of Voodoo priests, with O'Reilly declaring, "Behind all Voodoo there is grave punishment for wrongdoers. That punishment is to be turned into one of the living dead, to be turned into a zombie." O'Reilly then briefly mentioned the two popular cases of zombies, Francina Illeus and Clairvius Narcisse, saying, "Incredibly scientists have now proven that zombies do, indeed, exist."

In the remaining moments of the show, Turnbull was allowed to follow O'Reilly's notion that "the payoff comes when a Voodoo priest wants money from the peasants [and] almost always gets it." Turnbull indicted all Voodoo priests when he said,

He [the priest] will bleed them, just, until they have nothing left. They mortgage what's in the ground. So the poor people, who have very little to start with, will give the witch doctor anything he wants. Yes, and then he has nothing when he's finished. He usually is a drunkard and has women, so he, he's kept poor and maybe more ragged than his clients.

After the end of the material shot in Haiti, the viewer was brought back to O'Reilly in the studio, who intoned this final sentence with raised eyebrows: "Once again, there are those who say that Voodoo serves a legitimate spiritual purpose."

Paul Monaghan, Consultant to the University of Florida/Macaya Biosphere Reserve Project in Haiti, and I subsequently wrote a letter to O'Reilly complaining,

> We were very disappointed to see you drag out all the discredited cliches about . . . Voodoo and zombies. . . . The zombie stuff is, after all, at least four years old and not accepted by many scientists. . . . In addition, the "Inside Edition" rendition of Voodoo was at odds with all the scholarly work ever done over many decades by trained anthropologists.[94]

We also asked,

> Why was this out-of-date and misleading story shown just a few weeks after Haiti had installed the first popularly elected president in its entire history, at a moment when Haitians are trying to rebuild overwhelmed sociopolitical institutions and a shattered economy? Some people on your staff must be aware of the sensationalist and highly inaccurate . . . portrayals of Voodoo that have been used in the past to lay the groundwork for arguments against the ability of blacks to govern themselves.[95]

To his credit, O'Reilly did respond to our letter. He wrote,

> It is not our job to put any country or government in a favorable light. Our story concentrated on voodoo extortionists. . . . Surely you cannot argue that voodoo is [not] being used by criminals to enrich themselves.[96]

O'Reilly seems to be arguing that if there is even the hint of truth to anything that "Inside Edition" reports, then they are absolved from any damage that the impact of the report may have in its totality. In other words, his journalism has no responsibility for giving holistic portrayals of its subjects. And although Turnbull made a sweeping generalization that was obviously meant to indict all Voodoo priests, O'Reilly dismissed his journalistic responsibilities by arguing, "The Baptist minister who spoke in our story only addressed the economic and historical facets of voodoo and not the theology."[97]

It is just such coverage that has transfixed the notion of zombies in American minds. William Seabrook, the author of the most notorious book on Voodoo,[98] claimed in his autobiography, "The word *zombie* never appeared in English print before I wrote *The Magic Island*."[99] This is apparently correct, and since then the mass media has shifted its focus on Voodoo from cannibalism to zombiism. A few years after the publication of the shameless but commercially successful Seabrook book, the famous anthropologist Melville J. Herskovits, who wrote the first full-length ethnography of Haiti, stated,

> More than any other single term, the word "voodoo" is called to mind whenever mention is made of Haiti. Conceived as a grim system of African practices, it has come to be identified with fantastic and cruel rites and to serve as a symbol of daring excursions into the esoteric. Not only has emphasis been placed on its frenzied rites and the cannibalism supposed on occasion to accompany them, but its dark mysteries of magic and "zombis" have been so stressed that it has become customary to think of the Haitians as living in a universe of psychological terror.[100]

Modern reporting from Haiti has not improved over Herskovits's characterization of the western folk model. A journalistic and unreliable account by someone who is supposed to have special knowledge of Haitians has written about "that lawless vein of cruelty and abuse inherent in Haitian society since its foundation,"[101] and reported as fact an account of infant sacrifice in a Voodoo ceremony in the National Palace, a story repeated in the *Miami Herald* by a writer who claimed, "Such behavior had become mundane."[102]

Despite the popularity of such sensationalism, Voodoo is simply the name foreigners gave to the Haitian religion, a religion rich in symbolism and functionally satisfying for the large majority of Haitians. Although many of its beliefs and practices can be traced to African religions and to Roman Catholicism, it originated in eighteenth century plantations where black slaves reshaped these religions to meet their new needs and created what one Haitian intellectual called "the main achievement of rural Haiti"[103]

While many of the early writings on Voodoo concentrated on the preposterous notion that cannibalism was a primary focus of the ceremonies, most foreigners are now more aware of zombies. The most current writing on zombies is, in fact, the work of a foreigner and is a curious mixture of sensationalism and scholarship. As a doctoral student in botany at Harvard University, Wade Davis investigated the ethnobotany of zombification in Haiti. Although he spent relatively little time there and spoke no Creole, Davis had the good fortune to come across some informants who gave him information on the potions used by Voodoo sorcerers to poison people. Davis thought that he had discovered the active ingredient in the poison, tetrodotoxin, and wrote an academic article on his findings in the *Journal of Ethnopharmacology* in 1983.

Not everyone, however, accepted his scholarly conclusions; some toxicologists claimed that the tetrodotoxin in zombie potions was insignificant.[104] As if his pharmacological conclusions were not controversial enough, Davis wrote a popularized and fictionalized book in 1985 about his time in Haiti that reads like the first draft for a Hollywood movie, with Davis himself as an Indiana Jones–type hero. This book, titled *The Serpent and the Rainbow*, concentrates on his idea of the connection between zombies and secret societies.

The latest Hollywood insult to the Haitian people was released to theaters on February 5, 1988, and is, indeed, "inspired by the book by Wade Davis," as the credits read. Also titled *The Serpent and the Rainbow*, this film was, appropriately enough, made by the director of *A Nightmare on Elm Street.* For its scary scenes, the movie mostly uses dream sequences and encounters of the young white American hero with the tonton-makout—scenes that were not even in the book.

At any rate, Davis's scholarly explanation of zombification is plausible enough—although there are only two documented cases of "the living dead" in all the history of Haiti. A person is somehow administered a potion containing tetrodotoxin, which lowers the metabolic rate to a point near clinical death. The victim is assumed dead and is buried—within a few hours and without embalming. That night a sorcerer digs up the body and revives it by an antidote.

The person is presumably traumatized, probably brain damaged, and walks around "like a zombie."

I don't have any real problems with this. Poisoning has been common throughout Haitian history, beginning with slaves who poisoned their oppressors. As in any society of scarce natural resources, there are plenty of arguments over land, water, and food. Anyone can hire someone else to poison an enemy. Exactly why the poisoner would want a zombie, however, is not clear. Zombies aren't used as a warning because they are always taken out of the local community. They aren't used as slaves (a common notion in the Haitian folk model) because brain-damaged people don't make good workers. Presumably, most potential zombies died, either from suffocation in the grave or from the poison itself since the mixture cannot be accurately measured.

Where Davis runs into difficulty is, indeed, in his explanation for the creation of zombies. The major complaint is, of course, that his sample of two is too small for any conclusions at all. The other complaints are that Davis's "fieldwork" was too brief, his knowledge of Haitian history too simplistic, his experience in Haiti too shallow, and, if one takes his book seriously, his approach to religion rather too gullible.

Much of Davis's argument relies on undemonstrated historical connections, beginning with the notion that the structure of the secret societies of West Africa were transferred in Haiti to the mountain communities of escaped slaves (called *maroons*[105]) and continuing with a peculiar reading of Haitian history. According to Davis, during the Haitian Revolution the armies of the ex-slaves of the plantations turned on the maroons,[106] and, then, somehow, the maroon communities established their secret societies to maintain order in the ex-slave communities in rural Haiti.[107] Much of this section leans too heavily on the impressionistic historical research of Zora Neal Hurston into secret societies in Haiti.[108]

Davis's description of zombification, then, sees it as a device for social control, carried out by secret societies. Davis's conclusion is that these societies really do control rural Haiti. In his second book, titled *Passage of Darkness: The Ethnobiology of the Haitian Zombie* and billed as a scholarly effort, Davis makes clear that he thinks "zombification is a form of social sanction imposed by recognized corporate bodies—the poorly known and clandestine secret Bizango societies—as one means of maintaining order and control in local communities,"[109] though in the only one really well-documented case of zombification the person "stated that he had been made a zombie eighteen years before by his brother because of a land dispute."[110]

Much of the Davis thesis sounds like a repeat of earlier insulting notions that Haitian peasants are pawns of superstition and have no understanding of the social forces of their own society. Such a thesis depends without support on the division between the ex-slaves and the maroons and as well as "between the representations of the urban-based authorities on the one hand and the traditional leaders of the vodoun society on the other."[112] In addition, such a thesis exaggerates the fact that people often do not have a thorough knowledge of the seats of power in their community. Their lack of detailed knowledge does not, however, mean that secret gatherings constitute the totality of social control in the community—any more than the selection of political candidates in smoked-filled back rooms constitutes the totality of power in modern democracies.

Besides having only two documented cases of zombification, Davis apparently attended only one meeting of an alleged secret society.[113] The account of that meeting actually reads just like a Voodoo ceremony. The groups Davis discussed are neither as secret nor as powerful as he suggested. They also vary tremendously by region in structure and purpose. Many of these groupings are remnants of reciprocal work groups.[114]

I could conduct an unwary non-English-speaking visitor on a highly structured and tightly guided tour around my city, Gainesville, Florida, the home of the University of Florida, to the fraternities at the university with their secret handshakes and rites and to the Masonic Lodges and other allegedly secret societies, and the visitor could well conclude that these organizations exercise some strange power in Gainesville. My visitor's story would not, however, appear in the popular news magazines in this country, though Davis's story appeared in *Time*[115] and *Newsweek*.[116]

It is fitting that Davis's books, especially the popular *Serpent and the Rainbow*, should be so fictionalized; in an insightful review of the fiction produced about Haitians by Americans, J. Michael Dash demonstrated that "what beckons or revolts Americans is Haiti's impenetrable mystery, its irredeemable strangeness, its unpredictable 'Otherness.'"[117] As Davis himself states, he was, in fact, actively looking for something "ancient and tribal."[118] He produced a variation on the notion of terrified peasants ruled by their own uncontrollable superstitions, a folk model found in such turn of the century publications as the *National Geographic*.[119] Indeed, his folk notion was a common component of the initial European view of ancient and tribal Africa, as I will demonstrate in chapter 2.

2 | A cooperative labor squad turning the soil in order to plant sweet potatoes.

Origins of the Biases

Despite the isolation and ill will of the surrounding white world, Haitians have continued to maintain their independence and an amazing amount of international fiscal responsibility. Haitians themselves thought of their country as a center for freedom in a world of oppression, and throughout the nineteenth and twentieth centuries they progressively supported many of the independence movements in South America and elsewhere in the world. Indeed, some white commentators could not help but be impressed by the extraordinary accomplishments of the Haitians, and a few accounts of Haiti have been laudatory.

Unfortunately, the majority of accounts have not, and contain deep biases against Haitians. Most biases of North Americans against Haitians come from the long-standing racial prejudices of Europeans, particularly the English. While most of continental Europe had traded in white slaves for centuries, almost all of these slaves were captives from various battles and territorial expansions, and notions of inferiority were not extended toward these slaves to the same extent as blacks. By the time England became involved in the slave trade, however, most of the slaves were black Africans, and slavery itself required some justification other than war. The rationalizations centered on the supposed mental inferiority of blacks and their alleged suffering under the savagery of their own leaders in the interior of a diseased and untamed Africa.

The folk models of Africa were probably first reinforced among the English by popular travel accounts in the sixteenth century. These accounts were very inaccurate in their descriptions of black peoples. Not only were blacks inferior in every way except perhaps brute strength, but also the writings posited that whites had a mission to save blacks from their uncivilized selves. The slave uprising in the

French colony of Saint Domingue (now Haiti) and the subsequent independence of Haiti in 1804 made it clear to many English writers that white Europeans must be portrayed as the saviors of black Africans. Most accounts of the Haitian Revolution, therefore, emphasized the brutality and treachery of the ex-slaves and the subsequent failure of Haiti to become a materially rich nation.

Even into the twentieth century, travelogues have continued to be as insulting to Haitians as those in previous centuries had been to Africans. Most of the accounts of Haiti up to the second quarter of the twentieth century were, indeed, based on impressionistic travel journals, missionaries' reports, biased accounts of the old French colonial planters, and various other unsystematic historical records.

In fact, nineteenth century anthropology itself was often a second-hand, armchair affair based on these biased sources. Anthropologists have not always gathered their data through firsthand participant-observation in the field. Modern fieldwork may be dated from the work of Franz Boas and Bronislaw Malinowski.[1] After the introduction of professional fieldwork, commentators should have had little excuse for paying any attention to irresponsible reports about Haiti and should have been able to apply some standards by which to judge the reporting. Folk models die slowly, however, and twisted readings of the political, religious, and economic scene in Haiti continue to this day.

From Darkest Africa

Slavery in earlier times in continental Europe was not connected with black skin.[2] In tenth century Europe, white slaves were traded from Slavia all the way across Europe to Iberia. Indeed, the word *slave* itself was first applied to captives of Slavic origin in southeastern Europe. In the thirteenth century, Italians brought slaves from their Black Sea colonies. England was not involved in this slave trade of white peoples, and the English traffic in blacks did not start until the fifteenth century.

Although images of light and darkness as analogous with good and evil were frequently found throughout Europe in Christian and even pre-Christian cultures, most North Americans seemed to have received their basic racial prejudices from England. The English had already attached certain negative values to the color black apparently before they actually saw any black people. In the folk models of southern Europeans, blackness did not carry such strong connotations. For the English, however, blackness "was an emotionally partisan color, the handmaid and symbol of baseness and evil, a sign of danger and repulsion."[3]

After already having developed a prejudice about the color black, the English transferred the prejudice to black people even before the institution of slavery forever stamped "inferior" on the skins of blacks. In fact, the English discovery of black Africans happened during a time when the English folk model of beauty consisted of pasty white skin and rosy cheeks. The rather sudden appearance of black Africans in England probably came about in the mid-fifteen hundreds,[4] and although the English were struck by the color, it was only in the eighteenth century, when slavery required some justification, that white writers thoroughly emphasized the alleged savagery of Africa.

The notion of a connection between black and evil and African savagery grew throughout the sixteenth and seventeenth centuries.[5] Then as now, popular books, especially travelogues, were among the least trustworthy representations of truth and the chief purveyors of ethnocentric explorations of the unknown, and "printers hoped to generate quick profits from sensational world-wide discoveries."[6] And to the English, one of the most arresting characteristics of the newly discovered peoples of Africa was color. A study of sixteenth century travel books pointed out, "One common motif in the travel literature of the sixteenth century is an interest in and recording of color differences among non-whites."[7]

In a review of travelers' notes from the European age of discovery, two scholars wrote, "Most accounts of primitive peoples were tinged with ethnocentrism, but nowhere was the assumption of superiority clearer and the critical observations harsher than in the African accounts."[8] *The Universal Modern History* of 1760 characterized Africans as

> proud, lazy, treacherous, thievish, hot, and addicted to all kinds of lusts, and most ready to promote them in others, as pimps, panders, incestuous, brutish, and savage, cruel and revengeful, devourers of human flesh, and quaffers of human blood, inconstant, base, treacherous, and cowardly; fond of, and addicted to, all sorts of superstition and witchcraft.[9]

By the late seventeen hundreds, Europeans "believed that African skin color, hair texture, and facial features were associated in some way with the African way of life (in Africa) and the status of slavery (in the Americas), according to an investigation of the historical British image of Africa.[10] With the independence of Haiti in 1804, it became increasingly important to depict white Europeans as the saviors of black Africans.

Europeans remained, however, relatively ignorant of Africa. For the most part, contact was limited to the west coast and a few navigable rivers. The European image of "darkest Africa" comes both from the color of its people and the fact that little was known about the interior until late in the eighteenth century. Although some specialized accounts of Africa did exist even in the early seventeen hundreds, the public had much easier access to popular accounts, such as William Snelgrave's *A New Account of Some Parts of Guinea and the Slave-Trade*, which focused on human sacrifice, cannibalism, and the sensuality of black women.[11] The alleged cannibalism of Dahomeans was emphasized again in Archibald Dalzel's popular 1793 *History of Dahomey: An Island Kingdom of Africa*. These and similar reports on Africa had the purpose of justifying slavery, claiming that it had already existed in Africa, that people in the interior of Africa lived under horrible conditions, and that the transport of Africans to the Caribbean saved lives.

On the island of Hispaniola, it was the Spaniards who first began importing slaves. Slavery in North America has long had close ties with this Caribbean island. Some authorities believe that the first blacks to reach the United States arrived as part of a Spanish expedition in 1526 from the port of La Plata on the northern coast of Hispaniola and landed at Cape Fear, North Carolina.[12] The Treaty of Ryswick in 1697, however, required Spain to cede the western half of Hispaniola to France, which then established one of history's cruelest slave states under the name Saint Domingue.

In a brazen 1790s document, the French planters of Saint Domingue attempted to justify their cruel sugarcane plantations by claiming, "The situation of the negroes, in Africa, without property, without political or civil existence, continually a prey to the weak capricious fury of tyrants, who divide among them that vast uncivilized country, is changed in our colonies for a condition of comfort and enjoyment."[13] As though slaves enjoyed anything resembling freedom, the document went on to say that "well-informed men are not to be persuaded that the negroes in Africa have the enjoyment of freedom."[14]

Thereafter, from the antiabolitionist propaganda to the postslavery antiblack racism of travelers and politicians, the writings about black peoples were infused with allusions to Africa and its barbaric savagery. Apologists for slavery in the American South remarked about "the stifling grasp of African barbarism."[15] After the American Civil War, when slavery was no longer an option for suppressing black peoples, the British consul in Haiti warned, "In spite of all the civilising elements around them, there is a distinct tendency to sink into the state of an African tribe."[16] Later, American observers of the Haitian scene echoed this refrain, claiming, "Without the white man, the blacks have been gradually sinking to their original savagery of the African jungle."[17] A popular travel guide to the West Indies and Bermuda published just after the turn of this century prattled about "African savagery" in Haiti[18] inherited from "their barbarous ancestors in Africa."[19]

A 1920 article on Haiti in the widely respected *National Geographic* claimed, "Here, in the elemental wildernesses, the natives rapidly forgot their thin veneer of Christian civilization and reverted to utter, unthinking animalism, swayed only by fear of local bandit chiefs and the black magic of voodoo witch doctors."[20] The anonymous author cited for authority a previous article in the *National Geographic*[21] that had made the same claims.

Some travelogues and publishers in the twentieth century continued to be as irresponsible as those in previous centuries. In 1920 Harry Franck emphasized the negative aspects of Africa in his travel books about Haiti and the Caribbean by observing "the close relationship of the Haitians to their savage brethren in Central Africa"[22] from which the Haitians had apparently received "the primitive instincts of the African."[23] Franck was openly amused at the poverty of the Haitian people, stating that "Bare feet were as general as African features"[24] and "that lack of the sense of personal dignity characteristic of the African came to their rescue in the abjectness of their condition."[25]

Another observer wrote about a Voodoo dancer "in [whose] expression shone the ancient fires of Africa."[26] Edward Brathwaite accurately summed up much of the white world's view of Haiti in his 1970 introduction to Herskovits's ethnography of life in a Haitian valley:

> Haiti for most of the world... still is a mysterious distant hump of green somewhere in the Atlantic; an island of savage incompetent Blacks who had rebelled against Napoleon during the French Revolution and had continued doing it ever since; who had produced one leader, Christophe—or was it Toussaint—whom Wordsworth had written a romantic sonnet about; and after that nothing; or, if not nothing, then darkness; rumor and darkness. The darkness of the night of ignorance, of voodoo drums and human sacrifice, of zombies, Congo gutturals.... It was all of a piece, really, with what the Establishment thought of Africa and Africans in the New World; dumb, drumming, demoralized and up to no good.[27]

An analytic model of Haiti would, in contrast to these denigrating opinions, concentrate on the genius of deracinated peoples in maintaining enough morale to create a new culture from African and European elements. This genius is even more striking when the peoples are involuntarily removed from their original cultures and placed under some of the most severe restrictions and the most brutal conditions known in human history.

To Blackest Haiti

In the Caribbean, the folk models that whites had of blacks were as distorted as those in Europe, and the brutal demands of the slave system indurated the behavior of the misplaced Europeans toward the extirpated Africans. Reflecting the common prejudices of the white residents of the Caribbean in the last quarter of the eighteenth century, the widely read Edward Long described blacks in Haiti as "brutish, ignorant, idle, crafty, treacherous, bloody, thievish, mistrustful, and superstitious."[28] Just before the opening of the nineteenth century a widely read writer complained, "The Africans transplanted to Saint-Domingue remain in general indolent and idle, quarrelsome and talkative and liars, and are addicted to stealing."[29]

This same observer also recorded that "two-thirds [of the blacks in Haiti]. . . come from Africa."[30] Indeed, at least two-thirds of the slaves on the island had been born in Africa when revolution began breaking out as early as 1789. With a slave population of five hundred thousand, a freedman population of twenty-eight thousand, and a white population of only forty thousand, the colony of Saint Domingue was ripe for a slave revolt and the departure of the French.

The combination of the large numbers of recently arrived slaves, the maintenance of African culture, and the purposeful extermination of most whites and many mulattoes during the Revolution and immediately thereafter gave the particularly African and black form to the nation of Haiti that has always startled white visitors. Even before independence, a visitor arriving in the soon-to-collapse capital of the colony from elsewhere in the Caribbean exclaimed, "How it differs from the places one has left! You see four or five black faces, or at least shadowy ones, for each white one."[31] Over a century later a writer of books on the Caribbean complained about Haiti that "ragged blacks swarm everywhere,"[32] just as a journalist a few years earlier had grumbled, "There are Negroes everywhere, in rags, moving slothfully."[33]

The surprise of whites over the blackness of the people of Haiti has been a constant theme in travelogues, such as one that claimed Haiti's population was "so black that the darkest resident of Chicago's black belt would have been suspected there of being a white man."[34] The book is filled from beginning to end with references to "naked black boys"[35] and "fuzzy black heads."[36] Similar comments on the hair are found in many other travelogues, such as in a description of a female as she "tossed her crinkly head."[37] Another traveler, who may have been confusing Haiti with the Hollywood movies of the 1920s and 1930s, found that "all around us was a mass of black, woolly heads, white rolling eyes, and ivory teeth."[38] In an adventure story set in Haiti, the author commented on "the angelic faces of their children, black as shadows."[39] And a journalistic account of current political events in Haiti has commented, "Above all, it is the blackness of the population . . . that evokes another continent."[40]

Some of these heavy-handed writers of travelogues had to reach into rather ludicrous corners of their imagination for the appropriate metaphors for blackness, such as the one who saw the Haitian people as "blacker than the shades of a rainy-season midnight."[41] The travel guides are written more prosaically, referring simply to "savage blacks"[42] or complaining simply that "black faces are everywhere."[43] Travelers are continually assured and warned, "This fact [that the republic is black] will be strongly impressed upon the stranger at first sight of any of its ports, with their wharves swarming with black and coloured people."[44]

Journalists rarely fail to note the blackness of the population, whether they are commenting on the common people—"These stevedores are naked to the waist, and their black bodies glisten"[45]—

or about the ruling elite—"François Duvalier is a small, black-skinned man."[46] The *National Geographic* has referred to Haitian peasants as "unthinking black animals in the interior."[47]

A wide variety of other writers have used blackness as the identifying characteristic of Haiti. Missionaries have described the younger population of Haiti as consisting of "kinky-headed, tarry-black youngsters."[48] Perhaps thinking that he was making a compliment, Arthur Cox, an Episcopal bishop, described one of the presidents of Haiti in these terms: "His white hair is only a little crisped, and, though he is quite black, his countenance is most intelligent, his features regular."[49]

In a novel, Russell Banks has his hero, a white American, express astonishment at how black Haitians are.[50] In this novel the blackness of Haitians is associated by whites with a mystery unfathomable for whites in its evil darkness. For example, the hero thinks,

> This is crazy, they don't know anything about me that isn't obvious to anyone willing to take a quick look at me. He insists to himself that he's making it all up. It's only because they're so black, so African-looking, and because they don't speak English and he doesn't speak Creole, that he's attributing awesome and mysterious powers to them.[51]

Even contemporary social scientists seem occasionally awed by Haiti's blackness. Several that I have talked with at universities in Florida—all white people of good intentions—have expressed in confidence to me how ill at ease they felt in Haiti and how they always thought something else was going on behind the surface greetings and conversations. One white university administrator who makes frequent professional trips to Haiti confessed to me that he felt uncomfortable there precisely because everyone was black. Another thoughtful professor speculated that his own discomfort stemmed from the hundreds of miles of Hollywood film he had seen in his youth depicting Africans as sorcerers and witch doctors.

Less sophisticated travelers to Haiti have written explicitly about the reversion of their thoughts to Africa, as, for example, when a well-known writer of travelogues about the Caribbean fantasized upon reaching Haiti that he "might have been in the heart of the Congo."[52] Others have made it a theme of their works to compare Haiti with Africa and to claim that Haitians "have reverted to almost pristine African savagery"[53] or that "the manners [of Haitians] are as depraved, brutal, and savage as in Dahomey."[54]

But it is the color black that remains impressed upon the minds of these whites. In the words of a widely read travelogue, it is the impression of a somehow topsy-turvy, upside-down, inside-out, and incomprehensible world of "dazzling white tropical suits, dark heads and hands [that] resemble a photographic negative."[55] This negative to the white world, this proliferation of black, is the negation of what the white world most fervently wants to believe in, that is, the good will of whites in an essentially black world. Unfortunately, the parochial minds of the whites can only perceive that Haiti "certainly *is* black in morals, instincts, conditions, and the colour of its people."[56] The myth of blackness combines with the blindness of racism in the statement that "above and over all, however, is the fact that Haiti is 'black,' that there is no guiding hand of the Caucasian to lead the Haitians on their way; no firm, benign power to rule and protect them; no superior intellect to advise or direct."[57]

The move from darkest Africa to blackest Haiti involved both the uprooting and enslavement of people and the transformation of a folk model applied to blacks in Africa to one applied to blacks in the Caribbean. These European writers and observers in the Caribbean brought with them their negative baggage derived from the associations of black with Africa and slavery and assumed that, because Haitians were black, they were less than human. The folk model of the whites, in fact, prevented most of them from even seeing the humanness of Haitians—only their blackness.

The Slave Uprising

In 1789 the black slaves of the French colony of Saint Domingue began their five-year struggle for freedom. In August 1791, two years after the French Revolution—and fed, in part, by the rhetoric of that revolution—the slaves in Saint Domingue managed a major uprising that could not be contained. In that year, Saint Domingue was easily the richest colony of the French empire—its wealth built upon the labor of about five hundred thousand blacks.

By 1796 white supremacy was at an end and black rule was established under the leadership of Toussaint Louverture, an ex-slave, within the framework of the French Republic. In 1802 Napoleon tried to retake the colony and reenslave the blacks, but the blacks were led by some people with considerable charisma and amazing military skills. By 1803 the Haitians had defeated the best troops of Napoleon, who were, for most of the war, under the command of Napoleon's brother-in-law, General Leclerc. On January 1, 1804, Dessalines proclaimed the independence of Haiti, an event that has to be understood within the context of economics and the folk models of racial superiority and inferiority.

Since the Haitian Revolution, the United States has had its own Civil War, there have been two world wars, the United States has suffered a stalemate in the Korean War, a defeat in the Vietnam War, and won a war with Iraq. Many Americans have lost sight of the great significance of the Haitian Revolution. It has, nevertheless, been often recounted, recently by Thomas Ott, who has put his finger on precisely the importance of the event in saying, "The Haitian Revolution had the distinction of proving that the Negro was, after all, a man."[58]

Not only did the black slaves defeat the armies of Napoleon, but they also maintained their independence and governed themselves despite their isolation from the surrounding white world. An early attempt by a Haitian to counter the bad press pleaded,

> To fully appreciate the origin of the unceasing and persistent calumnies of which Haiti has been made the target, one must go back to the very first days of her existence and call to mind the circumstances under which she started life as an independent country.[59]

Much of the anger directed toward Haiti was a reaction to the Haitians' revolution, and can be described as a fear of black independence and self-determination elsewhere. The white world's folk model of the Haitian Revolution characterized the victory of Haitians over their white slave owners as something odious, complaining, for example, about "the foul butchery of the entire white population by the frenzied negroes."[60] This insult is compounded by the constant references to one of the national heros of Haiti, Jean Jacques Dessalines, a military genius who led the defeat of Napoleon's armies, as a "monster."[61]

In addition to Dessalines, at least two other Haitians captured the imagination of historians and others. Some writers referred to the three black leaders of the Haitian struggle for freedom as a triumvirate.[62] One doctoral dissertation consisted of three original plays about Toussaint, Dessalines, and Henri Christophe.[63] Some writers included the mulatto leader Alexandre Pétion,[64] and others, especially those more sympathetic to the French, made Pétion a major hero.[65] Several books have been written about the flamboyant Christophe, who declared himself king of Haiti and caused a split between the north and south just after independence.[66] No Haitian leader, however, has received the attention lavished on Toussaint.

Despite the adverse folk model that whites had of blacks, many commentators could not help but be captivated by the extraordinary achievements of these ex-slaves. Although most of the writings on Toussaint are laudatory, some of the early works of French authors were adverse, treating Toussaint as a criminal and tyrant.[67] Nevertheless, after the martyrdom of Toussaint in a French dungeon and the successful completion of the Haitian struggle for independence, books on Toussaint became almost a separate publishing industry. *Toussaint L'Ouverture* was first published in 1863 and contained an English translation of Toussaint's autobiography.[68] *Black Liberator* is the English abbreviated version of the French literary account of the life of Toussaint by the Haitian writer Stéphen Alexis.[69]

Books about Toussaint were sometimes written by missionaries, such as an early American black missionary that referred to him as a soldier, statesman, and martyr.[70] Books were written about him using the label attributed to Napoleon, such as the one titled *This Gilded African*.[71] Others referred to him as *The Black Napoleon*.[72] Some books on Toussaint were large,[73] and some were small.[74] There were, of course, the inevitable collections of writings by and about Toussaint.[75] Toussaint figured prominently in both Marxist[76] and non-Marxist[77] interpretations of the Haitian Revolution. The juvenile literature based on the life of Toussaint had a definite viewpoint, as is illustrated by the titles of two books, *Black Patriot and Martyr*[78] and *The Black Liberator*.[79]

William Wordsworth best romanticized Toussaint's martyrdom in the last lines of his poem "To Toussaint L'ouverture."[80]

Though fallen thyself, never to rise again,
Live, and take comfort. Thou hast left behind
Powers that will work for thee; air, earth, and skies;
There's not a breathing of the common wind
That will forget thee; thou hast great allies;
Thy friends are exultations, agonies,
And love, and man's unconquerable mind.

In contrast to Toussaint, no full and authoritative biography of Dessalines yet exists, probably related to the fact that Dessalines is forever associated with the slaughter of whites. The white world recoiled with horror at the news of blacks killing whites. The slave-owning planters capitalized on this revulsion, and in their report to the French government at the beginning of the Revolution, these white planters referred to their ex-slaves as "cannibals"[81] and "barbarians,"[82] and greatly emphasized the rape of white women.[83]

White refugees from Haiti fled to North America, and, beginning in 1793, newspapers first reported plots of black slaves against whites in the United States.[84] "The popular press regaled its readers with tales of horrible atrocities [in Haiti]."[85] Racist accounts of the Haitian Revolution concentrated on "the tragedy of the annihilation of the white population."[86]

Contemporary accounts sympathetic to the Haitian Revolution were quite rare.[87] Within a few years of the establishment of the independence of the Haitian people, however, James Barskett chronicled the horror for blacks in the last months of the French in Haiti, stating that "Almost all the male negroes and mulattoes, of whom the French could obtain possession were coolly murdered, and often with circumstances of shocking barbarity."[88] He goes on to list the numbingly large numbers of brutal beatings, tortures, drownings, the use of dogs, and so forth.[89]

Despite the attempt of some of the French-language schools to dilute its importance, most Haitians are quite aware of the great significance of their revolution. American education either dilutes or ignores the influence of Haiti on North American history, which includes significant contributions to the independence of the United States, such as the participation of about nine hundred Haitians in the Battle of Savannah in 1779.[90] In addition, with the defeat of the French armies in Haiti in 1803—and the French resumption of war with England—Napoleon's ambition to create an empire in the New World ended. A few months after the collapse of plans for the reenslavement of Saint Domingue, France sold the Louisiana territories to the United States, which laid the basis for the United States to become a world power.

The implications of Haitian independence, however, have far greater importance than its contributions to American history. The declaration of independence at Gonaives on January 1, 1804, "was declared and maintained by men who saw Haiti as a symbol of redemption for the whole African Race."[91] Haiti became the world symbol of anticolonialism and racial equality, and Haitian writers have never tired of reminding the white world that Haiti defeated the armies of Napoleon.

As two contemporary scholars of the Caribbean have pointed out,

The Haitian elites viewed their country as a beacon of freedom for the colonized of the world and as a black republic carrying the traditions of France into the New World. Thus, they supported the Greek independence movement. They supported Simón Bolívar who took refuge in Haiti, and they expressed their enthusiasm in 1898 for the freedom movement in Cuba while expressing their fears of U.S. intervention which might abort it. Dantès Bellegarde and Nemours Auguste denounced white South Africa and Fascist Italy in the League of Nations.[92]

Indeed, in the first constitution of Haiti, Haitian citizens of whatever color—including Germans and Poles given Haitian nationality—were officially labeled "black." The Creole word *blan* (from the French word for "white") still is used to refer to a foreigner—of whatever color. A black from the United States, for example, would be a *nwa blan,* a "black white" or, more accurately, a black foreigner. In other words, Haitians use color distinctions but not race distinctions. The traditional Haitian saying is that a rich black-colored person is a mulatto and a poor mulatto is black. Haitians have a pride in all things *culturally* black but not necessarily in all things *colored* black.

> Haitians have continued to take a special interest in the affairs of the Black race throughout the world; as President Geffrard had ordered a special requiem mass at the death of John Brown in 1859, so [François] Duvalier declared several days of national mourning after the assassination of Martin Luther King more than a hundred years later.[93]

And two major thoroughfares in Port-au-Prince are named after John Brown and Martin Luther King, Jr.

This greater significance of Haiti is also recognized in the faded memories of the Revolution that may be found in the folk models of Haitian history. The peasants in the regions surrounding Cap-Haitien on the north coast told many tales to me about the battles for independence and especially about the role of the maroon communities.

Some of the most ferocious fighting in the battles for independence took place around Cap-Haitien. At that time Cap-Haitien was known as Cap Français, and it was the capital of the French colony. Among the many atrocities that the French committed in this lovely city, Ott recounted: "The French carried 6000 blacks out to ships in the harbor, bayoneted them, and kicked their bodies into the sea. Around the hull of one ship alone bobbed 240 human buoys."[94]

In Port-au-Prince, a city later to become the capital of Haiti, the notorious French general Donatien Rochambeau carried out a "program with an almost diabolical ingenuity. There he employed a ship named *The Stifler*, its hold converted into a gas chamber through the use of noxious fumes."[95] Few wars have been as destructive as was the one in Haiti. Ott estimated, "The population fell from about 500,000 people to about 250,000, or less"[96] and said that for the French, the Haitian War "was something of an eighteenth-century Vietnam."[97]

The peasants spoke to me about more than the bloodiness, however. Their memory of the events has not been continually renewed by studying the written record; they are, for the most part, illiterate. However, these unlettered, rural-dwelling farmers are well aware that their ancestors defeated the best that white Europe sent against them. And, in doing so, they made Haiti the stage for the ensuing arguments about the effect of freeing slaves and the capacity of blacks for self-government.

It is well known that "the Haitian phenomenon strongly influenced England's pioneers of the abolitionist movement."[98] Although the English abolitionists were cheered by the liberation of Haitians from slavery, their attitude toward the violent military force employed by the slaves against legitimate white government was somewhat ambivalent. "No major figure appears to have openly approved of violent self-liberation by the blacks."[99] "In the late 1790s the entire antislavery movement was clearly being debilitated by the news from St. Domingo."[100]

After the independence of Haiti became an incontrovertible fact, the arguments in the white world shifted to the capacities of blacks for self-government. "Most defenders of slavery depicted in great detail the former prosperity of the French system in St. Domingue, contrasting the 'happy past' with the poverty, ignorance, and disorder of tyrannical black and mulatto rulers in free Haiti."[101] Several years after Haitian independence James Franklin, an influential opponent of emancipation, wrote, "Hayti affords us a strong instance of what may be expected from the emancipation of slaves before they have been previously prepared to receive this boon by moral and religious instruction."[102] At the same time, W. W. Harvey, an advocate of emancipation and a sympathetic English adviser to the ruler of northern Haiti, Henri Christophe, wrote that the blacks showed admirable abilities to govern themselves.[103]

Before the American Civil War, advocates of slavery wrote about the alleged misgovernment in Haiti by blacks (but not by mulattoes), both as a reason for continued enslavement of American blacks and for shipping the free American blacks to Haiti. These advocates proclaimed, for example, that

> The African race here [in the United States] must remain a servant to the white man, as a necessary condition of the preservation of our civilization and liberties, or be removed altogether beyond the limits of the United States.[104]

The opposite lesson was drawn by the American abolitionists who wrote, for example,

> There is only one country in the Western World...where the insolent question, so often asked of us, "What would become of the Negro if Slavery were abolished?" is answered by the fact of an independent Nationality of immovable stability, and a Government inspired with the spirit of progress.[105]

The argument continued after the Civil War with M. B. Bird, a Methodist missionary in Haiti for thirty years, writing, "Hayti has at least demonstrated the existence of sound mental material in the African."[106] In contrast, the representative of the British government in Haiti stated,

> As long as [the black] is influenced by contact with the white man, as in the southern portion of the United States, he gets on very well. But place him free from all such influence, as in Hayti, and he shows no signs of improvement; on the contrary, he is gradually retrograding to the African tribal customs.[107]

And, again, an American writer, suggesting a racist rationale for the coming American Occupation of Haiti, wrote, "Haiti...proves that the Negro as a race, when left alone, is incapable of self advancement."[108]

Bird's work represents a subplot to the argument about the competence of blacks, which revolves around the notion of the emigration of American blacks to Haiti. Racists in the United States viewed such emigration as a solution to the perceived problem of freed blacks on American soil. The early Haitian leaders viewed such immigration as their duty to the oppressed peoples of the world.

> One of the first acts of [the newly independent] government in [1804] was to encourage the return of negroes and mulattoes from the United States..., offering to the captains of American vessels the sum of forty dollars for each individual native black or man of colour whom they should convey back to Hayti.[109]

Later Haitian leaders seemed to be more interested in the skills that American blacks might bring with them.

Bird was following a tradition began by James Redpath, a protege of Wendell Phillips, who was a colleague of the famous emancipationist John Brown (who, not incidentally, modeled himself after the great Haitian leader Toussaint). Redpath's book extolling the advantages of Haiti was originally published in 1871 by the Haitian Bureau of Migration as *A Guide to Haiti* for American blacks. Redpath's objective was not limited to helping Haiti but was directly tied to emancipationist aims, as is clear when he wrote, "With the lever of an enlightened immigration to Hayti, the colored men of America could greatly aid in overturning the system of chattel Slavery in the South."[110] He recommended that cotton, sugar, and rice be grown in Haiti with free people to economically exhaust the American South. Redpath's book followed a call in 1859 for immigration to Haiti issued by the Haitian Secretary of State for the Interior for "members of the African race, who groan in the United States."[111]

Some whites in the United States saw this call for immigration to Haiti as a way to get rid of potentially troublesome free blacks. Some blacks saw it as a way to participate in the building of a new black nation. Although records are scarce, it is clear that a few black Americans did migrate to Haiti. The American Civil War and the subsequent westward expansion of the United States, however, soon overshadowed any interest in migration to Haiti.

Nevertheless, throughout the nineteenth century North American blacks viewed Haiti as the center of black resistance, first to slavery and then to discrimination. Certainly the Haitian Revolution had an effect on slaves in the United States. In a well-researched article on the repercussions of the Haitian Revolution, John Baur wrote, "Apparently American Negroes, free and slave, had an astonishingly well-broadcast and accurate knowledge of Haitian affairs."[112] He goes on to list many slave insurrections that were consciously modeled on the Haitian example.[113] These fears were especially evident in Louisiana, where many of the French planters had fled from Haiti with their slaves. In fact,

> at the plantation of the wealthy Julien Poydras at Pointe Coupé, 150 miles from New Orleans, a conspiracy, probably inspired by the Haitian precedent, was hatched in April 1795. It called for the massacre of local whites. The plotters quarreled among themselves, their secret leaked out, and the revolt was quickly smothered.[114]

Fully a century after Haitian independence, an article in the popular *National Geographic* darkly warned, "It is well to consider whether we too may not expect some such acts of savagery [as in voodoo] to break out in our own country if our own colored people are not educated for better things."[115]

Favorable accounts of the Haitian Revolution are difficult to find as more and more groups depended on advancing their own nefarious interests through denigrating the black struggle for freedom and Haiti's subsequent struggle for survival in a hostile white world. Only a few groups with specialized knowledge and objective perspectives handled the reporting of Haiti in anything approaching an even-handed manner—at least before the rise of black consciousness in the United States during the 1960s. One such group was the Foreign Policy Association, whose information service explained in 1929,

> The case of Haiti seems to be the only one in modern history in which a Negro population, previously subjected to a slave system marked by terrorism and brutality, has suddenly been obliged to organize a

government and an economic system of its own. In view of this historical background, it is perhaps remarkable not only that the Haitian peasant should possess the qualities of gentleness, charm and hospitality so frequently attributed to him, but, also, that the Haitian people should have been able to maintain an independent existence for a hundred years.[116]

During that hundred or so years—up to the American Occupation in 1915—Haiti was effectively isolated as a black nation in a white-ruled world by official trade embargoes and the lack of international diplomatic recognition. "The very existence of a free and independent Haiti defied the international system to which it belonged; the country was ostracized and isolated."[117]

The United States, Haiti's most important neighbor, refrained from diplomatic intercourse with Haiti until 1862 when President Lincoln recognized both Haiti and Liberia. Although the merchants of New England wanted to use Haiti as a trade base—and, in fact, did carry on a great deal of illegal trade there—the official policy of the United States toward Haiti bowed to the interest of politicians from the slave states of the South and to the hysteria of French diplomats.

French Foreign Minister Charles Talleyrand wrote to Secretary of State James Madison in July 1805 discouraging the establishment of relations:

> The existence of a Negro people in arms, occupying a country it has soiled by the most criminal acts, is a horrible spectacle for all white nations. . . . There are no reasons...to grant support to these brigands who have declared themselves the enemies of all government.[118]

From the very top layers of the policymakers of North America to the very base of society, then, there prevailed a folk model based on ignorance and self-indulgence. Over the next century and a half after the Haitian Revolution, these parochial notions ruled the commentaries on Haiti.

3 A Haitian farmer and his wife, living near the Pic Macaya region on the southern peninsula.

*D*evelopment of the Biases

Chapter 1 contained several themes of contemporary North American biases. Many people continue to hold to a folk model that denigrates Haitians, imagining, for example, a connection between AIDS and Haitians, or that Haitian religion is filled with real cannibals and zombies. It is noted in chapter 2 that these biases had their origins in the long-standing European prejudice against the color black. Both colonial Haiti and black became inextricably connected to an unknown and mysterious Africa and the institution of slavery for Africans. The successful slave uprising in Haiti focused many outsiders on that little nation in a way clearly out of proportion to its size. Almost all that anyone hears about Haiti is filtered through various attempts throughout recent history to put Haiti back "in its place" as black, backward, dangerous, and savage.

The development of these biases is seen most clearly in several areas that most writers select when they write about Haiti. In this chapter I'll make the connection between writings from the several decades immediately after Haitian independence and modern writings by journalists and others. It will be clear that there is a continuity in thematic biases that spans almost two centuries. These biases are most evident in writings about politics, racism, sexuality, laziness, religion, and language.

For the English-speaking public, the biases against blacks in general and Haitians in particular were originally centered on the great debate on the abolition of slavery and the ability of blacks to govern themselves. Although the abolitionists in America and Britain were adamant in their opposition to slavery, few were as equally enthusiastic in their arguments about blacks being in charge of their own fate, and they preferred to see blacks led by whites[1] or, more particularly, white missionaries.[2] And fewer abolitionists still ever

51

showed any great enthusiasm for blacks expressing their desire for freedom through violence against whites.

These arguments about the self-determination of blacks are explicated through two books on Haiti published just a few years apart. Both of these books came out in the middle of the emancipation argument in Britain. Harvey's *Sketches of Haiti,* published in 1827, presented a fairly optimistic view of the ability of the Haitians to govern themselves from his perspective as an English adviser to Henri Christophe, one of the great generals of the Haitian Revolution. Harvey gave a detailed account of Christophe's rise to power in the north after independence and of his feud with the leader in the south, Pétion.[3] Harvey thought it was clear that the Haitians were advancing toward civilization, and he reacted strongly against the European, ex-colonial criticism leveled at the struggling nation. In particular, he attacked the notion that Haitians had behaved like savages in their fight for freedom and independence. Harvey suggested that they were only reacting against the barbarous effects of the institution of slavery.

Three years later, Charles MacKenzie published his two volumes entitled *Notes on Haiti.*[4] He was the British consul-general in Haiti in 1826 and 1827 after the north and south were reunited. His racist account and his pessimism about the ability of blacks to govern themselves obviously fit the folk model of white Europeans much better than did Harvey's concept of Haitians overcoming the scars of slavery. Unfortunately, most of the subsequent writing on Haiti followed MacKenzie's lead. Another fairly widely read book came out at the same time and supported MacKenzie's views.[5] So, although there were other accounts sympathetic to the Haitians,[6] MacKenzie's book dominated the day and was often referred to with approval by St. John, whose destructively influential book fifty years later was the most popular book in English on Haiti until the writings of Americans in the 1920s.

St. John was intermittently in Haiti from 1863 to 1884 as minister resident and consul-general, and his total time there was about twelve years. His book gave the first blood-curdling account of Voodoo and cannibalism, although St. John admitted in his book that he had never attended a Voodoo ceremony. His account of a famous cannibal trial in Haiti in 1864 became widely read. This account included a reference to "Congo stew," a dish supposedly made out of Congo beans and human flesh and eaten by Haitian cannibals. Many subsequent travelogues and novels about Haiti have made use of his fanciful image of Haitians eating Congo bean stew.

Actually, most of the book chronicles the nineteenth century regimes in Haiti. St. John concluded that blacks were incapable of governing themselves and, of course, came out strongly against the black governments and in support of the mulattoes as the lesser of the two evils.[7]

The year 1910 saw the revised edition of *Where Black Rules White*, one of the more outrageously racist travelogues about Haiti. The author very bluntly stated that blacks cannot rule themselves even though they had the opportunity to build upon a French governmental system.[8] Interestingly, the book mentioned only St. John in its list of literature on Haiti.

One more book rounds out the foundation for the subsequent flow of hysterical and racist travelogues about Haiti. In 1837 an Englishman, Jonathan Brown, published two highly ethnocentric volumes based on his one year in Haiti.[9] Brown's last chapter contains much of the material that readers had come to expect from travelogues about Haiti, such as the characterization of Haitians living in a state of fear, the notion that Creole is not a real language, and that beggars covered the land.

Much of the offensive material on Haiti published in the twentieth century came from North Americans, such as the ones who were part of the American Occupation of Haiti from 1915 to 1934,[10] and others who traveled through Haiti with no other apparent aim than to ridicule the country and its people.[11] Still others took their turn at imitating St. John and playing on the appetite of the lay public for fanciful stories about Voodoo.[12]

Haiti was not without its defenders. Some of the Haitian elite wrote books attempting to set the record straight.[13] Occasionally an American journalist wrote a decent work.[14] And, of course, anthropologists such as Melville Herskovits[15] and Alfred Métraux[16] were trying to tell the real story of Haiti. In addition, the beauty of the land and the people was being shown through various picture books.[17]

Almost all the nineteenth century commentators agreed that the regimes dominated by mulattoes were superior to those dominated by blacks, since many whites believed that mulattoes were not quite as inferior as blacks. This viewpoint has been worked into various modern analyses of the Haitian political scene in some subtle ways, and is an old and important part of the political history of Haiti. The first look at one of the components in the development of the biases will, therefore, focus on black politics.

Black Politics

One of the best known "color" analyses of Haitian politics, positing a peculiar caste interpretation of Haitian society, is the 1941 book by the North American sociologist James Leyburn.[18] Although criticized by some Haitian intellectuals, such as Jean Price-Mars, the book became extremely popular among the Haitian elite—mostly because it reflected their own notions of Haitian history as a struggle between the blacks and the mulattoes. Such an interpretation of history is constantly professed by members of the elite in their conversations with foreign observers and was put into print once again in the 1980s by a Haitian writer whose book is appropriately subtitled *Class and Color Politics.*[19]

The notion of the division of Haiti into a mulatto class and a black class certainly did not begin with Leyburn. Brown, in his 1837 two volume history, interpreted Haitian society as divided into castes.[20] Gustave D'Alaux wrote extensively on a black-mulatto caste system in his 1856 book. And St. John's 1884 chronicle of nineteenth century regimes in Haiti summed up the consensus of the white world by supporting mulatto governments against the black ones.

Another, related view existed among some foreign observers, primarily abolitionists and ersatz nationalists. In his 1853 *Toussaint L'Ouverture*, John Beard blamed the mulattoes for most of Haiti's problems, labeling them colonial sympathizers, thus inverting the perspective most outsiders held.[21]

Like most folk models, the black-mulatto interpretation of history is based on some surface truths. Beard, for example, pointed out that color distinctions were extremely important to Haitians themselves, and he included an appendix with several charts on color types in the Haitian population.[22] Even the one-time president of Haiti, Leslie Manigat, installed in office in February 1988, lectured in the mid-1960s at North American universities in terms of these color distinctions, saying,

> On the one hand, there has been the light-skinned elite, claiming to be ideologically liberal, in reality, politically autocratic, economically conservative, socially sectarian, and culturally pro-European. When in power, this elite has represented the interests of the urban, moneyed oligarchy. Against its traditional hegemony, on the other hand, there has been a coalition led by the dark-skinned elite. Although socially progressive because of the need to maintain solidarity with the middle classes and masses through the common denominator of color, this coalition was also politically autocratic, ideologically authoritarian, economically quasi-traditional, and culturally nationalistic.[23]

In the campaigning for the aborted November 1986 elections, the first free political expression in Haiti in thirty years, the "color issue" was nowhere to be found. Ironically, Manigat was originally a candidate in this election. The absence of the color issue is, in fact, illustrative of the ephemeral value of basing analyses on folk categories. In actuality, almost all families in Haiti can claim members whose skin color ranges from light to dark.

Many have claimed, even recently, that the racial distinctions have been historically important. In particular, the power elite gained an advantage by presenting a picture of Haiti to the white world as a caste society divided into a small, sophisticated, westernized mulatto segment, and a large, dangerous, Africanish black segment. The "mulatto elite" could then request outside help in their efforts to rule the unruly masses.

There are historical facts on which this folk model may be based. The greatest accomplishment of the early Haitian nation was total land reform, and the country's greatest fear was that the French would return and reenslave the population. Land reform divided the land among a largely black peasantry, who have always regarded the government as having little relevance to their lives; these peasants simply wanted to farm their small plots and practice their religion. In striking contrast to the rest of the Caribbean and to Latin America, the largely mulatto elite simultaneously retreated to the cities and, with no land, made their living from taxing peasant markets and the nation's foreign trade. In other words, the elite made their living through their control of the government apparatus, a situation that one contemporary Haitian scholar has referred to as "state fetishism."[24]

The elite also practiced Roman Catholicism, the religion of the slave owners. Fear of a potential return by the French caused the bulk of the population to retreat into the mountainous interior of the country inside a ring of forts. The nation became literally divided, then, into a very small, European-oriented, Roman Catholic, mulatto elite located in several regional urban centers set against a rural, scattered, black farming population that worshipped in the ancient African manner.

It is the Africanness of the Haitian population that is so striking to most foreigners. At the time of the Haitian Revolution, fully two-thirds of the slaves had been born in Africa. By the end of the revolution, virtually all the whites had been eliminated, and there were several massacres of mulattoes. After the revolution, Haiti was isolated by the white world. The United States blocked Haiti's invitation to the famous Western Hemisphere Panama Conference of 1825 and refused to recognize Haitian independence until 1862. This isolation was imposed on Haiti by a frightened white world, and Haiti became a test case, first, for those arguing about emancipation and, then, after end of slavery, for those arguing about the capacity of blacks for self-government. Great Britain was one of the few nations that had diplomatic relations with Haiti, and it is from the writings of the English racists and antiabolitionists that Haiti began to get its widespread bad press.[25]

These earlier writings focused on two things. One was "the foul butchery of the entire white population by the frenzied negroes."[26] The other was the savagery of Voodoo, especially the alleged ritual cannibalism. Actually, Haiti is the only case in modern history in which a slave population was suddenly faced with organizing a government and an economic system of its own. It is a remarkable tribute to the genius of the Haitian people that they were able to maintain an independent existence at all—much less expect them to be able to provide a decent standard of living to the population at large. The press on Haiti, however, continued—and continues—to depict in great detail the former prosperity of the French system in Saint Domingue and to contrast it with the poverty, ignorance, and disorder of tyrannical rulers in independent Haiti. This depiction conveniently overlooks the fact that the wealth of colonial Saint Domingue was enjoyed by only a small percentage of the population—and, in fact, a small percentage of the Haitian population still enjoys considerable wealth today.

More recent writers make little distinction between blacks and mulattoes. When the distinction is made, the blacks are usually depicted as stupid, brutish, deracinated Africans addicted to incomprehensible cults, while the mulattoes are characterized as pretentious buffoons hopelessly attempting, on the one hand, to imitate their white superiors, and on the other, tending toward a macabre savagery more in tune with their brothers in the interior.

As if the historical folk model of Haiti did not contain enough imaginative misinformation, Haiti itself in the latter half of the twentieth century supplied a figure that the western press could use as a caricature of the Third World in general and Haiti in particular. François Duvalier, sometimes known as Papa Doc, became an integral part of the bad press of Haiti, and his regime forever clouded the notions of the "color" model of Haitian politics.[27]

Duvalier's father was a minor jurist, teacher, and journalist, and his mother was a baker. He had an urban background and went to school in Port-au-Prince. One of his teachers was Dumarsais Estimé, later to be president of Haiti, a champion of the underprivileged black majority and a hero for Duvalier. Another of his teachers was Price-Mars, whose writings romanticized Voodoo and the Haitian peasantry.

Duvalier went on to medical school in Haiti. In 1939 he married a nurse, and they had four children. Their only son, Jean-Claude, would succeed his father as president.

In the 1940s Duvalier took courses in public health at the University of Michigan and returned to Haiti as a major participant in the highly successful campaign against malaria and yaws. He practiced primarily in the village of Gressier, just a little south of Port-au-Prince. Duvalier would later claim that his knowledge of rural Haiti came largely from his work there.

Duvalier was, however, never simply a country doctor; he was somewhat of a black-power nationalist. Early in his career Duvalier contributed patriotic articles to newspapers that opposed the American occupation of Haiti.

In 1938 Duvalier was involved in the founding of a journal called *Les Griots*, from an African term meaning storytellers. The journal promoted Haiti's African identity, and Duvalier developed the long-standing color model of politics that all the progressive heroes of Haiti were black (especially Toussaint, Dessalines, and soon-to-be president Estimé) and the mulattoes had always held back the nation.

In January 1946 the army assumed power after a general strike, and in August Duvalier's former teacher Estimé was elected president. Among many other innovations the Estimé government introduced a graduated income tax, rural cooperatives and credit unions, and model farms. The government also expanded educational and social opportunities for the underprivileged, relaxing, in effect, the somewhat rigid class structure and refuting the imitative French culture of the elite. Astute observers of the Haitian scene labeled the Estimé government as "the Social Revolution of 1946 [and characterized it as] the culmination of the nationalist movement led by Haitian intellectuals during the American occupation."[28]

Estimé organized the 1949 Port-au-Prince Bicentennial to emphasize the African content of Haitian society, and the Estimé four-year rule saw the emergence of a politically powerful urban middle class that had little concern with the traditionally color-oriented folk model of an elite that thought of itself as mulatto. This urban middle class also did not think of itself as particularly oriented toward the peasant masses.

Estimé planned to amend the constitution to stay in office longer. That plan, combined with the general hostility of the traditional elite to his policies, led to the intervention of the army, and in May 1950 Estimé was ousted. In December, Paul Eugène Magloire, a former colonel in the army, was elected as president in what observers conceived of as a typical Haitian arrangement, that is, a black army officer representing the interests of the mulatto elite.

Magloire did enjoy the support of the upper classes, as well as of the United States. He even addressed a joint session of the American Congress and participated in a ticker-tape parade in New York City in January 1955. The growing classes of black urban merchants, along with various sectors of underprivileged Haitian society, had, however, tasted political power that they were not about to abandon. In the wake of widespread strikes and demonstrations, Magloire fled into exile, and the army was once again in the position of being a caretaker government. Several provisional governments rose and fell, and in September 1957 Duvalier emerged as the proclaimed heir to the Estimé social revolution to win the presidency with a decisive margin in an election closely supervised by the army.

Duvalier had been a minister in the Estimé government, and while a prominent member of the opposition to the Magloire government, he had cultivated ties with the army, the black middle class, and the rural poor. Despite some minor irregularities, the election of Duvalier featured universal adult suffrage and was truly a democratic event. Incidentally, the North American media consistently and erroneously refers to the election of Jean-Bertrand Aristide in December 1990 as the first free election in Haiti.

On October 22, Duvalier was inaugurated as president. He was regarded as a tool of the army by some and as a lackey of the American embassy by others. Duvalier, instead, proved to be extraordinarily astute politically, gaining the trust of the indigenous clergy, and bringing into his circle of advisers communists, North Americans, Haitian exiles, and others who represented various segments of Haitian society. To keep the army in control, he reduced much of its funding and created an alternative volunteer militia loyal only to him, the organization that came to be known as the notorious tonton-makout, named after a character in Haitian folklore who stalks bad children and carries them off in his basket.

The first few years of Duvalier's rule were marked by several attempted coups and invasions by Haitian exiles (see the Chronology). Duvalier soon became excessively concerned with the security of his administration and with his own safety. The result was a heightened campaign of oppression against opponents, real and perceived, and increased isolation from the international community. In April 1963 an attempt was made on the life of two of his children, Simone and Jean-Claude. Over the next year, Duvalier faced internal dissent that was growing into guerrilla warfare with several bombings and shootings in and around Port-au-Prince. Haitian exiles continued to mount invasions from abroad, particularly from across the border in the Dominican Republic. Duvalier's reprisals were swift, vicious, and widespread.

In June 1964 Duvalier staged a referendum in which he was approved as "President-for-Life." He remained in power until his natural death in 1971. He also provided the western press with an explanation for all of Haiti's problems[29] that was simpler than trying to explain the deep-seated ecological and sociopolitical nature of Haiti's difficulties. Even the novel by Greene was praised by some scholars, who claimed that it "captured the mindless terror and absurdity of the François Duvalier regime."[30] Some otherwise excellent scholarly accounts of Haiti did, indeed, engage in rather uncritical Duvalier-bashing, stating, for example,

Dr. Duvalier seems among the most bizarre and ruthless presidents of a country known for its erratic leaders. Conspiratorial, racist, paranoiac and reportedly drawn to the dark side of Voodoo, Duvalier was a master of political cunning and manipulation.[31]

There is no denying that Duvalier engaged in terrorist activities and that his tonton-makout was primarily an organization of extortionists. The Duvalier regime was, however, not without policy and not without support from elements in Haitian society other than gangsters. Duvalier did not stay in power only through the use of terror as some investigators have suggested.[32] An analytic model of Haitian politics must come to grips with the reality of these politics.

An article by the British historian David Nicholls provides a good antidote to those claims that a monopoly on terror maintained the Duvalier regimes.[33] Most writers trying to understand the Duvalier dynasty's staying power seem puzzled that the government excited any loyalty at all since it provided so few services to the general public. These writers overlook the fact that the masses historically expected little from the government, and in rural areas, people who bypass the traditional oral agreements and resort to governmental legalities are known as *moun ki pa konn viv* (people who don't know how to live). For their part, most Haitian administrations have assumed that by providing a minimum of local government they will be able to keep the peasants out of politics. Furthermore, as Nicholls pointed out, the black middle classes at the core of Duvalier's power rarely received any attention at all from any government and so their loyalty was bought with, for example, the installation of a piped water system in middle-class neighborhoods of Port-au-Prince—a price so low that foreign observers could not perceive the transaction.[34]

Most foreign observers also could not perceive the ideology of Duvalier, though in the early 1980s even the American ambassador spoke of "the Duvalier black populist revolution."[35] In addition to trading on the appeal of the Estimé social revolution, Duvalier adopted Dessalines as his personal hero, installing an eternal flame on Dessalines' tomb.[36] In the same way, Duvalier's internal repression imitated the example of Dessalines' mistrust of the army and his creation of an armed and personally loyal militia.

Mindful that Dessalines and other rulers of Haiti had usually succumbed to plots hatched by a traditionally mulatto-dominated elite, Duvalier was determined to break the hold of these elites. He practiced a sort of black populism, relying on his appeal to such amorphous groups as taxi drivers, Voodoo priests, black-power intellectuals, and, especially, his paramilitary volunteers, the tonton-makout. His populism worked to a degree, and I have talked with many Haitians who can recall that a genuine sorrow was felt throughout the nation when Papa Doc died.

However, I don't want to leave François Duvalier on a positive note. He was responsible for many unspeakable atrocities. Most of his policies lay the groundwork for the eventual downfall of the Duvalier dynasty. During the first years of Duvalier's rule, thousands of Haitian professionals fled the political and economic tyranny and oppression to the United States, Canada, the Bahamas, the Dominican Republic, Venezuela, French Guiana, several African nations, and France. During the rule of his son, from 1971 to 1986, thousands of Haitians from all classes fled to Florida. The Haitian diaspora greatly influenced politics back in Haiti. The Haitians abroad, especially those in the United States, tended to have little patience with the notion of a French-oriented elite. They used Creole and were more socially mobile than the Haitians in Haiti. Most importantly, since blacks and mulattoes overseas mixed extensively, Duvalier could find little international support with his form of black nationalism.

Internally, much of the movement against the Duvaliers came from outside Port-au-Prince. Haiti traditionally has had regional centers of proud and influential intellectual and political importance. Duvalier's practice of concentrating resources in Port-au-Prince increased the resentment in these regional centers, and many of the forces that combined to oust his son found their strength in these regional capitals.

For the most part, the Duvaliers paid off the urban elites by taking from the rural areas. Expecting the peasants to endure this exploitation as they always had, the Duvaliers, for example, skimmed the export taxes on crops grown by the peasants and took some of the basic products sold by local industries. It really didn't amount to much compared to some of the great world-class thieves, such as the Marcoses of the Philippines and some of the Mexican presidents, but it was more than the relatively small economy of Haiti could tolerate, especially since agricultural development was almost totally ignored by the Duvaliers.[37]

The appeal and durability of Duvalierism has eluded journalists and others surveying the Haitian scene, most of whom predicted year after year that "Haiti has just about reached the end of its frayed and rotten rope."[38] It was a prediction based on a lack of understanding of black politics in Haiti. And this lack of understanding has often been based on an overt or covert racism.

Always Racism

Most of the materials reviewed in this chapter have been discussed within the framework of racism. Too much has been written on racism for me to pretend that I can now add any additional insights or create any new general analytic models on the subject. An interesting book on racism in the United States in relation to Japan and World War II suggested that racism in the United States tends to lump other people into stereotypical groups and then denigrate them, while Japanese racism tends to elevate Japan by stressing its purity and the superiority of its mission.[39] The American folk model of Haiti seems to contain both elements of racism. At any rate, I must emphasize that the intensity and depth of racist feelings associated with Haiti surpass most types of ordinary ethnocentrism. And this racism is certainly not limited to Euroamerican whites or to the distant past.

In a novel that features the smuggling of Haitians into Florida, Russell Banks had one of his Jamaican characters say,

> You can never rely on Haitians the way you can rely on other people. They're different somehow, almost another species, it sometimes seems, with their large, innocent eyes, their careful movements, their strange way of speaking.[40]

In a case of life imitating art, some of the most blatantly racist remarks that I ever heard about Haitians came from a dark-skinned Jamaican stranded in Cap-Haitien with a broken boat engine. He sought me out, he said, because I was a white American and would understand his complaints. He constantly referred to Haitians as "niggers," and claimed, "None of them are bright enough to fix my engine. They just give me that dumb stare and smile. They're all after my money. That's all their race ever thinks about. Money and sex. And the women are so ugly."[41]

The Jamaican continued to complain that the Haitians did not understand English and that they did not have "English civilization like Jamaica." He speculated, "They probably have too much nigger blood in them to be able to learn anything properly. They're all so black."

St. John made the biological component of this type of racism clear when he wrote,

> Constant intermarriage is causing the race [Haitians] to breed back to the more numerous type [blacks, as opposed to mulattos], and in a few years the mulatto element, which is the civilising element in Hayti, will have made disastrous approaches to the negro.[42]

Contrary to all the evidence available even in the nineteenth century, St. John agreed "with those who deny that the negro could ever originate a civilisation, and that with the best of educations he remains an inferior type of man."[43]

St. John certainly was not the first racist, though he was one of the most prominent of the early racists writing on Haiti. He also was among the first to proclaim in the very midst of his racism that he was a man without color prejudice, writing most brazenly, "I do not remember ever to have felt any repugnance to my fellow-creatures on account of a difference of complexion."[44]

His denial of racism has been followed by others and has, in fact, been part of the myth of the American Occupation of Haiti from 1915 to 1934. John Houston Craige, an American marine captain and the chief of police in Port-au-Prince, was as straightforward a racist as one can find—as he himself admitted—writing, for example, "In backbone, courage, initiative and intelligence they [that is, blacks] lag a long way behind their white brothers."[45] Later Craige espoused his belief not only in white supremacy but in American white supremacy, writing,

I believe that the white man of western Europe is the most able and progressive of earth's types, and that the men of the United States are the most able group of the western European stock. I believe that the yellow and red men are less able, and the black men least able of all.[46]

Yet he states in the next paragraph, "I have no color prejudice."[47]

Craige continued the insult by announcing his love for these inferior people, saying, "I had grown fond of my primitive black children."[48] Their very inferiority brought out his paternal feelings, for even though "their modes of thought were different from those of people whom we call civilized, yet after all they were simple enough when one understood their environment and heredity."[49]

W.B. Seabrook, the author of *The Magic Island*, perfected this type of frustrating insult, saying,

I have a warm feeling toward Negroes. They're perhaps by and large less intelligent than whites,...but I often think they're superior to us emotionally and spiritually.... I'd like to go down to Haiti or some-where and turn Negro.[50]

The American Occupation of Haiti is widely regarded as reflecting the racism of white Americans in general and of the Marine Corps in particular.[51] Even before the Occupation there were articles suggest-ing that the United States had a mission to civilize the Haitians.[52] "The United States' refusal to recognise Haitian independence until 1862 was largely determined by [racial] prejudice, as was the failure to invite Haiti to the Panama conference of 1825."[53] In addition to Craige's books,[54] several other Marines have written revealingly racist accounts of their rule in Haiti.[55] The Marines in Haiti habitually referred to the population with the terms *nigger*, *gook*, and *coon*, while "for many Haitians the Marine initials U.S.M.C. meant *Un Salaud Mal Costumé* (a sloppy bum)."[56]

The period of the American Occupation saw the publication of a large amount of literature on Haiti perhaps best exemplified by Franck's book, which is replete with flagrantly racist statements such as "[Haitian servants] are usually stupid beyond words, with the mentality of an intelligent child of six, but they are sometimes capable of great devotion, with a dog-like quality of faithfulness."[57] Franck continued,

> They have not a trace of gratitude in their make-up, no sexual morality, unbounded superstition, and no family love. Mothers gladly give away their children....They have a certain naive simplicity and some of the unintentional honesty that goes with it; they have of course their racial cheerfulness.[58]

And like many writers of his time Franck made comical comparisons with the blacks in the United States, concluding, "More temperamental than our own negroes, the Haitians are incredibly childlike in their mental processes."[59]

Some American writers of this period even displayed a prejudice against the landscape of Haiti, writing that "gaunt, shadowy Haitian hills rose up mysteriously and menacingly."[60] Such a notion is also found in novels written by Americans and set in Haiti, such as one description of the first sight of Haiti, in which "it rose out of the sea like a gaunt-boned savage beast, aloof, forbidding, furred with a coat of rough, bristling, blackish green."[61]

Unfortunately, it is not necessary to return to the 1920s and 1930s to find these prejudices against Haitians. In 1986 the television tycoon Ted Turner was quoted as warning a group of Miami bankers that the city might end up "knee-deep in Haitians" because "it's like kittens. If you have two kittens and you don't spay them, pretty soon you have more kittens than you can handle."[62]

Sex and Rhythm

Turner was obviously misinformed by the basic white racist belief in the heightened sexuality of blacks. In one scene in Ralph Ellison's novel *The Invisible Man,* two black prostitutes are discussing the sexual characteristics of an elderly white man, and one of them tells the other, "Girl, don't you know that all these rich ole white men got monkey glands and billy goat balls? These ole bastards don't never git enough."[63] Kenneth Roberts had one of his white characters in Haiti exclaim in the novel *Lydia Bailey,* "By God, Hamlin, you can talk about women, but you don't know anything about 'em till you've had colored ones!"[64] These passages vividly illustrate the socioanthropological axiom that most folk models contain the notion that members of other ethnic and racial groups are sexual athletes. For whites, the ultimate sexual athletes have often been blacks.

This notion does, indeed, seem to have reached its heights when used by whites and applied to blacks. The stereotype of the black sexual animal is inextricably tied to the concept of the innate sense of rhythm in blacks. The most offensive book in this regard is Richard Loederer's *Voodoo Fire in Haiti*—published in 1935 by the highly respectable Literary Guild of New York City.

Loederer wrote about his boat trip to Haiti that:

The remaining two passengers were pure-blooded negroes who with their ultra-European bearing and appearance were both incongruous and entertaining.... Their western culture lay deeper than might at first sight have been expected and on only one occasion did the primitive African break through the shell of civilized convention. When someone put a record on the ship's gramophone the studied calm of the two black stoics vanished. Consciousness of rhythm submerged the veneer of civilization. Indeed, so strong was the primitive urge, that a complete physical change transformed their bodies.... The music seemed to surge, compelling responses in shoulders, hips and thighs— swaying, flexing, vibrating, in complete surrender to the throbbing rhythm. For the first time I realized what *rhythm* meant to the negro.[65]

Fifteen years later another traveler to Haiti echoed Loederer, saying, "Rhythm and the dance are probably the single most pressing need in the organism of the Negro in his primitive state."[66] Similiar writing can be found even in the journalism of the 1980s. A freelance journalist who visited Haiti for the first time in 1984 described a night out on the town in these words: "A band was playing exuberant, drum-filled music; on a large platform, couples were dancing with an elegance and eroticism that would shame most American discos."[67]

Loederer's description of night life in Port-au-Prince is to go from journalistic blandness to the ultimate in scandalous purple prose.

A full-blooded negress appeared suddenly in the middle of the room— black, naked, a statue carved from polished ebony miraculously endowed with life. Her short curling hair clung in tight ringlets round her Ethiopian skull, giving the appearance of a miniature beehive. There was carmine rouge smeared on her pulpy lips and on the nipples of her heavy tip-tilted breasts. Great golden earrings glittered against her polished sable neck, sparkling in the lamplight and matching the reflections of her high-heeled slippers. Round her waist a short, all-revealing grass skirt hung from a narrow belt, and jumped up and down with every movement of her hips. Her projecting buttocks swayed and rolled; her stomach undulated and twisted in a wild umbilical dance. She displayed all the unbridled vitality of a young jungle queen resolved and sublimated into swelling waves that rippled snakelike down her pliant body. And yet she was no black goddess of voluptuousness, but only a high-spirited child of nature at play.[68]

Loederer seemed obsessed with the notion of sexuality in very young black women, as when he writes in another passage:

Two negro girls strolled slowly along the road below and gazed at the white stranger with ogling curiosity. Coquettishly they let the tops of their dresses slip down from their shoulders showing beautiful black satiny bodies. Whenever my glance caught theirs, they smiled with happiness and amusement. Then they laughed out loud and executed a little dance, bending and swaying their bodies enticingly. When this performance was over they turned round and walked back to their huts, every now and then turning their heads to look back at me with open invitation.[69]

As a final touch the book carries illustrations from wood block with captions such as "I saw the naked figures of a young negress....The young negro when he woos a girl; a typical example of the innocent, naked eroticism of the African native."[70]

The Indolent Native

Instead of engaging in constant sex, however, the life of the average Haitian peasant and urban proletariat is one of almost ceaseless toil in an only partially successful effort to survive amid dwindling natural resources. The Euroamerican folk model of Third World peoples in general and blacks in particular, however, portrays them as indolent. The presentation of Haitian work habits in popular writings exhibits, therefore, a certain ambiguity—for Haitians are obviously a hard-working people. They are, nevertheless, poor, and it is difficult for middle-class writers to understand how people can be both hard-working and poor, and so they generally assume that the poor must also be lazy.

In the eighteenth century during the time of slavery, an observer wrote with injustice about a people who were quite literally worked to death when he said, "Indolence...is the favorite state of the negro."[71] A century later the iniquitous St. John continued along these lines, writing, "Habits of idleness and rapine...have continued to the present day."[72]

In the 1820s much of the discussion of the indolence of blacks revolved around the justification for slavery and the denigration of free Haiti. One observer made such a purpose very clear when he wrote to the British secretary of state to explain the Rural Code of Haiti and spoke "of the utter hopelessness of obtaining from the Negroes, without compulsion, that degree of regular and steady exertion, which is indispensable to secure a fair profit on fixed capital invested by European Planters in the West Indies."[73] Another bluntly claimed, "Constituted as he now is, the Negro will not work but under coercion. Hayti proves it."[74] Still another observer claimed that Haitians felt "only the few wants characteristic of the savage, and [that with] those wants easily supplied, they are careless of all consequences, and never bestow a thought on the future welfare either of their posterity or their country."[75]

Even after the end of slavery this notion of indolence continued with an article on Haiti in the widely read *World's Work* being subtitled, "A Land of Misery Amid Opulence, Where Childish Negroes Play at Dignity, Spill Blood, and Do No Work."[76]

The objection to the portrayal of Haitians as lazy was accurately lodged by a highly placed elite Haitian politician when he wrote, "Those detractors who persist in representing indolence as one of the principal features of the Haitian peasants either know nothing of them or have not taken the trouble of observing their customs."[77]

The charge of laziness, which is usually made by travelers leisurely passing through foreign countries, is often based on ignorance of customary work habits. The mistake can be seen at other levels of interaction. Day workers at my university often complain about the laziness of the students whom they see out tanning in the noonday sun, not knowing that these same students may begin studying in the afternoon and stay in the library until midnight.

In an extension of this curious misunderstanding of work habits, poverty, and natural resources, a North American author of travelogues wrote, "[In Haiti] natural harbors abound, which are hardly occupied, which, if they belonged to a civilised people, would teem with commerce and be alive with ships and sailors."[78] The implicit notion here is that Haitians could become wealthy if only they really wanted to work at it. Such a misunderstanding of exploitation and the international division of labor is found in this peculiar passage by a former American financial adviser to Haiti:

> The peasants...are enviably carefree and contented; but, if they are to be citizens of an independent self-governing nation, they must acquire, or at least a larger number of them must acquire, a new set of wants.[79]

This sort of blame-the-victim approach twists the situation completely to the opposite of reality and posits that people are poor because they are satisfied with their poverty. For example, an article in the once-popular *New England Magazine* stated that Haitians are "usually content to work only enough to receive a sufficiency of coarse food, tapia, and tobacco."[80] The explicitly racist Franck even goes to the extreme of stating that Haitians would rather starve than work: "So lazy have they become in their masterless condition that this one meal a day has come to be the habitual diet of the masses."[81]

The myth of the indolent native has a long history. A book on this topic is fairly well summed up by its subtitle *A Study of the Image of the Malays, Filipinos, and Javanese from the 16th to the 20th Centuries and Its Function in the Ideology of Colonial Capitalism.*[82] The book contains an overwhelming collection of remarks from the pens of travelers, administrators, and respected scholars. The original function of this image of laziness was, of course, to justify the European colonial exploitation of the land and labor of the indigenes, whether they were imported slaves or the original inhabitants of an area. Lazy people do not deserve land, and the initial colonial response to the lack of eager labor to work the stolen land for colonial enterprises was forced labor through a slave system.

After the collapse of the slave system, the myth of the indolent native persisted; where the indigenous agricultural systems were land extensive, the indigenes had no interest in working the labor-intensive colonial cash-crop systems so that the elite in some distant land could become rich. One specific problem for capitalist England centered on getting the indigenes to work hard on the cash crop plantations owned by the Europeans.[83]

Anyone who has observed Haitians cannot but be impressed with their energy as they go about the task of survival in a bare environment, and, therefore, even casual observers display a certain ambiguity between the received myth of the indolence of blacks and the activity they can see before their own eyes. A study of tourists in Haiti reported, "'Everyone seems so busy and hard at work' is a...frequent comment, usually accompanied with an expression of mystification as to why, then, the people look so poor."[84] My own observations of Haitians both in Haiti and in Florida have sometimes left me dizzy at their never-ending motion even though some of them are obviously suffering from malnutrition.

Different evaluations of Haitian work habits show up clearly over the years in different writings. By the end of the 1920s Haitians still lived "indolent and shiftless" lives,[85] but by the 1960s the typical peasant woman had become "an indefatigable laborer."[86] In the early 1970s the Haitians were "indubitably lazy,"[87] but by the late 1970s they were "strenuously toiling" in the agricultural fields.[88] Of course, they did not really change their work habits during these fifty years. The explanation for the discrepancy in the accounts comes from the fact that the negative reports are based on folk models and the positive ones on analytic models. The negative quotations are by a journalist and by an ideologue, and the positive quotations are by a sociologist and by an economist.

Although not as flexible or as amenable to facts as analytic models, folk models can change. The historical notion of Haitians as lazy, for example, currently finds no support among those whites who hire migratory workers for stoop labor. Indeed, contemporary writers often comment on the industrious characteristics of Haitians.[89] Richman, the anthropologist who did fieldwork "among Haitian farm workers who travel from Florida to New York in the 'eastern stream' of migratory agricultural labor,"[90] speaks of Haitians as "the preferred prey of labor contractors...since they are intent and arduous workers."[91]

Land of Voodoo

Few words in the English language have the immediate power to produce images of revulsion and to convey notions of irrational behavior. As was noted in chapter 1, *zombie* is an example. *Voodoo* is another. These words are, of course, connected to each other and to Haiti. In the minds of the lay public these words evoke thoughts of the living dead, secret rituals, cannibalism, wild and drunken orgies, and odious doings by incomprehensible black people. The word *voodoo* has become a singularly derogatory term in English, and it is often used simply to conjure up abstract negative images.

People who would not think of publicly using other ethnic terms pejoratively, such as "jewing someone down," use *voodoo* with no concern at all about its meaning to Haitians. For example, in the 1988 American presidential campaign, both Michael Dukakis and George Bush used the phrase "voodoo economics," the editor of the *Atlanta Constitution* editorial page characterized a White House study as "voodoo social science so mad-dog it bays at the moon,"[92] and a regional columnist referred to Reagan as "a voodooist who dispels hunger with TV-borne chants."[93]

Careful scholarship has revealed that the word *voodoo* actually "refers simply to a type of dance often held in the Haitian country-side, which does not necessarily occur in conjunction with religious ceremonies."[94] This particular meaning of the word is no great secret. In the late 1700s in what is probably the earliest published account of Voodoo, Martinique-born Médéric-Louis-Elie Moreau de Saint-Méry referred to "Vaudoux" as "an African dance," though he went on to label the entire religion Voodoo.[95] In fact, "the word 'voodoo' is an outsider's term, a Euro-American word of Dahomean origin."[96]

Since the English pronunciation does not quite match the Haitian one, scholars have often given the word different spellings, such as *vaudou, vaudoun, vudu, vodun,* and *vodoun.* Many Haitians, of course, recognize that much of the outside world refers to their religion as "voodoo," and however incorrectly others may use this word, Haitians that deal with tourists and other visitors and Haitians that write about religion do use the word. I will follow this common practice and will refer to the Haitian religion as Voodoo.

Voodoo, then, is simply the religion of most Haitians, especially the peasants and the urban proletariat. Many of its beliefs and rites come from Africa, but others have a Roman Catholic origin. As Métraux wrote in the first full-length anthropological study of Voodoo, "Its devotees ask of it what men have always asked of religion: remedy for ills, satisfaction for needs and the hope of survival."[97] Two decades earlier Herskovits had described Voodoo as "a complex of African belief and ritual governing in large measure the religious life of the Haitian peasantry."[98]

Contemporary anthropologists have concentrated on specific aspects of Voodoo. Glenn Smucker has written about the social context of Voodoo, which

> includes the household, the *lakou* [the extended household], the temple, the parish church, the cemetery, spirit *kapital* (spirit repositories), pilgrimage sites and public thoroughfares where processional societies dance along the paths and crossroads.[100]

He has very successfully shown the prime place that Voodoo occupies in Haiti with its beliefs and practices permeating "almost every aspect of daily life among peasants, from the household to the field garden and marketplace."[101]

The richness of Voodoo is perhaps best seen in the interaction Haitians have with the spirits, which are commonly referred to as *lwa*. Smucker pointed out, "Both human beings and spirits are able to shift quite easily back and forth between ordinary and extraordinary levels of being....As a consequence, reality is multi-layered and complex; appearances are deceiving."[102] Within this complex cosmos Haitians see themselves as followers or servitors of the lwa. Harold Courlander did extensive research on the Voodoo pantheon and compiled a list of lwa that covered twenty-one pages in his well-written book *Haiti Singing*.[103]

The lwa that the Haitians serve are conceived of as distant ancestors, and the major focal theme of Voodoo rituals concerns contacting and appeasing these ancestral spirits. In addition to serving the lwa, practitioners of Voodoo also pay various types of homage to their dead parents and grandparents. Voodoo can be seen, then, as a combined ancestral-focused religion and a worship of the dead. There are, of course, nonancestral elements in Voodoo. Some people literally purchase lwa to get rich, to do harm, or for a number of other reasons. For most Haitians, however, these are peripheral activities—though journalists focus almost exclusively on just these activities.

Anthropologists do not ignore the more malicious aspects of Voodoo—every religion, even Christianity, has various forms of witchcraft. Anthropologists do, however, study religion in its totality, pointing out, for example, "It is incorrect to define Voodoo in terms of witchcraft, but it is impossible to understand the ancestor cult without reference to the magical causation of illness."[104] Haitian believers in Voodoo are themselves "quick to denounce the practice of maligning magic, the purchase of *lwa* and the traffic in *zombi*."[105] To concentrate on the darker side of Voodoo is akin to writing a book on the satanic cults of southern California and presenting it as a study of Christianity.

In their investigations into witchcraft in Haiti, legitimate scholars have always been careful to present it within the larger sociocultural context. The anthropologist Erika Bourguignon wrote, "The belief in zombis is part of the larger context of belief in magic against which only counter-magic or the deities of the *vodun* cult are an effective defense."[106] Following the lead of Herskovits, Bourguignon has focused on the psychological aspects of possession,[107] a topic that has also fascinated journalists. She has, however, consistently interpreted possession within the wider context of an analytic model that can explain religion at large, focusing, in particular, on mental health.[108]

Other anthropologists, including Smucker, have, indeed, described Voodoo "as a cult of sickness and healing."[109] Sickness and death provide the major life crises during which many Voodoo rituals are undertaken. Much of Voodoo can be seen as a folk medical system that attributes illnesses to angry ancestors and that consists of rituals performed to appease these ancestors and to help cure the illness. Included in these rituals are divination rites, which are used to find the cause of illnesses; healing rites, in which a Voodoo priest interacts directly with sick people to cure them; propitiatory rites, in which food and drink are offered to specific spirits to make them stop their aggression; and preventive rites, in which ancestors are offered sacrifices to help head off any possible future trouble.

In addition to initiation rituals and the rites associated with health, Voodoo contains recreational rituals that permit the lwa to dance and have a good time by possessing the bodies of their followers. These ceremonies consist of the famous Voodoo dances that attract tourists who apparently think that they are seeing the real thing, when what they are actually witnessing is a sort of embellished version of a ritual that is traditionally a light-hearted social finale to the much more serious domestic rituals.

The anthropologist Gerald Murray has studied Voodoo's relationship with the ecological concerns of Haitians. He illustrated how Voodoo helps make adaptive changes in the resource control system. In particular, he focused on how Voodoo rituals help control access to land.[110] As with all good anthropology Murray's writings show how tightly Voodoo is interwoven into the fabric of Haitian life.[111]

Unfortunately, the anthropology of Voodoo is not popularly understood by the lay public. Foreigners' accounts of Voodoo apparently began with the voluminous writings in French of Moreau de Saint-Méry. Completed in 1789, his account gave a brief report of possession in describing what was apparently a serpent cult of Voodoo.[112] The snake was, indeed, an important feature in early Voodoo but seems to have almost entirely disappeared in Haiti today. In words that were to be repeated for almost two hundred years afterwards Moreau warned, "Nothing is more dangerous, according to all the accounts, than this cult of Voodoo."[113] The religion certainly was dangerous to the French slave owners. In his account of Haiti on the eve of the revolution, Moreau feared most that the slaves would "abandon the use of reason"[114] and do exactly what their black leaders told them to do—overthrow their masters.

In the times of slavery many of the Voodoo dances and rituals were held in secret because they were illegal and because many slave owners quite correctly viewed them as potential organizations for revolt and tried to suppress them. Moreau wrote persuasively about this.[115] The tradition of writing about Voodoo as a secret cult has remained,[116] though Voodoo is not usually practiced in secret except in periods of government suppression. Voodoo is usually practiced by households within their own family compounds.

Moreau's account, however, was not translated into English until 1985, and his French volumes were little read outside of academic circles. It was St. John who popularized the modern outsiders' folk model of Voodoo with his much-copied words from *Haiti or the Black Republic* on "Vaudoux Worship and Cannibalism."[117] Most of the chapter deals with the trial in February 1864 of eight people from Bizoton, a suburb of Port-au-Prince, who were accused of cannibalism. All eight were executed by Haitian authorities. Despite objections by more informed and less bigoted critics,[118] the book came out in a second edition in 1886 in which St. John expanded on his description of Voodoo as a cannibal religion in a savage country where every year children are sacrificed and devoured by worshipers of snakes.

St. John's book was widely read and was long regarded as the main authority on Voodoo. Métraux claimed that this essentially rural and rather obscure religion would probably have remained little known to the outside world if St. John's book had not been published. It is, indeed, regrettable that the first widely read book on Voodoo concentrates on one event to develop a misinformed description of the Haitian religion—a description that St. John himself intended to be used to support racist notions of the inferiority of blacks.

In fact, the use of Voodoo to illustrate this inferiority was not entirely new. For several years before the appearance of St. John's book, American Christian missionaries had made major contributions to these slanders. For example, after his visit to the Episcopal mission in Haiti in the 1870s, Bishop Coxe included lurid tales of cannibalism in his speeches.[119] Most of the writing by American missionaries continues to be terribly patronizing as they "patiently set about introducing these superstitious voodoo worshipers to the Christian way of life"—in the words of a book published by the Baptist Haiti Mission.[120]

Within a couple of decades after the St. John book, Americans became prominent in writing about Voodoo. An article in the widely read *National Geographic* discussed "the horrible sorcery called the religion of Voodoo" and repeated the misguided tales of St. John about orgies, cannibalism, and secrecy.[121] The racist content of his notions on Voodoo was made clear when the writer continued by saying, "The inhabitants themselves are naturally...gentle, except when overcome by the barbarous religious customs handed down from their African ancestors."[122] Another travel article in the same year talked about cannibalism and made the preposterous statement that "the taste for human blood may have been acquired at the time of the massacres of the French."[123]

The notion of the existence of widespread cannibalism in Haiti was repeated in such popular magazines as *National Geographic* even after the American Occupation of Haiti, when observers should have known better. In an article titled "Haiti and Its Regeneration by the United States" the writer speaks of "the sacrifice of children and animals to the mumbo jumbos of local wizards."[124]

It is clear that much of the American writing on Voodoo in the early part of this century was motivated by the fears about the spread of a rebellious religion among American blacks. An editor's note to an article in the popular *New England Magazine* that called Voodoo "a riot of debauchery"[125] warned about "the hold Voodooism has on certain colonies of negroes in the South to-day."[126] The notion of the powerful grasp of Voodoo on weak-minded blacks was publicly advanced as recently as the early 1950s in the widely read *Saturday Evening Post* when Haitians were characterized as being "enchained by voodooism."[127]

Many white writers tend to equate Voodoo with African savagery, such as the one who wrote,

> Wherever we find the African race we find gross superstition, and wherever the blacks are free from the restraint of the whites or of advanced civilisations, the natural superstition of the race find expression in witchcraft, idolatry, Obeah, or Voodooism.[128]

North American writings on Haiti and on Voodoo increased considerably as a result of the American Occupation of Haiti. Métraux commented on one of the writings that is typical of the United States military officers:

> During the American Occupation Voodoo was looked upon as a sign of barbarism and served as a butt for the spite of the military authori-

ties. One of the Marine officers, John Houston Craige, treats it in his book *Black Bagdad* with as much naíveté as horror. In reading some of his accounts, allegedly authentic, you cannot help wondering which is the more gullible and has the greater weakness for marvels—the unsophisticated peasant or the White chief of police.[129]

It is within this context that in 1929 one of the most popular books on Voodoo was published, Seabrook's *The Magic Island*. Seabrook was the son of a Lutheran minister and author of such sensationalist books as *Adventures in Arabia* in 1927, *Jungle Ways* in 1931, and *The White Monk of Timbuctoo* in 1934. One assessment of his writing called it "as sensational as compatible with accuracy."[130] One scholar of Haiti characterized Seabrook's *Magic Island* as "one of the most abominable books in the Haitian list of defamation literature."[131] A single quotation should be sufficient to give the flavor of Seabrook's writing. In describing a dance, which he thinks is the central component of Voodoo, Seabrook wrote,

> In the red light of torches which made the moon turn pale, leaping, screaming, writhing black bodies, blood-maddened, sex-maddened, god-maddened, drunken, whirled and danced with dark saturnalia, heads thrown weirdly back as if their necks were broken, white teeth and eyeballs gleaming.[132]

Just a few years later an even more strident book came out originally written in German.[133] Although not as well known as *The Magic Island*, *Voodoo Fire in Haiti* is perhaps the most offensive work on Voodoo ever published.[134] The author, Richard Loederer, was apparently an adventurer and artist from Vienna who spent several months wandering around Haiti—though some informed reviewers questioned whether he could have ever been to Haiti since the book contains so many factual errors.[135]

Loederer's book, nevertheless, received praise from the lay press, such as the August 3, 1935, edition of the *Boston Transcript*, which claimed, "This is a book of great charm and fascination. The author enjoys the wonderful sensations and experiences of penetrating an unknown corner of the earth."[136] Even the *New York Times Book Review* apparently took Loederer's sensationalist fantasies at face value.[137]

Reviewers who knew something about Haiti were not quite so generous, but their reviews appeared in publications of limited circulation, such as *The Nation* and *The Saturday Review of Literature*. Herskovits referred to Loederer's work as

> a combination of distorted borrowings from other works on Haiti, nonsensical reporting of what the author claims to have seen in the island, and attempted sensationalism that can only be regarded as a *reductio ad absurdum* of the "steaming-jungle, booming-tom-tom" school of adventure writing.[138]

Even untrained but sympathetic observers, such as Blair Niles, author of *Black Haiti*,[139] were appalled by Loederer's ridiculous distortions, writing, "It is a matter for regret that his book merely adds one more to the sensational travesties of which Haiti has long been the victim."[140] The book was, however, "circulated by one of the important book clubs,"[141] even though it was characterized by "rank sensationalism, cheap melodrama and an utter absence of seriousness and exactitude."[142] Informed reviewers wondered aloud, "When will the time come that visitors to this fascinating little republic will write sane and readable stuff that does not malign, calumniate or simply misrepresent the habits and customs of its people?"[143]

One writer of this period who should have known better and who did have some anthropological training was Hurston, who wrote a book about religion in Jamaica and Haiti titled *Tell My Horse*.[144] Although a slight cut above most journalism, the writing is contemptible of Haitians, and perhaps racist. Hurston calls Haitians untrustworthy and compulsive liars and talks about their enormous cruelty. She does have the dubious distinction of being perhaps the only black American who actually wrote approvingly of the American Occupation of Haiti. Her account of Voodoo is more gossip than scholarship, and certainly her notation of lwa names is careless.

In the years immediately following World War II Haiti was pretty much ignored. In the 1950s there was a rather strange book published that was not very different from the writings of Seabrook or Loederer but that was written by a professor of religion at the University of Iowa. On the flyleaf of *Strange Alters*, Marcus Bach is described as "America's foremost religious researcher."[145] He is actually known primarily for a dozen or so popular books on the minor faiths in the United States, as well as plays and other works of fiction. His *Strange Alters* is a trade book with none of the trappings of scholarship. He had apparently read almost nothing about Haitian Voodoo.[146]

Bach's account is not nearly as sensational as Seabrook's or as inaccurate as Loederer's, but it does have a quality of breathlessness that makes it seem parochial—especially from a professor of religion. A knowledgeable reviewer wrote, "The author does not have enough training in anthropology or cultural history to transcend journalistic observations."[147] The lay press took a different view. The reviewer for the *Chicago Sunday Tribune*, in a typical example, characterized Bach's book as "an unbiased look at a primitive form of worship."[148]

Popular interest in Haiti revived in the 1960s. Most of the writing of this period concentrated on the despotism of the dictator François Duvalier and expressed the traditional American fears of having a neighbor go communist. Writers in the ubiquitous *National Geographic* still spoke of "sinister voodoo."[149] Travel guides still employed purple prose to lure tourists with promises that

> Haiti the exotic, Haiti the bizarre has nothing more truly fascinating than the living practice of Voodoo. Voodooism is a barbaric African religion which flourishes in Haiti in spite of official condemnation by the Catholic Church. Answering some deep primitive need in the Haitian soul, it [offers] the visitor to Haiti...a basic primitive experience.[150]

Two of the magazines that were found on the coffee table of almost every middle-class American home in the 1960s, *Reader's Digest* and *Life*, carried articles with subtitles like "A Voodoo-Touched

Tyrant Exhausts Patience of U.S. and His People"[151] and "Murder, Torture, the Black-Magic Rituals of Voodoo—These are Among the Administrative Techniques of François Duvalier."[152] The article in *Reader's Digest* was replete with phrases such as "mumbo-jumbo sorceries"[153] and "weird, bloodletting voodoo ceremonies."[154]

Due primarily to the rise of black power, similar books were difficult to find in print after the 1960s in North America—though not in Europe or the Dominican Republic—and the *National Geographic* carried an unusually sympathetic article in 1976 on Voodoo. The journalist wrote that she went to Haiti with notions of Voodoo that "called to mind terrifying ceremonies, bloody with the sacrifice of animals—or, perhaps, humans—crazed dancing, possibly orgies, and mysterious miseries, even death, visited on an enemy by the sticking of pins into his image"[155] and instead she found the Voodoo religious meetings to be like "a Wednesday night missionary society."[156]

Nevertheless, the current Haitian government travel brochure emphasizes both the mysteriousness of Voodoo and the fact that it is a religion by saying "The ancient African religion of vibrant vaudou (voodoo), with its mysterious rituals, symbols, music and dances [is] a religion, however, and should be viewed as such."[157] A contemporary scholar of Haiti has written, "The foreign press is still prone to cite Voodoo as exotic evidence of Haitian backwardness."[158] Laguerre wrote, "Little reporting in the press about Haitian-Americans fails to make sensationalist statements about their voodoo practices. Voodoo has been evoked for its mysterious rituals, its exotic beliefs, its lascivious dances, and its criminal practices."[159] One president of the Dominican Republic, who assumed office in August 1986, wrote that Voodoo is "one of the most monstrous manifestations of African animism."[160]

White Euroamericans often emphasize the remoteness, strangeness, and alienation of Haiti by writing as though Haiti is knowable only to equally strange and alienated whites. While recognizing the pan-human components of all human beliefs and behaviors, anthropologists and others who do cross-cultural research also readily admit that there are certain components of every culture that are very difficult for outsiders to comprehend. These specific beliefs and behaviors, however, are usually patterned aspects of culture connected with cognition, such as numbering systems, temporal attitudes, and spatial orientations.[161] In other words, the unknowability of cultures is quite understandable and amenable to investigation. The "mysteries" of distant and inscrutable peoples are usually the creations of writers working from their own ethnocentric folk models.[162]

Writers of travelogues and adventure stories, however, continue to perpetuate the notion of inaccessibility. If they cannot find the appropriate expatriate, however, then they may invent him, as apparently Loederer did when he repeated the tales of human sacrifice in Haiti in the form of a conversation with a Sir Joshua Higginbotham, who supposedly attended the famous 1864 Bizoton trial as an adult with Spenser St. John—and who must, therefore, have been approaching one hundred years of age when Loederer "talked" with him.[163]

Even some of the more serious writers on Haiti fall into the trap of having everything interpreted to them by the "inside" outsider. This pattern seems especially strong in writings on Voodoo. Seemingly, all of Bach's information came from the knowledgeable white man who had lived among the natives for decades. In this case it was the American-born Stanley Reser, who came to Haiti as a pharmacist with the Marines and stayed there for many years. He was the superintendent of an insane asylum for some time. Later, he appears to have made his living from gullible tourists as a Voodoo expert, and he appears in several travelers' accounts.[164] Bach wrote,

> I had been told that he was the one man whom the black people of Haiti trusted and loved. He alone, among the three thousand whites on the island, had got behind the faces and the forms, behind the mountains and the jungle, behind the laughter and the shadows, the poverty, pain and glory, into the spirit of the people.[165]

Naturally the investigator of alien cultures has to start somewhere.

Anthropologists have a long tradition of gaining entrance to other cultures through people that they usually refer to as informants, and they make a distinction between informants and informers. Informants are people who have a special knowledge about some aspect of the culture and who become the liaison for anthropologists to other informants. Informants are rarely foreigners, and when they are, anthropologists quickly use them to gain assess to indigenous informants. For example, in the 1950s anthropologists and others very often were first introduced to a certain French woman who through marriage and study had become highly knowledgeable about Haitian culture. Métraux, for example, wrote, "I had the rare luck of meeting Mme Odette Mennesson-Rigaud. Few whites have ever succeeded in getting to know Voodoo as intimately as this French woman who became Haitian by marriage."[166] Filmmaker Maya Deren, author of the popular book on Voodoo titled *Divine Horsemen,* also acknowledged Mennesson-Rigaud as her major source of information.[167] Métraux, however, soon broadened his circle of acquaintances to indigenous informants.

Current writers depend heavily on a western-educated Haitian, "Max Beauvoir, a former biochemist who has become a voodoo priest."[168] Beauvoir oversees the performance of a commercial Voodoo ceremony almost every night for tourists in the Port-au-Prince area. He was the source for most of the information in the latest popularization of Voodoo, a fictionalized account by Davis of his search for the ethnopharmacology of zombification, which I discussed in chapter 1. Beauvoir's daughter Rachel apparently served as companion and interpreter for Davis's brief excursions into the countryside.[169]

A People without a Language

Popular notions about the Haitian language are often laughably false but have proved to be nearly intractable because they are based on a folk model not yet as widely discredited as racism. Disparities between folk and analytic models of language continue to plague linguists, who have been unable to establish the principles of language scholarship and relativism among the lay public. Ethnocentric and nonlinguistic writings on language abound in the popular media. Linguists generally label this folk model of language *prescriptivism*, an ideology of the existence of absolute, timeless correctness in language. In the words of a linguist, "Prescriptive grammar implies above all authority; it also implies order, stability, predictability and reason."[170]

Notions that are the linguistic equivalents of racism and intolerance appear regularly in print in the United States. Such notions are particularly prevalent in how-to-write books, which often propagate the belief in a formal, unchanging language.

Most people absorb their folk model of languages, that is, their notion of what a language should be, during their teens and early twenties. Without any training in the scientific analysis of language, many people often view language change in an unfavorable manner. Prescriptivists over the age of thirty often proclaim, "Language is in decline."[171]

In addition to the belief in an unchanging, correct form for communication, folk models of language contain often surprisingly precise notions about the characteristics of "primitive" and "civilized" languages. Primitive languages are simple, easy to learn (though not worth learning), poor vehicles for expressing refined thoughts, contain only a few hundred words, and have only a few constantly repeated sounds.

One common belief of adherents to this folk model is that people with a primitive language have to make up for the paucity of words by gesticulating. An eighteenth century observer in Haiti wrote, "Gestures or signs are many and form a basic part of their language."[172] And almost two centuries later in 1984 an agricultural scientist attached to a project of the Agency for International Development in Haiti insisted to me, "Haitians use a lot of gestures because they don't have enough words in Creole, and that's why they can't write it down."

In contrast, this folk model posits that civilized languages are those that have a printed literature. An accompanying notion is that only civilized languages have grammar. A self-contradictory example is a mid-nineteenth century comment on a linguistic analysis of the Haitian language verb *fè* (to make), which the writer introduced by saying, "the following [is the] conjugation of the verb *faire,* as it would be conjugated if the Creole had a grammar."[173]

Modern linguists recognize that all languages have structure, all languages change through history, and all languages are capable of expressing the full range of human emotions, needs, desires, skills, and experiences. In addition, it is known that since languages develop in a particular sociophysical environment, languages may describe their own surroundings more economically than outsiders' languages.

With their notion of the immutability of languages, adherents to simplistic folk models have difficulty tolerating language change or explaining the development of new languages, such as Haitian Creole. The very word used for the language—Creole—implies a sort of imitation, or, at best, a transplant of the original. The language that the Haitians are supposed to be imitating is, of course, French. In fact, until 1978 the official American government designation of Haitian Creole was "Haitian French."[174] Many educated Americans still refer to the language of Haiti as "French Creole," implying that it is a subset of the French language. Most dictionaries still give erroneous definitions such as "the French dialect spoken by Haitians."[175] Even the president of Haiti who held office briefly in 1988 misleadingly called Creole "the local dialect derived from the French language."[176] And a contemporary piece has claimed that travelers will hear "a Creole version of French...spoken in Haiti."[177]

Thus, in the eyes of the rest of the world Haitians are a people without a language—or a people who have been struggling to communicate with an inadequate and debased kind of French. Haitians, of course, do have a language, as do all peoples. It is commonly referred to as Haitian Creole, or when the Haitian context is clear, it may be called simply *Creole* (or *kreyòl* in modern Creole orthography). Calling the language "Haitian" would make more sense politically and linguistically, but I will follow the common social usage with the term Creole.

Misunderstandings of the Haitian language situation seem endemic among the lay public outside Haiti, among some scholars studying Haiti, and even among Haitians themselves. Some of these problems reflect the ambiguity of the Haitian elite toward their own language and toward that of their colonial masters, French.[178] Haiti has a very small pseudobilingual ruling class that supports its second language, French, as the official language in order to help to maintain its exploitative position. All Haitians speak Creole, which is an entirely separate language, and only about 8 percent of the population, the educated elite, speak French well. Even then, its usage is only as a second language. Another 2 to 7 percent use French with lesser degrees of competence.[179]

Even those who have spent years in Haiti often make misstatements about Creole, such as Rodman, who claimed, "To those familiar with French, Creole is not difficult to understand when spoken slowly."[180] Creole does share a considerable amount of its lexicon with French but phonologically and morphologically it is a completely independent language. Since some of its vocabulary is similar to French, some simple words, commands, and phrases are understandable in French, but no monolingual French person can understand a conversation in Creole no matter how slowly it might be spoken.

In fact, Creole was recognized as a separate language and distinct from French at least as long ago as the 1780s in a traveler's report on Saint Domingue that contains a Creole passage "followed by a French translation and by some general remarks about Creole."[181]

In addition to the erroneous notion that Creole is some sort of simplified or "a bastard kind of French known as Creole,"[182] the racial attitude toward the language was, once again, brought forward by St. John, who called Creole an "uncouth jargon of corrupt French in an African form."[183] One of the most explicitly racist statements about Creole comes from a surprising source, the introduction to a 1944 English translation of *Canapé-Vert,* a novel by the Haitian brothers Philippe Thoby-Marcelin and Pierre Marcelin. The translator, Edward Larocque Tinker, who is described on the jacket of the book as an authority on Creole, stated:

> French, which had taken centuries to develop into its present subtle, intricate form, was far too complex for these simple Africans. So they did their best and contrived a queer, simplified "pigeon" dialect of their own. It would be impossible to describe the myriad ways in which the tongues of African slaves mutilated and amputated the French language. But they all made for simplification, because the Negro, being adaptable, invariably chooses the easiest way. Not only was he handicapped by a primitive mentality but by differences of physical structure as well. His thick lips and unaccustomed tongue made it impossible for him to pronounce certain vowels.[184]

Another common notion—which actually contradicts the notion of Creole being a simplified version of French—is that Creole is an unmanageable mixture of several languages. Such an approach is found in the *National Geographic*, which told us that Creole

> is three quarters Norman French, brought to the island by buccaneers 300 years ago. Add to this a few words of modern French, some Spanish, and a little English, season it with Carib Indian and a hint of African, slur it with the softening influence of the tropics, and let the mixture age.[185]

Sometimes the claim is made that Creole is "a blend of French, Spanish, English, and Dutch, to which were added many words of African origin."[186] Another journalist wrote, "Creole...is a blend of the native Indian language and a French patois."[187] The highly respected *1988 Collier's Yearbook* referred to Creole as a "Franco-African patois."[188] Even with all the public focus on Haiti in January and February 1986 accompanying the downfall of the Haitian dictator Jean-Claude Duvalier, the journalists in their efforts to inform the public about Haiti seemed unable to write accurately about Creole, describing it, for example, as "a combination of

French, Spanish and English."[189]

Less than 1 percent of the vocabulary of Creole can be traced to Dutch or any native Amerindian language, and similar claims betray the writers' focus on the entymology of Creole words. In the absence of any historical context, these descriptions denigrate Creole as an illegitimate language. Would a journalist feel obliged to describe English as a mixture of Anglo and Saxon and Norman-French and some of almost every other European language and formed in "the 5th century A.D. when tribes from the northwestern Continental fringe, speaking a form of West Germanic, invaded and conquered Romano-Keltic England"?[190]

Sadly enough, the Haitians themselves are not always helpful in clarifying these misunderstandings. Haitians, of course, have their own folk models of language and may be particularly confused about Creole and French. I have been told by Haitian college students in the United States that Creole is not a "real" language and that it does not have a grammar. They were, of course, taught this in the French-language schools in Haiti, but it is not difficult to understand how their experiences support such a belief.

In terms of language, the educated elite in Haiti study French; very few schools, particularly the ones run by the French-language Roman Catholic orders, pay any attention at all to Creole. A student grows up knowing that French has grammar and a written literature, but that student has no linguistic sophistication about languages and certainly no analytic knowledge about Creole. Upon learning that I was studying Creole a Haitian college student once told me, "You don't have to study Creole, you just start speaking it. I had to study French and English but that's because they have grammar. Creole doesn't have any grammar. It's easy to learn." And, indeed, he had not "studied" Creole but had simply begun speaking it. Having expended a considerable amount of effort over several years studying several languages, however, I have become wary of people who speak a language from birth telling how easy it is to learn their language simply by listening to the sounds.

Writers of travelogues in trying to describe the sounds of Creole

have gone from essentially calling it a nonlanguage, such as the one
who wrote about "that strange series of noises which is dignified in
the French West Indies with the name of 'creole'"[191] to the one who
complained that "the air was thick with dust, and ringing with
incomprehensible and deafening Créole"[192]—though another writer
heard a "soft spoken Creole."[193] Most of these writers sometimes
seemed annoyed that Haitians speak at all, grumbling, "Their tongues
are rarely silent, and frequent cackles of unrestrained laughter sound
from the bundles beneath which their woolly heads are all but
invariably buried."[194]

In the introduction of a work in Haitian Creole in the United States,
the author calls Creole "a corrupt French, degenerated, but appropriate for soft sounds." Probably written by a white French planter who
spoke Creole from birth and learned French later from a tutor, the
introduction goes on to claim that ideas and poetry are difficult to
express in Creole. This essay, which reflects the folk model of the
French planters and is written in awkward, convoluted French, is
followed by seventeen pages of beautiful Creole poetry.[195]

Again in this context we find the journalists specializing in cute
phrases at the expense of deepening understanding and transmitting
information and describing Creole as "a quick-step French modified
by a heavy admixture of West African languages"[196] or describing it
as "a combined French-African language of deeply intoned words
that sound like the beat of a goatskin tambour drum"[197] or as a "vivid,
clipped patois."[198] Perhaps confusing the Caribbean with the mysterious Orient, one writer of popular travel books labeled Creole as an
"inscrutable French patois."[199]

Creole is, of course, mysterious to outsiders for many reasons,
most of them connected to folk notions of language. Its very
existence is threatening to some prescriptivists because it developed
in modern times and contradicts the notion of languages as being
timeless. Linguists themselves, as I briefly pointed out, have been
confused about the development of Creole. The first ones to study
Haitian Creole and other creoles simply expanded on the existing
folk models and assumed that the creoles were extensions of previ-

ous European languages. Such an extreme position is not taken seriously by scholars today.[200]

As I have stated elsewhere, "To understand Haitian Creole and its development, it is necessary to understand the evolution of creole languages in general."[201] I have, indeed, in a 1988 article, briefly reviewed hypotheses about pidgins and creoles; suffice it to say here that the newest and perhaps most interesting development in creole studies was foreshadowed by the pioneering insights of Melville and Frances Herskovits when they wrote:

> An analysis of some of the texts raised the question as to what cultural mechanisms operated to produce the linguistic elements that recur with such regularity, for even a first reading of the material made evident that we are dealing with an inner structure that was the result of something other than the blind groping of minds too primitive for expression in modes of speech beyond their capabilities.[202]

This new hypothesis has been set forth by Derek Bickerton from research done primarily in Hawaii. Bickerton makes the point that creoles arose out of displaced populations that spoke pidgins.[203] In other words, creoles are the languages of the children of immigrants and have strikingly similar structures whether their vocabularies are based on English, French, or Spanish. The creole of Hawaii, with a largely English lexicon, is structurally the same as Creole, with a largely French lexicon. Creoles, then, constitute a separate language family, and it makes little sense to attempt to link them to the established languages of landholders or slave owners.[204] Bickerton postulates that this structure, that is, this universal grammar of creole languages, comes from a common human neurophysiological component.

If creole languages truly do represent some manifestation of a neurologically determined program for language acquisition and development, Haitian Creole and other creoles should actually be easier for children to learn than other languages that have deviated through centuries of change from the original neurophysiological program. Bickerton does cite examples of mistakes that children make in the older languages and shows that these mistakes are actually correct creole grammar. I have asked many Haitian parents how they teach their children to speak Creole and how they correct their mistakes, and I have yet to have any parent tell me that they need to correct errors.

This contemporary research into creole languages carries many interesting implications, and I hasten to add that certainly not all linguists agree with Bickerton. One implication is that Haitian Creole and other creoles, far from being poor imitations of other languages or mixtures of languages, may address more directly the human experience, express more richly human emotions, and more appropriately reflect the human psyche than more-established languages. Established languages have been distorted by elites for their own purposes, made rigid by literacy, and ossified by prescriptive grammarians. Instead of being a people without a language, the people of Haiti may have a language that speaks louder than the languages of its detractors.

In the same way that the dynamics of language formation, change, and usage can never be understood from the perspective of an ethnocentric folk model, politics and religion also will always be distorted unless some cross-cultural analytic perspective is adopted. In particular, politics, religion, and language will always be infused with racist notions when Haiti is discussed by outsiders. As these biases continue to develop, to grow, and to assume the veneer of facts, it becomes all the more important for the educated public to question the documentation of Haiti. The first step in developing a counter-reactive analytic model is to develop an understanding of the process of behavior and beliefs within the context of the culture itself. Language, religion, modes of work, and interpersonal interaction make particular sense when understood against the historical processes that created a particular society. In the next two chapters Haiti is placed within the framework of the international situation, and the creation of Haiti as a colonial society is demonstrated.

4

A sacred tree in a cemetary near the foothills of Port-au-Prince.

*F*rance and Haiti

Even though Haitians defeated the armies of Napoleon and have been citizens of an independent nation for over a century and a half, many Haitians suffer from the same colonial inadequacies as many other citizens of Third World countries. The notion of the superiority of the colonial culture and an identity confusion are apparently difficult to overcome.

The pursuit of French ideas by Haitian intellectuals has been reflected by writers who emphasized the gap between the alleged richness of the old, white French colony with the poverty of the independent black nation combined with the aping of French manners by Haitian elites. Commenting on the success of the French plantations and the failure of the ex-slaves, an American southerner emphasized, "It was *French*—it is now *African*. This explains all."[1]

Others phrased Haiti's problems not so much as a loss of Frenchness but as a contest between Frenchness and an ever-encroaching Africanness, claiming, for example, "Haiti is . . . a country in which French culture is waging an unending struggle with the primitive instincts of Africa."[2] And in the words of the *National Geographic,* Haiti is "French in outlook and almost wholly Negro."[3]

There is no denying that members of the various Haitian elites did, indeed, turn toward France for education and guidance. In fact, until the early nineteen hundreds it was easier for wealthy Haitians from the important provincial centers of Haiti to reach Paris by ship than to travel to Port-au-Prince by land. Typical of the attitudes of these educated Haitians is the remark of Anténor Firmin, a late nineteenth century Francophile black politician, who wrote, "The Haitian who needs to evolve mentally could not have conceived of a better linguistic tool" than French.[4]

The ethnocentrism of the French themselves contributed both to the notion of the superiority of the French culture and the revolutionary reaction against France on the part of the former French colonies. The

Haitian scholar Patrick Bellegarde-Smith pointed out that the seminal works of anticolonialism all came from Francophone writers.[5]

French influence in Haiti has declined a great deal. This chapter will concentrate on the remaining Haitian ties with France in the forms of the French language and with the Roman Catholic church.

Abused by the French Language

One journalist stated, "The ruling class in Haiti speaks only French."[6] The television personality Barbara Walters suggested the same thing after her interview with the defenestrated dictator when she wrote, "Monsieur Duvalier spoke only French."[7] A modern nation in which members of the ruling elite are unable to communicate in the same language as the masses of people is difficult to imagine.

Journalists, however, may be forgiven somewhat since the first article of the 1979 law recognizing Creole as the language of Haiti and permitting it in the schools as a medium of instruction referred to Creole "as a shared language spoken by 90 percent of the Haitian population."[8] The *1988 Collier's Yearbook* stated that Creole is "spoken by *most* Haitians."[9] Even a member of the traditional Haitian elite has claimed that "less than 10% write and speak French and the other 90% speak Creole."[10] The member of the elite did, in fact, correct himself in the very next sentence, writing, "Creole is spoken by every Haitian."[11] In reality, 100 percent of the Haitian population speaks Creole and less than 10 percent uses French, and then only as a second language.

The strange attitude of the elite toward Creole has been noted by numerous visitors and researchers. Shortly after World War II an American educator wrote, "According to the testimony of many Haitian intellectuals, Creole is hardly rich enough to express certain ideas."[12] I was told the same thing in the 1980s. Many French-oriented Haitian intellectuals have, indeed, not progressed beyond the famous Haitian diplomat, educator, and Francophile Dantès Bellegarde, who wrote in 1948,

No other idiom, more than the French language, . . . possesses a literature richer in masterpieces, in no other has religious, philosophic, and scientific thought been expressed . . . with more clarity, force, and eloquence.[13]

Bellegarde did, in fact, lecture audiences in North and South America in French, though he spoke both English and Spanish.[14] Bellegarde considered Creole "as an inadequate patois" and opposed all Creole literacy programs.[15]

Many western-educated Haitians still seem ashamed of Creole, especially in comparison with French. My first Creole instructor once mentioned his objection to the approved Creole orthography by claiming that it did not have the aesthetic value of the French orthography. These attitudes are, however, rapidly changing—particularly among the new black middle class. Haitian students who have been in the United States for a few years and who, for the most part, are from the new black middle class, have told me of their surprise and delight at the new attitudes toward Creole when they go back to Haiti for vacations. Several students have mentioned to me that their younger relatives do not speak French at all and have no interest in learning it.

Nevertheless, when Haitians are asked what language they speak, they often answer French even though they might not speak French at all. A member of the educated elite who served as president of Haiti for a few months in 1988 once referred to his country as a "French-speaking republic."[16] Many of the Haitians that do speak French do not always concede right away that they also speak Creole. This misrepresentation has amusing results in the hands of non-Haitians. For example, one North American physician has written that "Many educated Haitians speak Creole in addition to French."[17] The correct statement is that many educated Haitians speak French in addition to (their native) Creole.

Daniel Dougé, a Haitian reared in an elite family, wrote, "Haitians generally regarded French as superior to Creole. Where the feeling of superiority of French was not so strong, there was still a belief that it was somehow more beautiful, more logical, better able to express important thoughts, and the like."[18]

While Haitians seem to admire French, they also have negative feelings about it. When Haitians say *Li pale franse* (He/She speaks French), they are often not talking about the language a person is speaking but instead making a derogatory comment on the person's character. The saying implies that French is used for deception and that people who have nothing to hide speak Creole. A researcher who did fieldwork among Brooklyn Haitians wrote about the prestige of French but then pointed out, "Strong feelings exist that French is the language of pretense, duplicity, deceit, and falseness; conversely the 'lowness' of Haitian Creole is identified with positive traits, such as truth, integrity, sincerity, and genuineness."[19] An investigator working on a survey in Port-au-Prince for the post-Duvalier government reported, "The official permission letter written in French from the Ministry of the Interior sometimes alienates people when the cartographer presents it to them."[20]

Many of the small minority who actually do use French that I have encountered have admitted to me that French makes them feel uncomfortable. For most Haitians, the use of French is contrived. A popular Haitian proverb cautions *Pale franse pa di lespri pou sa* (To speak French doesn't necessarily mean that you're smart). Many investigators—including myself—have observed, for example, that when Haitians speak French,

> they stiffen noticeably, subdue and control their gestures, modulate their voices and become very serious, conveying the impression that the conversational topic is of great import, even if they are merely discussing the weather. Haitians themselves are aware of this attitudinal and physical change.[21]

Much has been written about the various situations in which French is used and those in which Creole is used.[22] My own first hand experience with the relationship between French and Creole usage is most vivid in a meeting of the Rotary Club that I attended in the mid-1980s in Cap-Haitien, the second largest city in Haiti. The forty or so members gathered in the lounge of the Brise-de-Mer Pension before the meeting, and everyone conversed in Creole, telling jokes, laughing, and catching up on gossip. As I walked around introducing myself, most initially spoke to me in a rather stiff French, but when they realized that I was speaking Creole, they exclaimed with delight, "O-o, ou konn pale kreyòl!" (Aha, you know how to speak Creole!) and quickly switched to a friendly Creole.

The meeting was opened in French, and I was formally introduced to the club in French—with the acknowledgment that I spoke Creole and that everyone should talk with me in Creole because I dearly needed the practice. The last part of the introduction met with much laughter. During the meeting the men spoke French stiffly when they were standing and then a relaxed Creole to their tablemates as soon as they sat down. Several members of the elite of this important city had difficulty speaking French, and some of them explained out of the side of their mouth in Creole what they were trying to express in French—often to the amusement of their fellows.

One investigator straightforwardly declared, "While French may be the official language of Haiti, in reality most Haitians communicate best in Creole, the national language, in virtually all situations."[23] In talking about the programs for French-speaking students that the Haitian-Americans were put into in the public schools of a Chicago suburb, another investigator observed, "The irony is that French is as foreign to the Haitian students in the bilingual program as is English. They speak Creole only."[24] And in the clinics that serve Haitian-Americans, Creole is misunderstood by both French- and English-speaking physicians.[25]

The ambivalent attitude of the elite toward French and Creole is further illustrated by Dougé when he wrote about himself,

Ever since he was very young, his parents wanted him to speak French all the time. They spoke French around him as frequently as possible. He also had a baby-sitter who spoke French.[26]

In later years, his mother addressed him in Creole and still expected that he answer her back in French. He often spoke Creole with his brother and sisters and would switch back to French whenever in the presence of parents or relatives.[27]

As a member of the elite, Dougé attended a French-language school where all the students spoke French in class. French is celebrated in the private schools in Haiti that are run by French Catholic orders, and, of course, Creole is denigrated as a lesser dialect of French, as an interview with any student from one of these schools will quickly demonstrate. However, as Dougé described,

Once they were dismissed from the classrooms, they spoke Creole among themselves—they spoke Creole in the school yard during recess, on their way home after school, and so on. The students would change to French whenever an instructor approached them.[28]

The negative attitude toward French is clearly evident when Dougé continued his description of becoming an adult, stating,

The use of French was a formality that one sought to cast off as one became older. To do so was a sign of maturity and personal independence. The use of French in conversations with one's parents, one's relatives, and others was, in a way, a sign of submission to their authority; it was an acknowledgment of the higher status or seniority of these people who more or less demanded the use of French. When the children of the elite reached adult status, they were able to use Creole more often and more freely.[29]

The use of French as a sign of authority is, indeed, a prevalent theme. Both Haitians and Haitian-Americans see Creole as a political instrument identified with the aspirations of the people, and they identify French with the government and repression.[30]

Traditionally, members of the elite spoke French in formal situations, and they often used it in conversations with acquaintances. Even the traditional elite, however, used Creole "whenever there was," in the words of Dougé, "a breakdown in the formality of the situation."[31] That French is clearly a second language even for members of the Haitian elite is seen by the fact that they immediately switch from French to Creole whenever they are under any emotional strain, when they tell jokes, or when they wish to express intimate thoughts.[32] And, of course, the French of Haitians is a language without slang.

In fact, it is clear that Creole was the language of both the whites and blacks during the early days of the island as a French colony. A specialist in the colonial period pointed out, "Creole was widely spoken in Saint-Domingue and had become the language of choice even for the French colonials,"[33] though journalists continue to erroneously refer to Creole as "the patois of French and African dialects spoken [only] by the slaves."[34] Children of the white planter class learned French only from tutors or when they returned to France for schooling, and French was used in Haiti by the French, the "upper-class" slaves, and the freed slaves.

French is, then, clearly a foreign language for Haitians, and despite the fact that a good deal of literature exists in French written by Haitians, Haitians learn French only in school and use it with a certain amount of artificiality. French cannot replace Creole in the hearts of Haitians. For the Haitian elite to continue to maintain their position through the use of a foreign language not only retards the internal development of Haiti and abuses the Haitian people but can only damage the movement of Haiti toward a progressive political, economic, and cultural position in the world.

Catholicism in Haiti

Somewhat similar to Haiti's colonial relationship with the French language, Haiti's relationship with Roman Catholicism has also been curious. It was, after all, the religion of the slave owners. Before independence everyone was officially a Roman Catholic since the French king had ordered the baptism of all slaves. After independence in 1804 when all Haitians feared the return of the French, it was the religion of the enemy. Although the constitution established by Toussaint in 1801 declared the official religion to be Catholicism, Dessalines in 1804 declared that independent Haiti was to be unencumbered by an official religion, though he named himself head of his own version of the church and appointed his own priests. For the next half-century Haiti was isolated from the Roman Catholic church. The Vatican did not recognize Haiti, and no priests came from the Pope.

With all the legitimate priests gone, only renegade priests performed the sacraments. While the elites, nevertheless, remained nominally Catholic and retreated to the cities, the countryside turned wholeheartedly to Voodoo. In 1860 the government of Haiti and the Vatican signed a Concordat that reestablished Catholicism as the state religion run by foreign priests. For the most part this agreement remained the basis for the church-state relationship until the ouster of the Duvaliers. The agreement called for the Haitian government to support the Catholic church financially. According to a current book on Haiti,

> The 1981–82 budget allocated more than $400,000 to pay the Catholic clergy, who number about 150 priests in 132 parishes. There are over 600 nuns and brothers, and French historian Cornevin reports there are 20,000 students in Roman Catholic educational institutions.[35]

As a general statement, however, it is quite accurate to say that very few Haitians can be counted as practicing Catholics. According to a 1969 survey of religion in Haiti,

> After baptism at birth most have nothing to do with the life of the Church. The number of priests is woefully inadequate to care for the population, in spite of the help of the missionary orders.[36]

Various authorities have estimated that fewer than 5 percent of the Haitians attend mass more than once a year—and most of that percentage is confined to Port-au-Prince.

Peasants have always thought of the Catholic church as being part of the state, though they incorporate some of the church's rituals into Voodoo. Until the overthrow of Jean-Claude Duvalier, the church had always worked in collaboration with the urban governments. In 1941 and 1942 under President Elie Lescot the government engaged in the notorious "antisuperstition" campaign that was supposed to rid the nation of Voodoo forever. The Catholic church enthusiastically supported the campaign. Although earlier President Estimé seemed to favor Voodoo, it was only after François Duvalier became president in 1957 that the government clearly opposed the Roman Catholic church. When Duvalier's nationalist policies and the Catholic church clashed, the church excommunicated Duvalier, specifically over his expulsion of white bishops. In 1966, however, the president and the Vatican finally agreed on the appointment of five bishops and one archbishop, four of whom were black.

When Jean-Claude took over as dictator from his father, he put on the appearance of a good Catholic. By the 1980s, however, the Haitian Catholic church had become nationalistic—in contrast to and against the Duvalier-style of nationalism. During a seven-hour stop in Port-au-Prince on March 9, 1983, Pope John Paul II made a speech at the airport in Port-au-Prince in which he explicitly attacked injustice, inequality, oppression, and called for social change, saying, in an often-quoted phrase, "Something must change here." (The Pope also made unfortunate references to the "slavery of voodoo cults.") The homily was certainly not what the government expected, and it sent shock waves throughout the country.

Although the Haitian press censored the remarks by the Pope, the Roman Catholic radio station Soleil broadcast the words and everyone in Haiti knew what had happened within a matter of days. By April, 860 priests and others had signed a statement calling for more social change. In the next year Haitian Catholics held the first national meeting of the local organizations known in Creole as *Ti Legliz* (little church). These groups concentrated on grassroots economic projects and local political management, and they quickly became a focus of government oppression. Radio Soleil itself was destroyed on July 21, 1985, the day before the phony referendum on Duvalier's dictatorship. The Catholic church became instrumental in organizing the people to rally behind the movement that resulted in the expulsion of Duvalier in February 1986.

The flash point against Duvalier was reached on November 28, 1985, when militiamen fired on a student protest in Gonaives (the town where Haitian independence from France was declared in 1804) and killed three students. The protest was organized at the College of the Immaculate Conception and inspired by liberation theology.[37]

The Roman Catholic church in Haiti, however, had few structural components for its actual participation in political processes. Despite the rhetoric of its liberation theology no priests accepted government posts or ran for political office. After its initial role in organizing the protests leading up to the liberation of the country from the Duvalier dynasty, the church has appeared to have become irrelevant. It is difficult to gauge the influence of the Catholic church on the November 1987 elections since those elections were aborted, and the church seems to have had little influence on the January 1988 elections that were controlled by the provisional military-oriented government.

In the confusion following the fall of the Duvaliers, however, members of the Francophile elite and foreign missionaries attempted another anti-Voodoo campaign. A letter was published in the February 17, 1986, issue of the newspaper *Le Nouvelliste* calling for the provisional government "to issue a communication to organize the destruction of all Voodoo temples."[38] The Roman Catholic radio station, Soleil; the protestant station, Lumiere; and two independent stations, Caciques and Caraibe, joined in the call. During the next few days an unknown number of Voodoo priests were killed by bands of "Christian youths." Some of these priests may have been killed because they were also henchmen of the Duvaliers. The government, however, appeared to do little to stop the killings until foreign publicity later in the month forced the government to request the radio stations to cease their inflammatory broadcasts.[39]

Despite the laudable role of the Catholic church in opposing the abuses of the Duvalier dictatorship, the traditional alliance of the church with the elite continues to concern Haitian intellectuals. Foreign priests still control most of the best Port-au-Prince schools. Many of the priests still come from French middle-class Breton families and are trained for service in Haiti at a French seminary at St. Jacques near Quimper in Brittany. Many now also come from

Quebec in Canada. Most of the schools run by these priests have always encouraged conservative political beliefs and have "generally adopted a francophile position and ha[ve] helped to legitimate the claims of the elite."[40] They now send the same antiprogressive message to the last remaining hope of Haiti, that is, the children of the rising black middle class.

In addition to the *Ti Legliz,* which are usually run by Haitian and North American priests, the French priests show a clear preference for implementing economic projects through nonpolitical groups called *gwoupman agrikòl* (agricultural organizations). According to a recent study, these groups are "inherently less confrontational" in their approach to social change.[41] The preference for a nonconfrontational approach on the part of the French priests is a result of their conservative theology. The fact that non-French priests encourage confrontation, however, limits possibilities for change through compromise. Probably neither approach will be decisive in the long run, since economic, political, and ecological factors will play the most important roles in Haiti's future. In the short run, however, "the stress Catholic programs place on small-group autonomy and [the] training of local leaders limits the ability of the Church to truly control community movements."[42] As usual, after the colonial apparatus has had its impact, the Haitians are left to themselves to straighten out the situation.

photo by Joan Flocks

5 Haitians gather at a rally in Miami after the overthrow of Jean-Claude Duvalier.

*N*orth America and Haiti

As I pointed out in chapter 1, most of what North Americans have heard about Haiti concerns the boat people, the AIDS connection, and zombies. In all three cases most of the information generated for publication comes from biased sources, the overwhelming thrust of which is to add fuel to the already smoldering negativism of the common folk model of Haiti. I have uncovered the origins of these biases in chapter 2 and have traced their development in chapter 3. Haiti has also suffered from its colonial and neocolonial connections with France and North America. The exploitation of Haiti by France is historical; the exploitation by the United States, however, continues today.

The relationship of the United States with Haiti has admittedly never been a topic of great importance for most North Americans. I have even found that most incoming students at the University of Florida are quite surprised to learn that the U.S. Marines occupied Haiti from 1915 through 1934 as a part of the gunboat diplomacy the United States exercised throughout the Caribbean during the first half of this century. Good accounts of the historic relations between the United States and Haiti are certainly available, though they are, for the most part, rather obscurely published and rarely read.[1]

Even among Haitians themselves the folk memory of the American Occupation is rather dim. I could not find any peasants in the Cap-Haitien area who knew anything about the Occupation or its effects. Some of the educated Haitians knew about it but only through reading, and they had no emotional reaction to the straightforward exploitation that the Occupation represented and the underlying racism that it reflected.

The United States carried out the Occupation for pressing economic and strategic reasons, but the popular contemporary accounts of a Haiti characterized by cannibalism, violence, stupidity, wanton sex, and laziness that I documented in chapter 3 could only reinforce the notions of the North American public that authoritarian outside intervention was the only way to curb that nation's savage inclinations. Just a few years before 1915 writers had made a point not only of insisting that cannibalism was widespread in Haiti but also that "the United States should take this irresponsible island republic in hand and administer to it a salutary lesson."[2] Others, lamenting that in Haiti "one misses the lightheartedness of our own darkies,"[3] suggested that superior white nations were destined to rule rude black ones.[4]

Despite a racist folk model, however, not all the reaction to the Occupation was favorable. Black organizations, such as the NAACP, consistently opposed the occupation of Haiti.[5] Beginning in 1920 the American intellectual magazine *The Nation* carried many articles about the atrocities of the U.S. Marines in Haiti and other negative aspects of the American Occupation.[6] *The Nation* continued this education campaign through 1934 with a final article by the managing editor triumphantly titled "At Last We're Getting Out of Haiti."[7] *The Nation* also carried pro-Haitian articles by the famous black writer and adviser to Warren G. Harding, James Weldon Johnson.[8]

The semiofficial responses to these charges were carried in another intellectual magazine, *Current History*.[9] Reports by neutral organizations, such as the Foreign Policy Association, were generally sympathetic to Haiti.[10] The progressive views of *The Nation* and the reports of foreign policy organizations, however, were little-read compared to uncritically pro-American articles in such popular publications as the *National Geographic*[11] and *Review of Reviews*.[12]

The general attitude of the American government toward Haiti in the 1910s can be inferred from the response of the incoming secretary of state, William Jennings Bryan, to a briefing on Haiti in 1912: "Dear me, think of it! Niggers speaking French."[13] Such an attitude, coupled with an overtly racist president, Woodrow Wilson, and a U.S. Marine Corps dominated by officers from the southern states, led to the harsh treatment that Haiti received from the American Occupation. The degree of the harshness eventually prompted American elected officials to carry out a congressional investigation, which turned out to be largely a whitewash.[14]

Opinions of Haitians varied little among individual Marines. The highly placed Marine officer Smedley Butler referred to the leaders of the peasant resistance as "shaved apes, absolutely no intelligence whatsoever, just plain low nigger."[15] And a Marine colonel from Virginia writing to a fellow colonel described the Haitian elite in this way: "They are real niggers and no mistake—there are some very fine looking, well-educated polished men here, but they are real nigs beneath the surface."[16]

Despite the background of nearly two decades of intimacy during the Occupation, the American government has rarely exercised a progressive influence on Haitian administrations. Only two contemporary occasions come to mind. In August 1977 on a visit to Port-au-Prince, Andrew Young, the American ambassador to the United Nations, expounded on President Jimmy Carter's expressed interest in human rights and issued a warning to the Haitian government that economic aid would be directly tied to human rights. The consequent sociopolitical liberalization in Haiti lasted until the election of Ronald Reagan as president of the United States.

In the 1980s the Black Caucus of the American Congress developed an interest in Haiti that came about largely from the publicity surrounding the discriminatory treatment of Haitian refugees. In 1982 two black members of the American Congress, Walter Fauntroy and Shirley Chisolm, journeyed to Port-au-Prince as part of the Caucus Task Force on Haitian Refugees. Black members of the American House of Representatives have continued to show their concern for events in Haiti. Currently, the dramatic increase in Haitian refugees—at least 7,104 in the two months since the October 29, 1991, coup, according to the U.S. Coast Guard—has brought the immigration policy to the attention of national leaders such as Senator Edward Kennedy.

The Occupation affected Haitian intellectuals of the time and the reading public in the United States. The racial discrimination of the U.S. Marines forced the largely mulatto-dominated Haitian intellectuals to rethink their identity and to question whether they were imitation Frenchmen or transplanted Africans. The result was the negritude movement, a largely literary event that foreshadowed the black power and anticolonial post-World War II movements.[17] The Haitian intellectual and literary giant Jean Price-Mars was, for example, a leading figure in the early years of negritude.[18] The Haitian negritude movement also intertwined with the Harlem renaissance.[19] It was, indeed, an unlikely contribution of the American Occupation of Haiti that Haitians and black Americans came to reexamine their African roots.

A less savory literary consequence of the Occupation concerned the writings of U.S. Marines who had been stationed in Haiti. This literature ranges from the silly[20] through the fraudulent[21] to the racist.[22] Since the American Occupation brought Haiti to the attention of many writers, various scribes have used Haiti as an exotic background for adventure novels.[23]

Currently, however, Haiti is most directly related to North America through the fundamentally deleterious activities of Protestant missionaries, economic aid, and the treatment of Haitian immigrants. It is these three activities that I will examine in this chapter.

Protesting Protestantism

Few observers seem to have a clear idea of just what the Protestant churches are doing in Haiti. It is known that they have been having considerable success with superficial conversions at least. The Haitian perception of these conversions may, however, differ considerably from the expectations of the missionaries. Haitians are definitely interested in the handouts that come from the Protestant churches, primarily in the form of food and clothing. The ethnocentrism of the North American missionaries tends to interfere with an empathetic understanding of the Haitian people necessary for successful and compassionate missionary work.

Although there were Protestant missionaries in Haiti earlier, the invitation in 1817 from President Pétion to John Brown and others marked the beginning of sustained, semiofficial missionary work.[24] The earliest permanent Protestant church in Haiti was the English

Wesleyan Mission, now known as the Methodist church, which concentrated on the Catholic urban elite and grew very slowly. The Methodist church has, nevertheless, gained converts among some of the most influential segments of the elites. For example, the head of the Methodist church in Haiti, Alain Rocourt, was treasurer and apparent spokesperson for the 1987 Provisional Electoral Commission.

Traditionally, however, Protestant churches have been the least successful in areas where the Roman Catholic church has provided a sufficient number of priests, which is usually in the cities. The real growth in the numbers of superficial converts to Protestantism has come in the poorer rural areas since World War II. For example, one of the largest Protestant churches, the American Baptist Convention, has almost 80 percent of its Haitian membership in rural areas, particularly in the north. Members of some Baptist churches have become political leaders. For example, a Baptist minister, Sylvio Claude, was a leading presidential candidate in the November 1987 elections.

The Protestant denominations are overwhelmingly North American. In addition to the Baptists, some of the largest denominations include the Episcopalians, Seventh Day Adventists, and the Church of the Nazarene. An enormous amount of fragmentation makes documentation difficult. These denominations operate schools, hospitals, and various vocational training centers, and they emphasize the use of Haitian Creole. According to an investigator who surveyed the Protestant churches in Haiti in 1969 at the request of the West Indies Mission,

> No one knows how many different denominations there are.... There are a number of freelance missionaries who go to Haiti regularly as tourists.... Their missions are not registered with the government. There are also many national churches which are not registered either.[25]

Estimates of the number of Haitian Protestants range from 10 percent[26] to 25 percent.[27]

The major question about these numbers concerns just what they mean. The Haitians have their own folk models of religion, and they generally fit the alien religious beliefs and practices into the predesignated slots of their indigenous cognition system. The more sophisticated of the Protestant missionaries recognized that "Vodun represents a world view held by the majority of Haitians [and] is one of the most significant factors in Haitian life."[28]

One of the most common characteristics of Protestant missionaries in Haiti is that they regard Voodoo and Protestantism as mutually exclusive. These missionaries usually regard the lwa as demons and identify possession as demon possession. Protestantism in Haiti nearly always emphasizes to potential converts that they must totally renounce Voodoo in order to become true Christians. Such a presentation of Christianity combined with the world view of rural Haitians leads these Haitians to interpret the conversion experience in at least two different ways.

For many Haitians "conversion to Protestant Christianity in Haiti is primarily conversion *from* Vodun."[29] And, again, as some sophisticated Protestant investigators realized, many Haitians "are not interested in the positive content of the Protestant faith but only in the fact that Protestants are exempt in some way from the powers of vodun."[30] Indeed, "the church leaders [of the Association of Missionary Churches], who have made it a point to find out people's motives for becoming Protestants agree that the principal motive has been to find release from vodun."[31] The missionaries are apparently not so much aware that these converts are also exempt from the duties and obligations of Voodoo that cement the rural community into a web of mutually respectful and strengthening interpersonal relationships.

My own work in the Cap-Haitien area strongly suggested that most converts to Protestantism are, indeed, trying to escape the community obligations that they would have under Voodoo. Nevertheless, they interpret the conversion experience within the context of their Voodoo world view, a world view imbedded not only in the observable rites and ceremonies of Voodoo practices but also in the very cognitive fabric of their day-to-day interactions with their physical and social surroundings. Conversion, then, is often viewed as ritual for dealing with some extreme disease, discomfort, or malaise that has not been amenable to Voodoo cures.[32]

The endemic misunderstanding of Haitian life-styles by missionaries is, of course, imbedded in the missionaries' own folk model. The bigotry of many of the Protestant missionaries is well illustrated in the words of one who wrote, "Haiti is a land of contrasts . . . between the life of a born-again Christian and the life of a fear-ridden Voodooist."[33] The missionaries almost always refer to Voodoo as a superstition.[34]

Protestant missionaries from the United States have their own peculiar attitudes connected with their own peculiar American subculture, which is inextricably bound to the values of capitalism. In particular, evangelical Protestant missionaries in their attempt to restructure "the native conceptual universe [are laying] the ground[work] for its integration into the industrial capitalist world."[35] In a clear demonstration of the ties between the expansion of Christianity in southern Africa and the expansion of capitalism, it has been pointed out that Christianity "teaches the poor to be diligent, humble, patient and obedient"—and to make good factory workers.[36]

More than one missionary made it clear to me that they thought there was a definite connection between Voodoo and poverty in Haiti, and Christianity and wealth in the United States.[37] One stated to me,

> These people usually just want to do a little work on their own land, their own project, just for themselves, just enough to get along and then spend it all. They don't really understand the social power and dignity of work and cooperation. Part of the Christian message is to teach the dignity of working for others, the power of saving your money, investing in what your family needs, and not complaining all the time and fighting the government and trying to change things. When things get really bad, though, they'll get the point.

In looking for things to get really bad, that particular Baptist missionary understood more of the situation than he himself probably realized. In an earlier review of the Protestant churches in Haiti it was stated, "The failure of this [Voodoo] world view to deal with the complexities of modern life presents an opportunity for the preaching of the gospel."[38] It is, indeed, well documented that in those societies that have their indigenous culture still intact the proselytizing Christian missions enjoy a singularly striking lack of success.[39] Even the pioneering Protestant missionary in Haiti, John MacKenzie, acknowledged that Christianity's success was "the work of conquerors."[40] And a detailed study in Africa pointed out, "Only when Christianity followed on the heels of British military conquest did most Igbo people pay any serious attention to the new religion."[41]

The portrayal of Christianity as a religion that does little more than step into the void of imperialist devastation is not just an artifact of recent Euroamerican colonialism. In his authoritative seven-volume history of Christianity, Kenneth Scott Latourette, who described himself as "an active participant in the Christian [Protestant] missionary enterprise,"[42] gave the clear impression that all throughout its history Christianity has followed in the wreckage of cultures and appealed to those who have lost their cultural identity.[43] Latourette himself stated, "Never has Christianity been adopted where the pre-Christian culture remained intact."[44]

In a textbook used for giving missionaries background in the evangelical version of anthropology, Charles Kraft of the School of World Mission at the Fuller Theological Seminary (a center for the innovative training of Protestant missionaries) made clear the destructive necessity underlying proselytization[45]—even though "cultural disequilibrium is frequently the result."[46] And in a sentence that could well have been written for missionaries in Haiti, Kraft recommended, "Satan has so taken control of the operation of some cultures that rather sudden and total disruption of their world views is the only workable approach to Christianization."[47]

Although the Protestant missionaries may be allowed to disrupt the world views of the poor and downtrodden, they generally avoid questions of exploitation and tend to teach that their converts must obey the wishes of the state. At least one anthropologist has referred to evangelism as "a peculiarly anachronistic Christianity" and has pointed out that "it is ideologically opposed to confronting the issues of social injustice and capitalist exploitation."[48] Indeed, unlike many in the Roman Catholic church, most of the Protestant leaders in Haiti—with a few notable exceptions—have consciously tried to avoid politics. Protestantism has, therefore, often been viewed as part of the Duvalier regime, and several Haitian Protestants held high positions under the Duvaliers. Those associated with Protestantism were, for the most part, unable to take much credit for ending the Duvalier rule, and they currently have only a slim possibility of improving their image among the more politically active Haitians.

Exploitation and Development

The common American folk model of foreign aid is that such help actually does aid and develop the foreign country. An analytic model would more likely point out that the consequence of most foreign aid is the exploitation of the Third World by the First World. This exploitation takes several forms. One is the development of a market dependency, another is the growth of financial dependency, and still another is the exploitation of cheap labor. These and other forms of exploitation can be seen in the relationship of the United States and Haiti.

Although the primary player in foreign aid for Haiti is the U.S. Agency for International Development (A.I.D.), many other North American organizations play a role in the development efforts. One of the most progressive is the Inter-American Foundation, which was created by the American Congress in 1969 as a public corporation to support the self-help efforts of poor people in Latin America and the Caribbean. Congress acted out of a concern that traditional programs of development assistance were not reaching the poorest people. Instead of working through governments, the Foundation responds directly to the initiatives of the poor themselves by supporting local, private organizations.

Many Foundation grants go to grassroots organizations such as agricultural cooperatives, community associations, and small urban enterprises. Other grants go to larger organizations that work with local groups and provide them with credit, technical assistance, training, and marketing services.

Unfortunately, other American agencies are not so apolitical as the Foundation, and other governments send aid to Haiti for their own peculiar reasons. According to one specialist on foreign aid to Haiti, "In the late 1960s and early 1970s the Canadian federal government was eager to promote its bilingual image abroad and particularly to preempt growing Quebec initiatives in the field of foreign affairs."[49] Israeli aid is linked to its "desire to influence Haiti's vote in the United Nations."[50] West Germany, Belgium, France, and the Netherlands began sending aid to Haiti in the 1970s. And an examination of the financial difficulties of Haiti shows that

during the 1970's, in just seven years, Haiti's external public debt increased seven fold from $53 million in 1973 to $366 million in 1980. This represents almost twice the rate of growth of external indebtedness in Latin America, as a whole, over the same period of time.[51]

Since 1981, when A.I.D. began almost totally bypassing the Haitian government, there has been a proliferation of private voluntary organizations, sometimes known as nongovernmental organizations, and Haiti started suffering from "a wave of development madness."[52] I estimate that there are at least 250 of these organizations in Haiti—about one for every twenty-four thousand Haitians—spending a total of more than one hundred million dollars annually. A.I.D. even funded the creation of the Haitian Association of Voluntary Agencies to try to keep track of all of them.

The major source of foreign aid, nevertheless, is the United States, which encourages foreign investment with the policies of the Caribbean Basin Initiative (CBI), monitors foreign loans through its dominance of the International Monetary Fund and the World Bank, and provides direct aid through the A.I.D. The public face of these policies is seen in the statements of American officials such as Ernest Preeg, who was the American ambassador to Haiti from 1981 to 1983 during the launching of the CBI in January 1982. Preeg claimed that the CBI presented an unprecedented opportunity for Haiti to break out of its vicious cycle of economic distress and political isolation. Consequently, the past three years have been the most active period of relations between our two countries in a generation.[53]

The private face of these policies can be found in the internal documents of the A.I.D. For example, a revealing report prepared by the A.I.D. field mission in the early 1980s recommended the complete restructuring of the Haitian economy[54]—without any apparent indigenous input. The introduction to the report envisioned the consequence of American-prepared policies such as the CBI as "an historic change toward deeper market interdependence with the United States."[55] The more appropriate word in that quotation would, of course, be *dependence*. The introduction concluded by stating the real interest of the American government in "developing" Haiti:

> a lesser effort [than the total revamping of the economy] cannot be expected to make a measurable impact on the hemisphere's poorest nation nor upon the derivative problem of *illegal* migration to the United States.[56]

The meaning of the CBI is, indeed, the old story of First World industrialists searching for cheap labor and dependent markets. In Haiti the story has a subplot of racism with a fear of Haitian immigration into the United States. As an agency of the State Department, A.I.D. is, after all, an extension of American foreign policy. A.I.D. officials might even believe that their work is helpful to Haiti, as well as to the United States. In addition to the large number of racist-oriented remarks I heard from A.I.D. officials in Haiti, the director of the A.I.D. mission in Haiti from 1977 to 1979 has put his racism into print, stating, "The principal cause of Haiti's acute underdevelopment is a set of national values and attitudes dominated by traditional African culture."[57]

In the last ten to fifteen years over two hundred North American companies have set up assembly plants, creating about sixty thousand jobs at different times.[58] The policies of the CBI, under which most of these companies operate, is, however, a American-oriented investment program for foreigners whose only benefit to Haiti is the strikingly low wage of about three dollars a day for the relatively small number of workers. The manufacturers themselves were able to avoid nuisances found in the United States such as labor unions, rising taxes, and safety regulations. In addition, these assembly plants take people out of food production, and they don't create any additional indigenous industry. Almost all of the raw material, investment capital, machinery, and management for the assembly plants were shipped in from the United States. Almost all the products of the assembly plants, such as baseballs, textiles, electronic parts, and shoes, were shipped out to the American market. Haiti at one time produced upwards of 90 percent of all the world's softballs and baseballs, even though Haitians don't play baseball or softball.

When I was in Port-au-Prince in the mid-1980s, there were about 120 assembly plants employing about forty thousand workers. Interviews with the managers indicated that they were quite grateful for the compliant workers. Interviews with the workers convinced me that a majority of them were well aware of the superior working conditions in the United States and especially the higher wages for the same skills, and many of them were saving their money to emigrate to North America. This unexpected connection between "development" and migration is documented in great detail by the director of the Immigration Research Program of Columbia University.[59]

Meanwhile, A.I.D. policies and practices bolster American interests by imposing alien strategies for development. Most of the A.I.D. agricultural projects, for example, have focused on the development of export products like coffee and sugar, displacing Haitian peasants, sending them into the cities to join the unemployed (which keeps down the wages at the assembly plants), and lowering the production of subsistence foods. For the first time in its history, Haiti has begun to import a large percentage of its foodstuffs.

A classic case of the deleterious effects of development efforts in Haiti is the way foreign agencies have dealt with the Haitian pig. African swine fever reached Haiti in 1978 when Haitian peasants held an estimated one million pigs. The viral disease killed maybe four hundred thousand pigs, and another three hundred thousand may have been slaughtered and consumed. Perhaps three hundred thousand were still alive when the pig eradication program began in May 1982. It is not clear whether these remaining pigs were in any danger or the disease had run its course. Farmers that I talked with in the Cap-Haitien area vehemently claimed that their pigs had not been sick and that the pigs had stopped dying from the swine fever months before the eradication program started.

The main reason for the involvement of the United States in the pig eradication program was particularly self-serving and "seems to have been based upon the belief of the American Secretary of Agriculture, Bob Bergland, that the presence of African Swine Fever in Haiti constituted an 'emergency situation' that threatened the swine industry in the United States."[60]

Little attention was paid to the ecological and sociocultural context of the pig in Haiti though it was clear from any analytic perspective that the pig was an important feature in the peasant economy with about 85 percent of the rural population relying on the sale of pigs for additional income. And generally the poorer the farmer's household, the more important the income from sale of its pigs.

Many knowledgeable investigators have written about how the pig played several roles, such as a medium of exchange, a savings account, an insurance policy, a form of social security, and a retirement plan. As Jean-Jacques Honorat demonstrated, "Hog production is the bank account of the Haitian peasant."[61] The valuable cash income from the sale of pigs could be used for a variety of needs and situations such as marriages, funerals, modern health and dental care, and education. The pigs could also be bartered in the indigenous economic system for health care, particularly in the form of Voodoo curing ceremonies, and on the open market for farming needs, such as seed. It also proved to be a reliable resource in times of crisis, such as crop failures or food shortages.

The pig was, of course, a major source of meat protein, as well as the peasants' traditional source of grease. Some pigs were slaughtered as important elements in various religious rituals. Some of these rituals specifically require the sacrifice of a native black pig.

In addition to its strictly economic value, the pig was an important element in the ecosystem of the farm itself. As a nontoxic insecticide, the pig rooted out insects in the fields. As a substitute for plowing, the activities of the pig tended to aerate the soil. As a alternative source of inexpensive fertilizer, the pig provided a nitrogen-rich natural fertilizer.

Because of its superb adaptation to both the Haitian social and physical environment—an adaptation that took several centuries—the pig required little care from the farmer and virtually raised itself. The pig did not compete with peasants for food but, instead, fed itself primarily through foraging for wild plants and crop residues. The pig also acted as a garbage collector, keeping the villages clean by consuming a variety of domestic wastes and incidentally eliminating niches from which disease vectors could plague the villagers.

None of this mattered much to the swine industry of North America, and no story in the international media took the time and space to explain things either from the Haitian peasant's viewpoint or from an ecological perspective. What mattered was that African swine fever is a virus that kills pigs, and the only way to fight the disease is through the isolation and eradication of all infected pigs.

By 1981 the Food and Agriculture Organization of the United Nations, the Inter-American Institute for Cooperation in Agriculture (an agency of the Organization of American States), the Inter-American Development Bank, and various units of the governments of Mexico, Canada, and Haiti launched a massive eradication project. Over fifteen million dollars of the total project price of about twenty-three million dollars came from the United States, and A.I.D. took a leading role in the project. The objective was to wipe out the entire pig population of Haiti.

As is common with these types of projects, rural leaders, local organizations, and the peasants themselves were left out of the planning stage and, in fact, were never fully educated about the disease or its prevention. Few of the Haitian farmers were aware that African swine fever itself does not infect people, and that the meat from infected pigs can be eaten by humans without any injurious affects. Consequently, when rumors about the disease and the forthcoming eradication program began to spread throughout rural Haiti, many farmers killed their pigs without using the meat, assuming erroneously that it was bad. Some of these inopportune killings were made under threats from local authorities who themselves were not correctly informed about the project. The eradication project ended in June 1983, and in August 1984 Haiti was declared free of African swine fever—and of pigs.[62]

Although A.I.D. made promises of remuneration, apparently only limited compensation to selected peasants was given. All of the people in rural areas that I talked with complained of not being remunerated for their lost pigs. The increase in poverty in Haiti due to the pig eradication project has yet to be fully documented and probably never will be; the agencies involved in the project have now moved on to other things, and the international press has never displayed an interest in digging into the real causes of poverty in rural Haiti.

One obvious consequence was that many peasants were forced to move into the already overcrowded cities and join the ranks of the unemployed. Many of these added themselves to the crowds whose widespread protests contributed to the downfall of the government in February 1986.

The pig eradication project was supposed to be followed by a repopulation project, guided by the ubiquitous A.I.D. with the participation of the American Department of Agriculture and the Inter-American Institute for Cooperation in Agriculture. Despite the obvious drawbacks that could be identified by any college freshman with one semester in an introductory ecology course—as well as by any illiterate Haitian farmer—A.I.D. officials insisted on importing American breeds into Haiti in an attempt to modernize the swine industry.

White pigs from Iowa were chosen for their high breeding capacity, good health, and high feed-conversion rates. They were not, however, chosen for their adaptability to the Haitian environment. These "bourgeois" pigs, as the Haitians have labeled them, required, in fact, the kind of care that is simply extraordinarily expensive in the Haitian context.

The first bunch of imported white pigs were housed in concrete shelters, given imported fortified feed, and supplied with fresh drinking water. In other words, they lived better than most Haitians. Next, the first generation of piglets bred in these palaces were distributed to regional centers where they were kept under similar conditions.

The final part of the repopulation project was supposed to involve getting the pigs into the hands of the peasants. However, this stage of distribution has fallen far short of expectations. Most of the farmers are too poor to meet the requirements for receiving pigs, such as having approved pig pens. The high cost of feed is probably the major limiting factor. The diet of the imported pigs costs about one hundred dollars a year, more than the income of most Haitians. A journalist well-versed in Haitian life stated, "The 13-month-long, $23 million slaughter [was] a disaster so devastating that it has ended a way of life for the Haitian peasant."[63]

Apparently, Haitians with means have been obtaining the pigs that were meant for the peasants. Many of the pigs are now in the hands of wealthy elites and foreign religious and other private voluntary organizations.

The pigs that have gotten into the hands of peasant farmers have not fared well. Farmers told me that only about 50 percent of the sows in rural areas were in good enough condition to reproduce. These imported pigs have few immunities against local diseases, and it is often commented that their light skin does not protect them from the hot sun. Some of my informants estimate that 40 percent of the imported pigs have died.

One of the major consequences of the "development" and "modernization" of the Haitian swine industry has been to make Haiti more dependent on American foreign assistance. The original pigs were imported. The technical assistance all came from foreign agencies. Now, all the pig feed has to be imported.

Provincial cities throughout Haiti experienced riots and protests in May 1984 in the beginning of the end for the Duvalier government. Interestingly, the food riots in Cap-Haitien in that same month were directly concerned with pig feed. The local prefect, Auguste Robinson, told me a few months later that he was greatly saddened that people were fighting over pig feed but that it was to be expected since the A.I.D. program required that the pigs be better fed than the people. By this time the A.I.D. officials had become very defensive about the entire pig affair. Displaying an embarrassing ignorance of ecology, one of them exclaimed to me in September 1984, "What's the fuss! A pig is a pig." Then in June 1986, several months after the end of the Duvalier regime, the interim government announced that it would reintroduce the Haitian black pig, pointing out that some had survived in Haiti and some would be imported from Guadeloupe and Jamaica.

The obvious inference from these events—and there are many other similar ones—is that Haiti would be better off left alone and that Haiti should develop its own self-sufficiency. There are several analytic models that attempt to explain why countries in the Third World are essentially not allowed their self-sufficiency. None of these are ever given any play in the popular media of North America, but they do provide fresh perspectives. One of these goes under the label of the world-system model. There were earlier variations of it, usually known as "dependency theory," but rather than talk about all the variations I will concentrate on some of the fundamental propositions that help explain the relationship between development and exploitation and between Haiti and North America.

We are indebted to Immanuel Wallerstein for the notion of a world-system approach explicated in his 1974 book *The Modern World-System*. The approach focuses on a single world economy with a single division of labor. This division breaks down into three spatial zones—the core states, the semiperiphery, and the peripheral areas. The core consists of negotiating states, and the periphery of competing areas. The core features diversified industry and agriculture, is capital intensive, and has a work force of skilled wage laborers. The periphery is characterized by assembly industry, labor intensive agriculture, and a monocropping labor force. These three zones are tied together through the world market in an unequal exchange, so that the core becomes increasingly developed and the periphery increasingly undeveloped.

At first the control of the core over the periphery was accomplished through blunt, coercive force. I'm referring here, of course, to the colonial era in which the periphery was simply robbed of its available resources literally at gunpoint. This same end is now accomplished through neocolonial economic control, which is more subtle and therefore more difficult to detect and combat—especially so when the process is obfuscated by folk models.

The unequal interrelationship of the core and the periphery is seen in a peculiar interdependence. The core and the periphery both depend on each other, but the core depends on the periphery in the aggregate, not individually. The United States, for example, depends on "guest workers" to do its stoop labor. Jamaicans pick apples in upstate New York and New England, and they cut sugarcane in Florida. If Jamaicans for some reason refuse to do this work, the United States just gets the labor from Trinidad or Haiti. Peripheral areas exist in abundance. An alternative to bringing in workers from the periphery is to set up assembly plants right in the peripheral areas.

The folk model of modernization assumed that the new postwar nations would travel the same path of development that the dominant North Atlantic nations had followed, namely toward a capitalist-industrial society. The world-system model, however, points out that the current well-being of the North Atlantic nations was due to their advantageous relationships with the less-developed states. Further, these advanced nations would not easily surrender their advantageous position and therefore the Third World would have to follow a different path and probably pass through different stages of development.

In other words, the analytic argument is that North America is economically powerful because it has the Third World to exploit, including, of course, Haiti. The particular type of capital-intensive enterprise that constitutes the modern First World, in fact, requires a periphery to exploit. The question is, what periphery does Haiti exploit? Of course, Port-au-Prince exploits the hinterlands, but there is really not much left to use.

World-system models rather gloomily do not allow for the possibility that the peripheral areas can ever extract themselves from their abject situation—short of some kind of apocalyptic change in the entire world system. Wallerstein does speak of an ideal type of world socialism, but he also seems to concede that world socialism is impossible. The notion is that not only are the peripheral areas not becoming developed but that they are becoming increasingly under-developed. This increasing underdevelopment is most immediately felt by the Haitians themselves, and their individual solution is to move from the periphery to the core.

The Hated Immigrant

In their dealings with Haitian immigrants, American government agencies are clearly characterized by "ideological and racial bias which continues to distort decisions as to which applications for refugee status or asylum will be approached," according to Walter Fauntroy, chair of the Congressional Black Caucus Task Force on Haiti and the expanded bipartisan Congressional Task Force on Haiti.[64] Most studies on the Haitian exodus to North America have, for example, pointed out the differential treatment accorded Cubans and Haitians.[65] Stepick reported,

> Cubans were quickly processed and released, classified as asylum applicants, while the Haitians were still classified as being in exclusion proceedings. Some of the Cubans were given cash gifts by the American authorities, while the Haitians were detained in jails.[66]

And a federal court noted, "All the Cubans who sought political asylum were granted asylum routinely. None of the over 4,000 Haitians ... were granted asylum."[67] A detailed review of the Haitian immigrant situation concluded, "Shared anticommunist objectives have taken priority over human rights."[68]

The blatant discrimination by the INS against Haitians as blacks has also been widely reported.[69] And, again, a federal court "documented the systematic violation of human rights that Haitians have suffered in the United States at the hands of the Immigration and Naturalization Service."[70] According to Judge James Lawrence King in Haitian Refugee Center versus Benjamin Civiletti,

> This case involves thousands of black Haitian nationals, the brutality of th[e Haitian] government, and the prejudice of ours [against] the

first substantive flight of *black* refugees from a repressive regime to this country.[71]

"In April 1983 the appeals court not only upheld the release of the Haitians but went even further than the Judge Spellman ruling—it found 'a stark pattern of discrimination' on the part of American immigration officials directed towards the Haitians."[72] The Civil Rights Commission noted that

the lack of minority representation and the apparent lack of sensitivity and cultural awareness on the part of some INS employees have resulted in some applicants from minority communities being treated contemptuously and presumed to be wrong until they can prove otherwise.[73]

Although New York City contains the oldest and largest Haitian-American community with probably over five hundred thousand in 1986, as pointed out in chapter 1, it is the Haitians coming to South Florida who brought the plight of these black immigrants into the national spotlight. The first boatload of Haitian refugees in December 1972 demonstrated that primitive sailing vessels could survive the 535-mile trip across the Gulf Stream. Many of the boat people who have migrated since then do not have proper travel documents, and government agencies cannot give an accurate count of them. Estimates for 1980—when the largest influx of boat people subsided—ranged from around fifty thousand, according to Bryan Walsh, director of Catholic Charities for the Archdiocese of Miami and a monsignor of Roman Catholic Relief Services,[74] to about seventy thousand, according to Thomas Wenski of the Pierre Toussaint Haitian Refugee Catholic Center in Miami.[75] Out of this number at least nine thousand did not have proper documentation before 1980.[76] The 1990 population of Haitians in southern Florida could well be more than one hundred thousand.[77]

The response to these boat people has varied as different groups have followed different components of the American folk model and their own interests. Some organizations have been forthright in their support for the rights of Haitian refugees. The state of Florida, various private organizations run by Floridians, and the federal judges have been trying to bring a sense of justice to the treatment of Haitian immigrants. The Florida newspapers, such as the influential *Miami Herald*, have been particularly helpful in bringing the plight of the Haitian boat people to the attention of the public. On the other hand, as Stepick reported,

Since 1972 national political authorities, goaded by local political groups, have attempted both to deter Haitian immigration and to deport those Haitians already in Florida. Members of southern Florida's political elite—including Democratic party members, elected officials, and some Cubans—believed that the boat people were a disruptive force, destroying the community and draining public resources. They appealed to their local Congressmen, who apparently pressured the INS into a response.[78]

"The record of the INS since then has been strikingly repugnant."[79]

Miller has found that they reflected American racial biases, and

even though the laws governing immigration in 1972 reflected vast improvements over the previous racist-oriented policies, they were, nevertheless, demeaning and tended to mitigate against black immigrants.[80]

Miller pointed out that in addition to racist laws and regulations "there was almost a total lack of blacks and other minorities in decision-making positions in INS."[81]

In dealing with the boat people the INS first tried to convince them to return to Haiti voluntarily, since the proper proceedings would be time-consuming and expensive. "Too frequently," Miller reported,

these non-English-speaking refugees have been pressured into signing documents that were incomprehensible to them, without having been informed of their right to have a lawyer or of their right to claim asylum.[82]

When such actions failed to get rid of the Haitians fast enough, the INS launched the so-called Haitian Program, which increased deportation hearings to an average of fifty-five a day—or about eighteen a day for each judge.[83] The federal judiciary finally had to order the INS to do its job legally and fairly, concluding that the INS had made the decision to expel all the Haitians no matter what credit any individual claim for asylum might have, and the federal court order itself characterized the Haitian Program as "offensive to every notion of constitutional due process and equal protection."[84] The order further stated, "The Immigration and Naturalization Service . . . violated the Constitution, the Immigration statutes, international agreements, INS regulations and INS operating procedures."[85]

As a result of the activities of the INS, many Haitians were illegally detained in American prisons and suffered much unnecessary abuse, "including the imprisonment [for about three weeks] of . . . an eight-year-old girl in a West Palm Beach jail."[86] Many of the boat people were kept in inhumane conditions in the Krome Avenue North Detention Center near the Everglades Swamp, which was ordered closed in October 1980 by the Dade County Department of Health but kept open by the federal government in clear violation of this order. In July 1981 the governor of Florida sued to close Camp Krome, noting that sixteen hundred inmates occupied facilities designed for 524 people. And still the federal government kept it open. The Haitians at Camp Krome staged several protests, and the Florida newspapers took up their cry for the closing of Camp Krome. The INS finally did reduce the number of detainees at Camp Krome and upgraded the facilities. A later federal district court order by Judge Eugene Spellman called for the release of Haitians pending adjudication of their asylum petitions. "During the reign of this illegal policy, however, the American government imprisoned nearly 2,000 Haitians, primarily in Camp Krome and in Ft. Allen, Puerto Rico."[87]

In a detailed review of the legal situation through the spring of 1982 Stepick found,

The various Democratic and Republican administrations have consistently deemed Haitians to be undeserving of refugee status. Haitian advocates have focused their challenges on procedural irregularities and the discriminatory treatment accorded the boat people by the INS. The challenges have apparently done nothing to alter the views of the INS or the administration. Under court pressure, policies, and less frequently practices, have been improved. Yet, whenever possible, at the lifting of a court order or the change of an administration, policy and practice have reverted to the former standards.[88]

In 1991, INS facilities and policies were still lacking. On August 7, 1991, Senator Connie Mack toured the Krome Detention Center and urged federal officials to speed up Haitian detainee cases.[89]

The Immigration Reform and Control Act of 1986 allowed many Haitians, especially those whose arrival had been recorded by the INS before January 1, 1982, to apply for permanent residency.

Haitians who did not have any record of their pre-1982 arrival or who had worked in seasonal agriculture for at least ninety days between May 1, 1985, and May 1, 1986, could apply (along with other undocumented immigrants) for temporary residency under two more complicated provisions of the new law.[90]

Unfortunately, a number of complications in this new law left many Haitians out in the cold.

Continued government discrimination against Haitians resulted in a May 8, 1986, letter to Attorney General Edwin Meese from Peter Rodino, chair of the House Judiciary Committee, stating,

I am compelled to express my strongest sense of outrage and protest over the continued discrimination accorded nationals of Haiti by departments and agencies of this government, particularly the Immigration Service.[91]

Haitians are, after all, unique among ethnic groups. In the United States they are black immigrants in a society largely dominated by whites, and they are speakers of French and Creole in an English-language nation. Although the Haitian-American population contains some highly educated members, most work at low-prestige jobs and live in low-rent neighborhoods. Laguerre estimated, "Roughly 70 percent of the Haitian population in New York belongs to the lower class."[92] It is clear that "Haitians arrive in the United States with a sense of being different from the other Caribbean immigrants due to their early independence, historical isolation, unique language, and African heritage."[93] And although legally vindicated in many ways, "socioeconomically they remain at a terrible disadvantage in Florida and nationwide."[94]

Haitians obviously suffer from something more fundamental than bungling bureaucrats and stupid government policies. Dougé's remark that "the fear of miscegenation, the fear of being overwhelmed by nonwhites, is a very important concern of white America"[95] pinpointed a deleterious component of the American folk model that cannot be overlooked. Haitians are the immigrants that Americans love to fear and hate, and yet Haitians continue to try to reach Florida. In January 1987 "more than 120 Haitian refugees found aboard two rickety sailing ships were intercepted by [the U.S. Coast Guard] and returned to their homeland."[96] By the end of the year the Coast Guard was still intercepting Haitians, having taken over four hundred Haitians from two overcrowded boats intercepted off eastern Cuba on Christmas Day 1988.[97] A few months later in March 1989 the Coast Guard cutters stopped 1,391 Haitians at sea, more than in any one month since the interdiction program began in 1981, and Coast Guard officials were publicly complaining that Haitian interception was hampering drug interdiction efforts.[98] Nevertheless, Haitians continued their perilous boat journeys with, for example, 136 in a forty-five-foot fishing boat in September 1990, and ninety-one crowding a forty-foot sailboat in October 1990—all caught and turned back by the U.S. Coast Guard.[99]

In the first half of 1991 the government apparently began changing the rules by which Haitians interdicted at sea might file asylum claims. Of the approximately twenty-two thousand Haitians turned back at sea since 1981, only twenty have been allowed to come into Miami to pursue political asylum claims, and of these twenty, twelve were admitted in the first few months of 1991. The number, however, still remains a small part of the total trying to get into the United States. In April 1991, for example, only nine of the 106 Haitians on one vessel were allowed to pursue political asylum claims.[100] In July 1991 people in Miami were shocked to see five Haitian men caged and shackled on the deck of a freighter awaiting deportation to Haiti. The reasons that Haitians continue to leave Haiti are obvious. The most accurate estimations suggest that at least 80 percent of the Haitian population is rural with an extremely high population density of about five hundred persons per square kilometer of cultivated land.[101] Rural Haiti does not provide many opportunities for a decent standard of living. The farmers have to grow their crops on very small and scattered plots of land, they are forced to cut valuable trees for cooking fuel, they do not have the capital to buy the resources (fertilizer, high-grade seeds, equipment) for intensive farming, they continually deal with the ever-increasing problem of soil erosion, and they suffered greatly from the eradication of their pigs. Fewer than 1 percent of the houses in rural areas have electricity, and education is so underdeveloped that about 80 percent of the adult population is illiterate. And as one might expect in such a poor country, "most of the rural population must still be classified as suffering from chronic malnutrition."[102]

Rural Haiti is a good place to leave, and there are very few opportunities for employment in the small, crowded cities of Haiti. It is only in comparison to the numbing economic hopelessness of Haiti that one can understand the joy with which the hardworking Haitians approach life in the United States—even the degrading life of the exploited migrant worker. As one investigator explained,

While sustaining their hopes for life in the United States, Haitians tolerate the degrading and oppressive conditions of farm labor. Inside dilapidated tarpaper shacks and crude cinder-block barracks, Haitian women proudly maintain tidy living quarters. They cannot, however, disinfect the stinking, disease-ridden latrines or the contaminated wells which have been approved for 'migrant use' by county health inspectors. Migrant farmworkers frequently suffer from dysentery and upper respiratory illnesses which directly result from the unsanitary conditions of the labor camps.[103]

Nevertheless, among Haitians in the United States "food stamps and welfare rates are very low."[104]

Despite their abhorrence of crime, especially violent crime, Haitians have become increasingly involved in the trafficking in cocaine in the American South. Very few Haitians use illicit drugs, but many have discovered that the retailing of crack cocaine is a way out of manual labor and a step toward the material rewards of the American dream. Although most of the new immigrants are in southern Florida, they had been fairly successful by 1987 in establishing a drug distribution network throughout Florida and into Georgia, retailing the drugs mostly in black neighborhoods. For the most part they purchase powdered cocaine from Columbians and then process it into crack, an inexpensive and highly addictive drug.

"In 1986 and 1987 some law enforcement officials in east and central Florida claimed that from 70 to 90 percent of the crack cocaine distribution was being controlled by four Haitian families."[105] Haitians have, indeed, been arrested and convicted in several north central Florida counties such as Alachua.[106] In May 1987 officials announced the arrest of nine people in busting one of the biggest cocaine rings in the American South—and six of the alleged dealers were Haitians.[107]

Nevertheless, as a response to the growing public recognition of discrimination against Haitian immigrants the new Cuban-Haitian Adjustment Act legalizes both Cubans and Haitians who applied for political asylum before January 1, 1982. Beginning in March 1987 with the announcement of the new regulations, many of the estimated seventy thousand Haitian refugees in Florida crowded immigration offices and community centers to initiate the process of becoming permanent American residents.

Still other Haitians have returned to Haiti to participate in the post-Duvalier politics. Some of these are interested in self-aggrandizement; others, in helping to develop the homeland. Most, however, will make their decision about where to live on an economic evaluation, and the basis for such a decision remains summed up in the words I've commonly heard from many Haitians *Ou pa kapab fè lavi nan Ayiti* (you can't make a living in Haiti).

Not only can Haitians not make a living anymore in Haiti, but since the October 29, 1991, military coup, the island nation has become highly volatile with at least one thousand people killed in the two months before New Year's Day. A steady stream of refugees has been intercepted by the U.S. Coast Guard, straining its resources to their limits. The United States temporarily housed over 5,500 Haitians in tents at Guantánomo Bay, the American base on the southeastern tip of Cuba, as American federal judges on Dember 13, 1991, for the third time continued to maintain that the Haitians are fleeing for economic, not political, reasons and therefore do not deserve asylum. Such reasoning became difficult to justify as both political violence and economic hardships increased in Haiti. Even the American press began to question the basic validity of American policy. A story in *Newseek* asked, "The awkward fact with which U.S. policy wrestles is that people flee the world's Haitis for a combination of motives. All are deserving of some compassion, but how much?"[108]

photo by Paul Monaghan

6 A vendor of household items at the livestock market in Croix de Bouquet.

*H*aitian Culture, Politics, and Prospects

Georges Salomon, former Haitian ambassador to the United States, once said, "In Haiti, with all our poverty and misery, we have had one striking success: we have been able to create a true elite. The talent and charm of this elite is something we should be proud of."[1] This statement does not dispute the ultimate wisdom of concentrating political power in the hands of a very small group whose interests are politically particularistic and personally self-aggrandizing. As a largely urban group with few profitable land holdings to support itself, the Haitian elite has traditionally used the government and its authority to tax as a source of personal income. Such a perception of government on the part of the elite has worked against the conception of public office as a public trust and even against the concept of social responsibility.

In contrast, the Haitian masses have for over a century been seemingly satisfied with their small plots of land and have expected nothing better from the government than to be left alone. A popular Haitian proverb, in fact, states, *Apre Bondye se leta* (After God comes the state), meaning that government is best left to others. In line with the arguments discussed in previous chapters, such a perception of government on the part of the masses has been misused by racists in their claims that blacks are easily manipulated and, therefore, innately incapable of stable self-government. Contemporary journalists have echoed this sentiment, saying, "For decades the mostly poor and illiterate people of Haiti have accepted their fate at the hands of corrupt dictators."[2]

The actual situation is, of course, much more complex. Dictators do not operate in a vacuum; certain groups in society support dictatorships because members of these groups somehow gain something from the existing government. A nation does not survive forever on charm alone. Of course, the talent and charm in Haiti are not at all limited to the elite. The political events following the ouster of the Duvalier regime have involved a very wide variety of urban and rural groups in an attempt to develop a progressive government. Even peasants in some of the most isolated areas of Haiti have come to think of the government as the cause of problems—such as obtaining potable water—and, conversely, these same peasants have come to think of the government as a potential source of solutions.

There is, however, no escaping the fact that governments in Haiti have been run primarily by members of the elite, and despite the early and heroic independence of Haiti from France—and from slavery— the attitude of the elite classes of Haiti has traditionally been a colonial one. The major event in the modern evolution of these classes has been what is usually termed the Haitian renaissance. Largely literary but definitely reflecting a sociocultural and economic context, the beginning of this renaissance is marked by the American Occupation in 1915 and the indigenism movement, a movement of intense self-examination, which developed the awareness of Haitianness, whether black or mulatto, urban or rural, elite or peasant. Beginning just after World War II and lasting to about 1953, the literary and sociopolitical movement known as negritude helped Haitians place themselves in a Caribbean and African context. The contemporary segment of the Haitian renaissance is the ongoing increase in the use of Creole as the appropriate language for Haiti.

The Haitian renaissance, then, consists primarily of intellectuals attempting to divest themselves of their assimilated French culture. As stated by Patrick Bellegarde-Smith, a perceptive student of the Haitian elite, "The psychology of colonialism had so affected the mentality of those who lived under it that the thinking of individuals confronting the realities of the world order were permanently distorted."[3] By changing their psychology, Haitians should be better able to approach indigenous problems with indigenous solutions.

This chapter looks at four aspects of the contemporary sociocultural and political scene in Haiti. All four—relations with the neighboring Dominicans, the use of Creole in public life, the place of Voodoo in the national psyche, and the development of political institutions—represent long-standing problems.

Living with the Dominicans

As might be expected, most of the Haitian emigrants go to their next-door neighbor, the Dominican Republic. The 193-mile border that Haiti shares with the Dominican Republic on the island of Hispaniola is largely unguarded and the neighbor has traditionally offered jobs to Haitians in sugarcane fields. The Dominican Republic has also traditionally offered some of the most venomous anti-Haitian racism to be found.

The roots of this semiofficial hatred are deep and tangled. Indeed, Dominicans have long been noted for the difficulties that they have with their own cultural and somatic identity.[4] Foreigners are often startled to find Dominicans with distinctly African appearances insisting that their background is Amerindian. As with other scholars, Lil Despradel locates this virile racism in the volatile history of Hispaniola and the peculiar class structure of Dominican society.[5] In addition, Despradel documents the cultural alienation of Dominicans from their African heritage and their racistly defensive nationalism.[6]

Europeans first established slavery in the Americas with the importation and exploitation of black Africans to the island of Hispaniola in 1510. With at least seven racial and sociocultural categories, Dominican society came to consist primarily of people who were constantly attempting to slip into the next higher and "lighter" category. In such a situation "the racist attitude of the Dominican mulattoes showed their cultural alienation" as they attempted to deny their African origins.[7]

Part of this denial focused on the muddled notion of Amerindian ancestry. Even though the Amerindians were exterminated in the sixteenth century, Dominicans created the myth of a cultural identity based on Amerindian ancestors to explain their dark color.[8] This highly vulnerable myth meant that the Dominican national identity became based on the fanatically held belief that they were not black and therefore not like Haitians,[9] so that "the racist ideology of the dominant classes, along with the myth about the presence of Indian blood, attempts to make people forget about their African origins."[10]

It should be stressed that it was the upper classes who felt most threatened by non-European cultural and somatic elements and who developed this antiblack folk model. Peasants in the Dominican Republic, whose skin was generally darker than members of the upper classes, had little antagonism toward Haitians throughout the first decades of the nineteenth century.[11] In fact, "certain groups manifested evidence of African culture in certain religious ceremonies, in music, in dance, and in cuisine."[12]

At the end of the nineteenth century, however, massive immigration of Haitians and other West Indians into the largely American-owned sugar industry put these black workers into direct competition with Dominicans. The result was racial antagonism. Before long, "all African cultural manifestations were considered savage and 'Haitian.' In particular, Voodoo attracted the attention of the dominant classes and was prohibited by law."[13] Dominican newspapers made much of the preposterous notion of Haitians eating children in their Voodoo rites.[14]

As of 1990, about 90 percent of the cane cutters in the Dominican Republic were Haitians; about four hundred thousand Haitians lived there. Nevertheless, according to Martin Murphy, an anthropologist who has spent many years in the Dominican Republic and several among the Haitian workers in the Dominican sugarcane fields, although anti-Haitianism exists nowadays among lower-class Dominican sugarcane workers, it is not anywhere near as virulent as that of the dominant classes.[15]

The tenuous cultural alliance between the lower classes of the Dominican Republic and Haiti does not mean that the Dominican power elite simply lets these people fraternize with each other. As recently as 1963 paramilitary Dominican troops slaughtered a group of Dominicans and Haitians in a frontier town—apparently for practicing Voodoo together.[16] Many upper-class Dominicans will even claim that Voodoo does not exist on the "civilized" side of the island, though Dominican social scientists themselves have made studies of Dominican Voodoo and have often compared it with the Haitian variety.[17]

The historical origins of the anti-Haitian elements in the racist folk model of Dominicans may be found in the Haitian occupation of the present-day Dominican Republic from 1822 to 1844, as well as in the earlier invasions of the Spanish-speaking side of the island by Haitians under their revolutionary leader Dessalines.[18] During this occupation the Haitians upset the upper-class Dominicans by abolishing slavery, proclaiming sexual equality, requiring French in official communications, redistributing the land to the lower classes, glorifying blackness by placing blacks in important positions, and using Dominican resources to pay Haiti's French debt. Although the United States has occupied the Dominican Republic twice since then, Dominicans frequently refer to the Haitian ordeal as "the Occupation."

By the turn of the century, professional Dominican historians themselves repeated the myths of this folk model and produced anti-Haitian textbooks proclaiming, for example, the importance of "maintaining the purity of the [Spanish] language and the morality of [Hispanic] customs."[19] Around the mid-1940s the famous Dominican historian Américo Lugo wrote about the need for a "de-Africanization" of the Dominican Republic.[20] A Dominican president has claimed, "The Dominican Republic [is] the most Spanish of the nations in the Americas."[21]

One of the most disturbing characteristics of this racist folk model is, indeed, its official nature and the expression of its most odious features by the leaders of the Dominican Republic. For example, Rafael Trujillo, Dominican dictator from 1930 to 1961, "exhibited what can only be described as a pathological phobia toward Haiti, Haitians, and everything of Afroamerican origin."[22] As if personifying the antiblack myth of Dominicans, "Trujillo used cosmetics to disguise the phenotypical features that he inherited from his Haitian grandmother."[23]

In terms of relations with Haiti, Trujillo is best known for having approximately thirty-five thousand Haitians killed in the rural areas near the border during a thirty-six-hour period beginning on October

2, 1937. He is reported to have responded to questions about the massacre by saying, "Haitians are foreigners in our land. They are dirty, rustlers of cattle, and practitioners of Voodoo. Their presence within the territory of the Dominican Republic cannot but lead to the deterioration of the living conditions of our citizens."[24] (The argument that the massacre never occurred is made in very racist terms by the former president of the National Frontier Commission.[25])

Just a decade ago a student of Dominican anti-Haitianism wrote that it "continues in all sectors of Dominican society."[26] The images of Haitians as inferior are certainly still evident in Dominican popular literature.[27] This racist folk model recently found expression in the 1986 election, and 1990 reelection, of Joaquín Balaguer as president of the Dominican Republic. Secretary of State George Schultz attended the 1986 inauguration and applauded its proceedings, seemingly implicating the United States in the Dominican folk model of Haitian-hating.

In a 1949 book (and again in a 1984 book that is mostly a reproduction of parts of the 1949 book) titled *La Isla al Revés*, Balaguer repeats as official ideology the most outrageously racist elements of the Dominican folk model. Pierre Hudicourt, a Haitian who has held diplomatic posts in the Dominican Republic, called the book "200 pages of insults to the dignity of the Haitian people."[28] It is no doubt one of the most racist tracts written by a head of state that could found in the second half of the twentieth century.

Balaguer referred to Haitians as "a people of primitive mentality"[29] and claimed, "The Ethiopian race is indolent by nature."[30] In his fear of the growing population of Haiti, Balaguer wrote of "the fecundity which characterizes the negro."[31] And he abhorred the possible "Africanization of the [Dominican] race owing to the proximity of Haiti."[32]

Haitians still migrate to the Dominican Republic for work, especially to cut sugarcane. In June and July 1991 the new Haitian government requested talks with the government of the Dominican Republic to discuss the possible repatriation of Haitians working under the harshest conditions, which are often found on state-owned plantations. The response of the Dominicans has been to deport Haitians to Haiti in a seemingly arbitrary manner, breaking up families and including troublesome Dominicans of Haitian descent, as well as unwanted Dominican criminals.

By August 1991, three months after the talks, the number of Haitians deported from the Dominican Republic had gone over ten thousand, according to Haitian authorities.[33] It seemed clear that the expulsions were partially "an effort by the Dominican Government to arouse racial and nationalistic passions as a distraction from its difficulties with striking labor unions, high unemployment, steep inflation and failing public services."[34] Shortly after the election of Aristide and his subsequent allegations of human rights abuses in the Dominican Republic, Balaguer had ordered the expulsion of all Haitian plantation workers under the age of sixteen and over sixty, apparently in an effort to forestall punitive trade sanctions from the United States for the Dominican state-owned sugar industry's low wages and its widespread use of child labor.

Interestingly, cutting sugarcane is regarded by Dominicans as work fit only for slaves, and the work conditions of Haitians in the Dominican Republic do, indeed, approach those of slavery. The Haitian government itself has contributed to these conditions through the unfavorable bilateral contracts and rapacious graft perpetrated by the Duvalier family and its associates. Research on the Haitian cane cutters in the Dominican Republic, sponsored by the Anti-Slavery Society in London, has pointed out that "for the immediate future the cards lie mostly with the [new] government of Haiti,"[35] which carries the responsibility for negotiating the contracts and controlling the supply of workers.

In recent years Haitians have also been supplying much of the labor for the growing Dominican construction industry, and many Haitians have moved into the Dominican cities, controlling much of the petty marketing. Clearly, Dominicans and Haitians have their destinies bound together and must work together to solve similar problems of surviving on the same island. It is particularly important that Dominicans overcome their racist folk model.

Solving the Language Problem

The power of the Haitian language in the minds of Haitians may be glimpsed through the well-known proverb that proclaims, *Kreyòl pale, kreyòl konprann* (Creole speaks, Creole understands). And if you, as a Haitian, want to be understood, you must speak Creole. Creole is the language of emotion, especially love and compassion. The real dynamics of life as experienced in the depths of the Haitian soul are expressed in Creole. Creole is the only first language of Haiti, and it is inconceivable that Creole could be supplanted by any other language. It is only with this paramount fact clearly in mind that one can sensibly approach the language problem of Haiti.

Haiti does have a language problem, but the problem is not difficult to understand, only difficult to solve. As I demonstrated in chapter 3, Haiti is neither bilingual nor diglossic,[36] nor does Haiti contain various ethnic groups that have different languages, like the Philippines.[37] The problem lies strictly in weighing the relative advantages of French and Creole. The power elite in Haiti exacerbates this problem by selfishly attempting to maintain French as the language of high-level communication despite the fact that the Haitian language is viewed by all Haitians as one of the primary symbols of national unity and cultural uniqueness.

Although all government documents are in French, Creole is widely used in conversations, even within the government itself. Much like the Rotary Club in Cap-Haitien, official government meetings are often opened in French, but the participants soon switch to Creole.[38]

Despite the efforts of the Haitian elite and the foreign-operated schools to denigrate Creole and elevate French, Creole continues to gain in popularity as the language through which Haitians communicate on all levels of interaction. With the introduction of a widely accepted orthography in 1979 the written literature in Creole has grown considerably—much of it coming from publishers in New York City and Miami. Support of Creole as the official language of Haiti has always had a political component and has usually been associated with opposition to the elite-controlled government. Following the fall of the Duvalier dynasty in February 1986, Creole will no doubt become even more widely used to express the ideology of liberation.

The better-known newspapers published in Haiti and New York City, such as *Le Nouvelliste* and *Sommaire* in Haiti and *Haïti-Observateur* in Brooklyn, are entirely in French (except for occasional cartoons and advertisements in Creole). Some newspapers, such as *Haïti Progrès*, published in Brooklyn and distributed in Haiti, have some articles in French and others in Creole. Some of the better-financed newspapers that have sprung up since the fall of Duvalier are in French, such as *Haïti Libérée, Journal d' Opposition*, and *La Pintade Enchaînée*. Most of the less well-financed newspapers, however, such as *Libète* and *Jounal Moda* (an acronym for Mouvman Ouvriye e Demokratic Ayisyen, or Haitian Labor and Democratic Movement) are in Creole.

Based on a study showing that out of one hundred recent political tracts sixty-two were in Creole and thirty-eight in French, one investigator stated, "We can say straightforwardly that the Creole language played a dominant role in the fall of Duvalier."[39] He goes on to illustrate that Creole was the language of popular uprisings throughout Haitian history, concluding, "Creole is the language of mobilization."[40]

The new feeling of freedom on the part of the Haitian people since the ouster of Duvalier has had its effect on Creole. New words have sprung up, many of them related to English—very few to French—and still others being what Haitians call "real Creole words," that is, words that are combinations and recombinations of indigenous Creole sounds, many of them with sociopolitical meanings. Haitians seem to delight in their ability and freedom to play with their own language.

Even before February 1986 a number of major periodicals were published exclusively in Creole. For example, the monthly magazines of religious organizations headquartered in Port-au-Prince are written in Creole and include the widely read Roman Catholic *Bon*

Nouvèl and the popular Protestant *Boukan*. Popular literary presentations in Creole have always been wildly popular with Haitian crowds, even though as recently as the 1950s

> Haitian Francophone intellectuals argued . . . that Haitian creole was not a suitable idiom for expressing abstract thought or high, dramatic action. [Félix] Morisseau-Leroy's response was a creole adaptation of the Sophocles tragedy, *Antigone*, set in rural Haiti. Performed at the Rex Theatre for the first time on July 15th, 1953, before a middle class and elite audience, *Antigone in Creole* [c.1953] proved the efficacy of creole as a dramatic language.[41]

Frankétienne's 1978 play *Pèlin-Tèt* "was presented about 50 times to packed houses in the Rex Theater located in midtown Port-au-Prince. The enthusiasm of the audiences and the very indirect references to politics led the government to forbid further presentations after March 1979."[42] In addition to his *Pèlin-Tèt*, Frankétienne has written other plays in Creole,[43] and, indeed, a number of other successful productions for the Haitian theater have been written by such authors as Morisseau-Leroy[44] and Nono Numa.[45]

A good deal of strikingly effective poetry is now available in Creole by modern writers,[46] but perhaps the height of power and flexibility of Creole is reached in the novel. The best-known work in modern Creole is Frankétienne's *Dézafi*.[47] Another important Creole work is Emile Célestin-Mégie's *Lanmou pa gin baryé*.[48] Jean-Baptiste had two novels published in the late 1970s, *Peyi zoulout*[49] and *Sogo nan kwazman granchimin*.[50] Carrié Paultre's very popular novels *Ti Jak*[51] and *Tonton Libin*[52] were serialized in the magazine *Boukan* in the 1960s and 1970s.

Although these examples are modern literature written with widely accepted spelling systems, Creole draws its real strength from the fact that it builds on the traditional oral literature of the Haitians, which sophisticated investigators have always noted for its power of expression.[53] In fact, one of the earliest known examples of written Haitian Creole published in the United States is a small booklet of folklore under the French title *Idylles et chansons, ou essais de poësie creole*.[54]

Despite the backwardness of the literary elite and the government of Haiti in failing to promote Creole, the sustaining ideology of language comes directly from the people who strongly support Creole as the language of communication. Those who recall the language attitudes of the mulatto elite in the past stress the emphasis that these families placed on speaking French—in the home as well as in school—and write about how they denigrated Creole.[55] Scholars have, indeed, noted that some Haitians "tend to have an almost fetishistic attitude toward the French language."[56] Members of the rising black middle class, however, do not have any such attachment. While they recognize that French is necessary for advancement in business and government and, therefore, send their children to French-language schools, they themselves speak Creole almost entirely—using French only for writing and when their job requires it. The black middle-class families that I lived with in Port-au-Prince and Cap-Haitien, however, never spoke French to each other or to their children, and they found laughable the notion that Creole might be inadequate to express anything they would ever want to say.

The nation's sentiments are well mobilized in favor of Creole, though admittedly Creole has had image problems in the past. The technical difficulties of implementing Creole as the national language are, however, overwhelming.[57] Illiteracy in Haiti approaches 90 percent, funding for education is minuscule, the government is ineffective, and the power elite is committed to French.

It certainly is possible to have education in Creole, and, in fact, the Section for the Education of Adults under the director general of national education has published textbooks in Creole.[58] The Division of Rural Development under the Ministry of Agriculture has also published textbooks in Creole for elementary schools.[59] More recently, the government has been publishing manuals on health in Creole.[60]

Much of the publishing of textbooks in Creole is being carried out by private organizations, particularly religious ones. Protestant groups publish textbooks for all levels of education including secondary schools.[61] Catholic groups have concentrated on books for adult education and rural development,[62] as well as using radio broadcasts in Creole to reach rural people.[63] Some overseas Haitian groups are also publishing books in Creole on, for example, Haitian history and geography that could be used as textbooks.[64] Some bilingual programs in the United States are publishing textbooks in Creole under grants from the U.S. Department of Education.[65] In August 1979 the Haitian Institut Pédagogique National (the National Institute of Education or IPN) hosted a conference on the language problems and adopted a standard orthography for Creole. Attended by scholars from France, the Creole Institute of Indiana University, and other interested scholars and educators, the conference was sponsored by A.I.D. and the Haitian Ministry of Education. At the opening session, Joseph C. Bernard, the minister of education, announced the government's decision to use Creole as a medium of instruction, saying, "The government's goal is to provide relief from an old injustice perpetrated against 90 percent of the population which has been kept in ignorance and illiteracy."[66] The government then reorganized the Department of National Education and began a general reform of public education. Four years of experimentation were financed by the World Bank and began with about one thousand pupils studying in Creole instead of French.

The initial plan was for all subjects to be taught in Creole for the first four years with French taught as a second language. Beginning in the fifth year, French would be used as the medium of instruction. Such a plan is not entirely original. In 1919 the famous Haitian intellectual Jean Price-Mars called for the use of Creole as the language of instruction in the elementary schools since they overwhelmingly served a monolingual population. He suggested that French be taught as a foreign language in the later grades.[67] In fact, many studies have shown that children learn most effectively when instruction is in their native language.[68]

Unfortunately, the French-speaking elites felt threatened by the potential of an educated Creole-speaking mass of people, and these elites pressured the weak presidency of Jean-Claude Duvalier. By June 1982 the opposition to the education reform had focused on the use of Creole as a language of instruction and had spilled over into public debate in the newspapers of Port-au-Prince.[69] Duvalier fired the talented Bernard, and the government effectively ended all support for education in Creole.

Despite the backward attitude of the Haitian government and the apparent personal ambiguity toward Creole of Jean-Claude Duvalier's fifteen-year dictatorship, the publishing of works in Creole has been rapidly expanding since 1979. By 1981 a preliminary dictionary in the IPN orthography had been produced.[70] Although some of the religious groups in Haiti waited a few years, the major overseas publication in Creole, the defunct journal *Sèl* from Brooklyn, quickly adopted the new spelling system.[71] The difficulty in agreeing on a spelling system stemmed from the indefensible notion that Creole should be spelled like French in order for the people to more easily learn French in higher education.[72] Actually, the notion that the "inclusion of several very specific common notational conventions between Creole and French [will] facilitat[e] the acquisition of any sort of functional proficiency in French" has no linguistic legitimacy.[73]

The question of an appropriate orthography for Creole seems to be settled now, and this obstacle should no longer impede progress toward making Creole the language of record as well as of fact in Haiti. The legal progress toward the recognition of Creole as the appropriate language for Haiti can be traced in the changes in the language sections of the various recent constitutions. Article 35 of the 1980 constitution permitted the use of Creole to "safeguard the material and moral interests of those citizens who do not have a sufficient knowledge of the French language."[74] Article 62 of the 1983 constitution of Haiti declared both French and Creole to be national languages. Article 5 of the 1987 constitution, which is distributed in both Creole and French, states simply and in its totality, "A common language unites all Haitians, and it is Creole. Creole and French are the official languages of the Republic."[75]

The often-noted reluctance of the government to promote Creole as a legitimate language combines with an appalling lack of educational resources. An optimistic estimate concluded that only about 10 percent of the children in rural Haiti complete primary schooling.[76] A more recent and more realistic estimate has only 14 percent of all school-aged children attending school in rural Haiti, and almost all of them are in the primary grades.[77] In fact, only about 4 percent of children in primary schools nationwide finish their studies, and only 2 percent complete high school.[78]

In addition to the low investment by the government, other factors figure into this low attendance, including unaffordably high tuition, the use of children in agriculture, the generally poor health and nutrition of the children, and the fact that "95 children per classroom is not uncommon in rural areas."[79] Also, there is a very "high teacher attrition, estimated at 9–10% per year,"[80] mainly because teachers are paid less than secretaries.[81]

Despite some of the educational reforms in the early 1980s students for the most part are still taught in French by teachers who often have only a tenuous grasp of French themselves. Promotion to the next grade is based more on the learning of French than on mastery of the subjects. As one Haitian wrote,

> The French language in Haiti operates as an absolute value in and of itself; to such an extent that Haiti is perhaps the only country in the world where the primary objective on the elementary and secondary school level is the initiation to *language*.[82]

The result is that many children repeat grades until they drop out, tired of having the subjects presented to them in a foreign language.

A contemporary observer of the Haitian education system characterized it by saying:

> The present primary school curriculum copies the early twentieth-century French model, using the same textbooks and teaching techniques of one-way classical exposition by the teacher to passive students. Memorization is the key factor in both instruction and students' evaluation. This anachronistic curriculum is geared toward the children of the elite, who successfully fulfill the academic requirements to go on to secondary and university level education. The premise of academic progression and the materials presented based on French circumstances are alien to the Haitian world, especially in the rural areas.[83]

Indeed, a common sight that I witnessed many evenings in the wealthy Port-au-Prince suburb of Petionville is that of students pacing under lampposts memorizing passages from French textbooks. The promotion of the French language is clearly the most serious obstacle in solving Haiti's language problem. This fact is recognized by sophisticated Haitians writing on the problem, such as one who bluntly stated, "One of the most tragic and unfortunate mistakes of Haitian leaders, throughout Haitian history, has been their adamant refusal to consider anything but French as the *language of the country*."[84] Most surveys and interviews, however, indicate that Haitians prefer for their children to be educated in French,[85] but such feelings are only a function of their awareness of the current structure of Haitian government and commerce in which proficiency in French is needed in order to advance. This current structure, however, does not reflect the real world language situation. Certainly the post-World War II decline of French as the international language of diplomacy and commerce needs no documentation.

A progressive government can change Haiti's dependency on a declining language. The poverty of Haitian education means that the nation has not yet invested its educational resources in French. The lack of governmental archives means that the government has not yet invested its archival resources in French and still has a chance to set things right. In fact, the widespread illiteracy itself means that Haiti still has a real chance—now rare in the Third World—to make a rational decision about the national languages that it will use to conduct its own government and business and its transactions with the rest of the world.

The obvious progressive decision is to eliminate French as a national language and to proclaim what is already true in fact, that is, that Creole is the primary national language of Haiti. The French culture as well as the French language belongs to the colonial and neocolonial past of Haiti. Even a scholar of the French literature of Haiti stated, "The French heritage is becoming, it seems to me, a matter of historical interest rather than a living reality."[86] Creole is the language of the progressive and nationalist future of Haiti.

After making the decision to use Creole internally for all governmental, commercial, and social purposes, Haiti will be faced with the decision of what language to use with the rest of the world; obviously Creole is rarely spoken outside of Haiti. The fact that indigenous languages are rarely used outside of national boundaries is a problem common to the Third World. Not only is an international language needed but probably higher education in Haiti will have to be in an international language since it is fairly inconceivable that the world's literature can be translated into Creole.

In making a decision about the second languages, Haitians must consider the geography of Haiti and the languages of its neighbors. The most important trading partner and political ally of Haiti is the English-language nation of the United States. The second most important neighbor is the nation that Haiti shares the island of Hispaniola with, the Spanish-language Dominican Republic. In fact, if the myth of Haiti as a French-language country needs any further deflation, consider the following: Despite the fact that much of the literature of Haiti is in French, the most widely spoken second language in Haiti is Spanish, not French. Probably the most widely read second language of Haitians, if we include Haitian-Americans, is English, not French.

Over one million of the six million Haitians live in non-Creole-speaking countries. At least five hundred thousand live in the United States, maybe fifty thousand in Canada, and at least fifty thousand in the English-speaking Lesser Antilles and the Bahamas. More than five hundred thousand live in the Dominican Republic, Venezuela, and Mexico. Only between fifteen and thirty thousand live in France.

Except for Guadeloupe and Martinique, where the official language is French but where the people speak a creole mutually intelligible with Haitian Creole, all the neighbors of Haiti are English- and Spanish-language peoples. The conclusion, again, is obvious. English and Spanish should be the second languages of Haiti.

Since the end of World War II, American English has been the most rapidly spreading international language, and large segments of the Haitian population have found that they derive economic, social, and political advantage from using English. Another factor in the spread of English in Haiti is the television; not only is most of the programing in English but the very important black middle class shows a marked preference for programs from the United States. All of these households in Port-au-Prince that I knew demonstrated this preference. And finally, since the fall of the Duvalier dynasty more and more Haitians are returning to their homeland from the United States. Some of these were political exiles who will play important roles in future Haitian governments; some are fairly wealthy and will make important investments in the Haitian economy. Most of them have a commitment to English as the second language of Haiti, and many of them have little acquaintance with French. All of them are devoted to Creole as the language of opposition politics.

The "dean" of language studies in Haiti, Albert Valdman, wrote,

It is unlikely that the economic, social, and political forces that fuel the expansion of English or the extension of Creole will abate in the foreseeable future, or that countervailing forces will endow French with a newly found dynamic multifunctionality. . . . In the light of the current migratory, commercial, and cultural currents in the Caribbean, the dominance of English can only increase.[87]

In order to put the nation's ideological sentiment about language into effect, a new structure for the technical teaching of language and other subjects will be needed. This type of training could be accomplished with the four years of primary education entirely in Creole. Most students will not go beyond these first four years, so these years should be taught as a self-contained unit with a heavy emphasis on citizenship, including agricultural practices, Haitian history and literature, and, of course, literacy in Creole. At the completion of these four years Haitians should be able to participate in governmental processes, such as elections and judicial systems. Those students who continue will have three years of middle school heavily emphasizing acquisition competency in Spanish and English as second languages. Secondary education will have courses in the social studies in Creole and courses in the sciences in Spanish and English. Courses in the humanities should be in Creole, Spanish, and English—and perhaps even some in French. At the tertiary level the medium of instruction will be only in English and Spanish, though French, as well as other important international languages, may be studied—and certainly Creole may be studied linguistically and anthropologically for its continued important role in Haitian personality, folklore, religion, society, and culture.

The new post-Duvalier governments showed some signs of moving toward an emphasis on Creole. The famous Creole playwright Frankétienne was briefly named minister of culture. Perhaps the happiest sign is that the popularly elected President Jean-Bertrand Aristide read from the Creole version of the 1987 constitution when he took office on February 7, 1991, and gave his inaugural address in Creole.

In addition, Aristide and Education Minister Leslie Voltaire have announced the beginnings of a potentially massive literary program at the cost of about two hundred million dollars, with all of the literacy programs in Creole. It is obvious that Haiti does not have access to the necessary funding, so

> instead of undertaking an overall national program ...,the Aristide government has created a three-member National Bureau of Alphabetization that ... will develop a curriculum and teaching methods and then authorize and monitor any organization that wants to undertake a literacy project in Haiti.[88]

Restoring the National Religion

As demonstrated in chapter 3, popular writings on Voodoo have built on the Eurocentric equation of Voodoo with African witchcraft, the racist assumption that black religion must be inferior to white religion, and the christocentric belief that Christianity is an appropriate belief system for everyone. All three misconceptions ignore the importance of Voodoo as the only religion that has worked for most Haitians for most of Haitian history.

At least 85 percent of the six million or so Haitians are peasants in the traditional meaning of the term, that is, they are small landowners and largely subsistence farmers who are only tenuously connected to national and international markets. They are aware of themselves as members of a nation state, but their relative geographic and personal isolation means that, for the most part, they supply local solutions to local problems in the absence of any real integration into the national polity. A major component of these local solutions is Voodoo.

Several obstacles create difficulties in determining the number of servitors in Haiti. Most Haitians are aware of the bad press that Voodoo has received, and many deny their religion to outsiders. Another difficulty concerns the admixture of Catholicism. In fact, it is necessary to be baptized as a Roman Catholic in order to serve the lwa, and when some Haitians say they are "Catholic," it is not entirely clear what they mean. Those who explicitly deny Voodoo may say they are *katolik fran* or "pure Catholics." Others, however, may not be so explicit.

Combining the estimates of two North American anthropologists with many years of experience in Haiti, Murray and Smucker, with those of the Haitian anthropologist Max Paul, former Director of the Haitian Bureau d'Ethnologie, I would estimate that between 50 and 75 percent of the population of rural Haiti actively practices Voodoo. Whatever the percentage may be, it is clear that Voodoo is the indigenous creation of Haiti and that Voodoo comes far closer than anything else to being the national religion of Haiti.

In a detailed study of Haitian folk theater the investigator correlated the strength of Voodoo with the health of folklore and peasant culture, pointing out,

> In 1939, when the Catholic Church of Haiti led an anti-superstition campaign against Vodoun, . . . one could say that Haiti's folk life descended to its nadir. In the past thirty years during which time scholars have written and spoken of Voodoun as a bona fide religion, Haitian folklore has survived more comfortably.[89]

Similar to the Haitian elite's language ambivalence, there exists an essentially muddled notion that Catholicism—the religion of the slave owners—should be the religion of Haiti. Much of this attitude is based on the bad press that Voodoo continually receives in the foreign media. Haitians educated in schools run by foreign religious orders are always on the defensive about Voodoo. I have even heard these Haitians deny that Voodoo still exists. Others have claimed that it can be found only in very remote, "backward" villages.

The Frenchified elite find Voodoo quite threatening because Voodoo, like the Haitian language, is closely identified with the Africanized peasantry and the urban proletariat. It is the religion of the masses, the religion of slave revolution, and the religion of peasant uprising and labor unrest. The threat is social as well as political. Voodoo is egalitarian and democratic.

A study of the differing factions favoring the use of Creole or French in a Roman Catholic church in New York City clearly pointed out the attitude of elite Haitians, whose folk model associates Creole with Voodoo and French with Roman Catholicism.[90] The pro-French Haitian-Americans thought that a Mass in Creole meant desecrating the church with a "patois" suitable only for Voodoo rituals and would "deprive the parishioners of the more 'edifying' and 'civilized' aspects of Haitian culture by eliminating French from the Mass."[91]

> They further feared that the use of Creole would emphasize only the African component of Haiti's heritage and would thereby increase the isolation of New York City Haitian immigrants from the dominant white culture. To these Haitians being black and French was more desirable than being black and African.[92]

In contrast, the other side emphasized that Creole is the mother tongue of all Haitians and that French is used "as a tool of intimidation, exploitation and oppression in Haiti."[93]

In Haiti, members of the elite are not quite so worried about their identity. Smucker, a contemporary anthropological observer of Voodoo, stated quite clearly,

> As a belief system, the Voodoo religion crosses class boundaries; it is truly a national religion. In terms of ritual practice, Voodoo is largely

a folk religion of the peasantry and the urban poor. Middle- and upper-class families also participate, but rarely in public settings. Upwardly mobile families and the traditional upper classes tend to identify strongly with the Euro-Haitian cultural heritage. As a result, they avoid public affiliation with traditional Voodoo practice due to the social stigma imposed on Afro-Haitian cultural traits and the lower classes.[94]

In a study of novels written by Haitians another investigator revealed,

The official truth of the matter is that upper and middle class people are, by their very condition, Christian, more specifically Catholics who do not believe in *vaudou*, whereas the lower classes by and large practice *vaudou* only. In reality, however, these upper and middle class people who look down on the "vaudouisants" are often shown sneaking surreptitiously into the home of a [Voodoo priest] at night under the cover of darkness.[95]

In one of the novels by the famous Marcelin brothers the theme of the falseness of conversion to Catholicism as a mark of membership in the upper class is shown clearly when the father of one of the main characters pretends to denounce the lwa and accept Catholicism through a "conversion" that is purely for his own political and financial gain.[96]

The unfavorable stigma imposed on Voodoo by the Haitian elite's attempt to identify with essentially deleterious foreign beliefs and behaviors could be greatly relieved by official governmental recognition and aid to Voodoo. The Bureau d'Ethnologie has a traditional goal of creating Voodoo as a national religion, but so far it has made little headway for lack of funds and for political interference. Also, the lack of national leadership and even written records in the Voodoo church—while giving it strength in terms of flexibility and local diversity—detract from its proper role as a national religion.

There are no regional or national organizations of Voodoo priests, and little widely accepted theology in Voodoo. According to a specialist in the Voodoo of northern Haiti, "The ancient myths validating Dahomean and Yoruban religious beliefs have disappeared in Haiti."[97] Certainly there are no theological schools, and there is no Voodoo bible. Today, as in the 1930s, Voodoo "is informal to an extreme degree."[98]

Noting the localized character of Voodoo, an observer has written, "The patterns of life which radiate from its core substitute in Haitian rural existence for the kinds of formal or governmental institutions which are and have always been lacking in Haiti."[99] In terms of kinship and community, Voodoo enhances group solidarity, decreases anxiety in the face of uncertainty, offers entertainment and recreation, and provides Haitians with a coherent world view. Indeed, the Voodoo temple has been described as "sanctuary, clubhouse, dance hall, hospital, theatre, chemist's shop, music hall, court and council chamber in one."[100]

Voodoo, then, is essentially a family religion consisting of rites of homage to ancestral spirits. "In keeping with the pattern of spiritual inheritance and earthly kinship, the dead and other spirits are quintessentially local spirits. These spirits are inherited individually though they may reflect generalized archetypes which may be recognizable throughout different regions of the country. There are spirits, however, whose names are unknown outside a particular community."[101] Voodoo legitimizes a web of relationships with relatives, with the land, and with the experiences of growing up, becoming ill, getting cured, becoming ill, and dying.

The flexibility of its belief system among a largely illiterate congregation allows Voodoo to evolve to fit the needs of its servitors. Along with folk medicine, the religion provides avenues for prestige, the framework for small-scale credit organizations, interaction with supernatural beings, and the potential to become a participant in a multitude of ceremonies involving music, dances, songs, skits, crafts, and other entertainments.

Both the advantages of Voodoo for its adherents and the advantages of understanding Voodoo as a true religion are not entirely lost on the western press or on some members of the Haitian elite. One such member has written:

Voodoo is a very, very old religion. It is a religion, in the same sense as Islam, Buddhism, or Christianity are religions. It is a set of beliefs and practices, primarily of African origin, which came to the Americas with the slaves from Africa. . . . Voodoo is an integral part of the mental, political and moral structure of the West Indies and Central and South America—particularly in the peasantry and in the urban proletariate.[102]

And even the *National Geographic*, which in the past has so often pilloried Haiti, in the 1980s carried an article that explained,

While black magic still persists in Haiti and elsewhere, it is not the same as voodoo, which many sociologists and ethnologists now regard as a bona fide religion.[103]

Voodoo, then, stands as an independent religion and has no colonial necessity to lean on any other religion. While it is true that "official Catholic rites of the mass, baptism, communion, marriage, and burial are significant in Voodoo cosmology,"[104] it should be obvious that the religion of France, Roman Catholicism, is as alien and deleterious to a progressive Haiti as is the continuing use of the French language and a French-type educational operation.

Anthropologists themselves, especially the pioneering Herskovits and those who have followed him, have been guilty of viewing culture as a collection of traits, each of which may be traced to its origin. In this perspective Voodoo emerges as a syncretistic religion with parts of it being either more or less African or European. Just as the etymology of Creole words may be interesting so may be the history of Voodoo; the point, however, is that for its believers Voodoo is more than merely a collection of beliefs and behaviors. Voodoo operates as a fully integrated religious system giving meaning and comfort to the lives of its believers.

While "measuring the impact of *vodun* upon Haitian politics has always been an abstruse and doubtful enterprise,"[105] it is clear that the great majority of the Haitian population accepts Voodoo as the religion of the nation—granted along with "firmly believ[ing] in the existence of zombis, cannibalism, and the transformation of human beings into animals."[106] Nevertheless, a Haitian government that truly reflects the culture of its people must cease supporting imported religions and place its meager resources at the disposal of the Haitian national religion. I am not arguing for political suppression of Catholicism and Protestantism but simply for the curtailment of overt support for the Roman Catholic church and the tacit support for Protestant missionaries. After all, director Paul has been quoted as saying, "Catholics and Protestants want to reduce voodoo to a less significant role in Haitian culture."[107] Why should Haitians have to tolerate such interference? Freedom of religion should be maintained, but every nation must be allowed to control the importation of foreign proselytizers.

Indeed, Article 30 of the 1987 constitution forbids the establishment of any official religion in Haiti and declares, "All religions and all cults are at liberty."[108] The article also secures the right of anyone to hold to any religious beliefs, "provided that the exercise of this right is not contrary to the public peace and order."[109]

In the campaigns leading to the first two post-Duvalier presidential elections, that is, the failed one in November 1987 and the government-controlled one in January 1988, leaders in the Voodoo church and others connected with Voodoo increasingly played a role in representing the people as the Roman Catholic church began to fade into its own hierarchical labyrinth. The forthcoming presentation of the legitimate religion of the Haitian people can only have positive consequences and can help correct the folk model of the outside world.

Developing a Nation

After one aborted election, one faked election, several coups, successful and failed, and five different governments, Haiti, on February 7, 1991—five years after the end of a twenty-nine-year dictatorship—installed a popularly elected president. Jean-Bertrand Aristide, a thirty-seven-year-old charismatic priest, had been an activist in Haitian human rights movements for many years. In 1988 he was expelled by the Roman Catholic Salesian order for defying orders to abandon politics. He has, so far, escaped at least three assassination attempts, one by uniformed soldiers. Although he had an obvious and perhaps volatile appeal to many segments of the Haitian population, some doubted his ability to provide a stable government in the face of seemingly insurmountable problems. Aristide was, indeed, unable to bring together the various segments of Haitian society, and September 29, 1991, after a day of violent confrontation between soldiers and Aristide supporters that left at least twenty-six people dead, Aristide was ousted by the military. Such a turn of events seemed to validate the press's opinion that Haiti cannot govern itself.

The press coverage of Haiti in the last few years until the election of Aristide has apparently enjoyed reporting events within the framework of an implied comparison between the supposedly politically stable governments of Europe and North American and the unstable government of Haiti. The comparison, however, is anthropologically invalid because it is generally—and perhaps unconsciously—made between idealized political behavior in the Western world and actual political behavior in Haiti. To fully understand the performance of the press on Haiti, it is necessary, therefore, to make a final refinement in the concept of folk and analytic models. A major component of folk models may be referred to as idealized behavior, that is, behavior that conforms to normative expectations. It is also possible to examine actual behavior from a folk model perspective. What usually happens, however, is that those aspects of actual behavior in one's own culture that deviate from the norms are quickly forgotten or, in a sense, "edited" out of final consideration. It is much easier to observe actual behavior in other cultures and then point out how these behaviors deviate from normative expectations.

Such misleading perspectives were noted by the early nineteenth century Haitian politician J. N. Léger when he countered the complaints about Haiti's "unstable" governments by using twenty-five pages to briefly summarize the civil wars, revolutions, coups, and other rapid turnovers of governments in Germany, England, and France during the same period.[110] Although the United States has been extensively involved in destabilizing other governments—according to one count "excluding World Wars and expeditions to suppress piracy or the slave trade, the United States has made armed invasions and interventions in other countries on more than 130 separate occasions"[111]—North Americans tend to think of their own governments as highly stable.

While gaining my impressions of the press coverage of Haiti from an almost daily reading of a wide variety of North American newspapers and magazines, I could not help but notice that in the 1980s more than one hundred members of the United States federal administration were indicted for criminal activities or resigned under a cloud of suspicion. Most American state and local governments were also having their difficulties with self-aggrandizing and corrupt officials. In addition, many of the contemporary political problems of Haiti are the direct result of questionable dealings of the American government with nondemocratic forces in Haiti.

Apparently, the 1971 transition from Duvalier Senior to Duvalier Junior, for example, was part of a deal worked out between François Duvalier and the Nixon administration during Vice President Nelson Rockefeller's trip there in 1970.[112] The United States would support the continuation of the Duvalier dynasty, and Jean-Claude, when he came to power, would support a new economic program guided by the United States, a program featuring private investments from the United States that would be drawn to Haiti by such incentives as no custom taxes, a minimum wage kept very low, the suppression of labor unions, and the right of American companies to repatriate their profits—in other words, the sort of exploitation of Haiti that I described in chapter 5.

The foreign media seemed confused by the attitude of the American government, and, understandably, could not present a clear picture of the enigmatic Jean-Claude. Some journalists, especially Americans, who had written about the hopelessness of François Duvalier's Haiti,[113] began writing about the sudden improvement in Haiti after the death of Papa Doc.[114] Others, especially Haitians, claimed that repression was just as bad under Jean-Claude as it had been under François.[115]

The American Congress accepted the notion of a liberalization by Jean-Claude and endorsed the new investment plan, sending funds to Haiti to build a supportive infrastructure. Most of the projects, however, were left incomplete, and the development funds largely lined the pockets of Jean-Claude and his cohorts.

Under pressure from American president Jimmy Carter's emphasis on human rights, Jean-Claude did make some progressive changes. By the end of 1979, however, Jean-Claude's administration had slid back toward repression as the Carter administration became occupied with other matters. Correctly reading the incoming Reagan administration's lack of interest in human rights, the Haitian government increased its control of political, press, and labor groups. In fact, immediately following Reagan's election in November 1980, several hundred progressive Haitians were arrested and many were deported.

For the next six years Haiti was an example of what the United States will do for a pro-American, anticommunist country. With the help of various American government agencies the indigenous economy was destroyed and Haiti became economically dependent on the United States. With the aid of international lending enterprises, Haiti joined the ranks of the debtor nations for the first time in its history. And with the Reagan administration giving five times as much military aid per year to the dictatorship as Carter had, the army in Haiti finally regained the power it had lost under François.

During all this time the international press ignored Haiti. There were no calamities or coups, and there was no communism. However, a lot was going on: a compete restructuring of the Haitian economy, the impoverishment of the countryside, and the laying of the groundwork for an eventual military dictatorship. With the publicity of the boat people, the media in Florida and elsewhere did pay some attention to Haitian immigrants, but few if any reporters ever asked the basic questions about the creation of the crisis of poverty in Haiti.

Jean-Claude himself was an enigma to the press, as he was to most Haitians. François was rather affectionately known to Haitians as "Papa Doc"; and the foreign press gave Jean-Claude the label "Baby

Doc," though it was rarely used in Haiti. Born in 1952 (and now living in exile in Mougins on the French Riviera), Jean-Claude became president-for-life of Haiti in April 1971 when he was just nineteen. He was a plump, baby-faced, clumsy boy who had lived in isolation for most of his life and had developed a taste for fast cars. The western press never got beyond this image of Jean-Claude as a fat playboy. Even though he had slimmed down to an average weight (apparently prodded by his fashion-conscious wife) and had matured into a rather handsome man in his mid-thirties, the cartoons in North American newspapers in 1986 portrayed him as a fat-faced, bloated kid.[116]

Although Jean-Claude's serene face was on posters everywhere, few Haitians had any real affection for him, as they had had for his father. In contrast to his father, Jean-Claude had no ideology and no coherent policies. He did, however, have some support from the self-serving mulatto business community and the fickle young elite technocrats. His father, however, enjoyed solid support from the black middle class. Many Haitians have told me that the real beginning of the end for Jean-Claude was his elaborate wedding in 1980 to Michèle Bennett, the daughter of a mulatto business family, an event that alienated many of the black power followers of his father.

The frequent changing of personnel, including cabinet ministers, was a political device used by both Duvaliers to ensure their control over the government, but with the less-than-adroit Jean-Claude it also meant demoralization at the lower levels and incompetence at the upper levels of the government bureaucracy.

Both father and son used national funds like their household budget, but the shopping excesses of Michèle became highly publicized and destroyed whatever favorable public image the bland Jean-Claude might have created.

Neither of the Duvaliers seriously invested in their own country. And during the entire Duvalier dynasty the economic situation of most Haitians worsened by criteria such as per capita income, nutrition, infant mortality, and literacy. Under François, however, there were no promises of improvement and there even was some improvement for the black middle class, while the Jean-Claude regime actually promised economic improvement and then failed to deliver.

With little to show for fourteen years of rule by a second Duvalier, many Haitians finally reached the end of their patience with Jean-Claude, and in late November 1985 street protests began in Gonaives, mostly involving students. Many Haitians now think of these protests as marking the beginning of the modern era in Haitian politics.

A more economic perspective might choose the American-sponsored eradication of the pig population in Haiti in June 1983 as setting the final limits of endurance for the Haitian peasant. At any rate, it was, as usual, the overt and public political events that garnered so much attention from the media.

The violent police response to these November demonstrations, in which three students were killed and many others beaten, led to statements against Jean-Claude's regime from unlikely sectors of the nation, including, for example, the Haitian Association of Industrialists. By the end of December major readjustments had been made by Jean-Claude, including sending four powerful ministers away on ambassadorships and retiring twelve senior army officers. In a symbolic gesture in late January 1986 Jean-Claude formally abolished the small political police unit.

Nothing could stop the constant protests, however, and just a little over a year later at about two o'clock in the morning of February 7, 1986, an American transport aircraft arrived in Port-au-Prince from the American base at Guantánamo in Cuba. At 3:46 that morning Jean-Claude Duvalier left for France, and an era ended in Haiti. Haitians awoke that morning to what many of them thought was a revolution. Some of them were seen in the streets of Port-au-Prince that morning symbolically sweeping away the evil spirits of the Duvaliers with tree branches.

Later in the day it was announced that Haiti would be run by an interim government initially composed of a five-member council named the Conseil National du Gouvernement (National Council of Government or CNG). Headed by Lt. Gen. Henri Namphy, it was pared down to three members six weeks later.

A few days after the ouster of Jean-Claude the CNG abolished the widely hated tonton-makout, but the interim government did not pursue Duvalierists except under intense public pressure. Namphy and others still in power obviously did not view the end of Duvalier as a revolution signaling the end of authoritarianism in Haiti—they may not even have viewed it as the end of Duvalierism. While the CNG concentrated on controlling the political scene, social controls in the streets tended to break down. Informants constantly spoke to me about the lack of control in Port-au-Prince and Cap-Haitien and complained about the unprecedented occurrence of crimes in these two largest cities in Haiti. During the first week of October 1986 schools were scheduled to open, but the opening was delayed in Cap-Haitien because of rioting that included the sacking of the CARE warehouse. The main post office in Cap-Haitien was also ransacked. In November 1986 soldiers shot and killed a woman and a fourteen-year-old boy during anti-CNG protests in Cite Soleil, a Port-au-Prince slum.

Types of violence that are extremely rare in Haiti began to surface. Port-au-Prince was shocked by the report of several rapes in Port-au-Prince in February and March 1987. Various demonstrations and strikes continued throughout the year. As one of my informants put it: "There were people so frustrated by what they saw as a worsening situation here that rioting and burning barricades was their only means of expression." A returning exile is quoted as saying, "We have no work, nothing to live on; the country is in ruins."[117]

Despite these difficulties and the indifference of the CNG to the public welfare some of the processes of democratization continued. The 1987 constitution is a good example of the modern, liberal Haitian elite working at its best. The constitution is an indigenous document tailored to solve particular political problems that have arisen out of Haitian history. A highly progressive constitution even by world standards, it was, in fact, produced in opposition to the wishes of the CNG.

The referendum on the constitution was highly publicized and represented, in fact, the highest level of political participation by the

Haitian general public since the elections that led to the installation of the Duvalier dynasty in 1957. Many private groups and all of the political parties contributed to the public discussion of the constitution. The constitution was published both in French[118] and Creole[119] and was widely distributed in Creole for free. Several hundred thousand comic books and posters explaining the constitution were also distributed throughout Haiti. Several political groups prepared cassette tapes that contained the constitution in Creole so that discussion groups could be formed for the illiterate. Radio stations used many hours of their air time to the reading and discussion of the constitution.

The participation of the general public in learning about the proposed constitution proved once again what the nineteenth century abolitionists already knew, that Haitians are capable of governing themselves. The twenty-day period in 1987, from March 10 to March 29, the date of the referendum, was probably the peak of democratic activity since the ouster of Duvalier in February 1986, and one of the most politically exciting and profitable periods in Haiti's history. It brought the Haitian people together in a common cause.

The foreign press showed relatively little interest in this display of unity and political sophistication on the part of Haitians. The press did, however, become greatly interested in Haiti during the subsequent months of increasing calamity as the CNG did little to encourage further public participation in the political process and, in fact, began to erect barriers to free presidential elections.

The elections for president and for seats in the National Assembly were set for November 29, 1987, and by the end of April at least two hundred people had declared themselves to be presidential candidates, many of them returned exiles, and on May 5 formal filing for the presidency began. Through various constitutional processes this field was narrowed down to twenty-two for president and 328 for the 104-seat National Assembly. By the beginning of June, Haitians began experiencing the sort of wide-open campaigning that they had not seen for several decades.

Nevertheless, various thugs, include those identified as former tonton-makout, were emboldened by the lack of police and army concern for stopping political violence and began attacking those institutions identified with the new democratic processes. Two presidential candidates were killed, one in front of a police station clutching a copy of the constitution. One of the most popular candidates refused to campaign for lack of any discernible police protection. Just days before the scheduled elections the polling headquarters was burned down, the facilities for the popular Radio Lumiere were set afire by gunmen, and arsonists screaming "Long live the army!" destroyed a huge open-air market in Port-au-Prince.

On the morning of November 29 gunmen roamed the streets of Port-au-Prince firing at those going to vote and in at least one instance invaded a voting site to kill several people. Many in Port-au-Prince saw uniformed soldiers joining in the attack on voters. The trucks carrying ballots to the north were waylaid and the ballots burned.

At least thirty-four people were killed in the aborted November 29 election, and the CNG cancelled the elections later in the day. On the very next day an informant in Cap-Haitien wrote to me,

> For many months, November 29, 1987, has stood out in the hearts and minds of Haitians as a day of hope. Yesterday it became a day of deception. Yesterday, we saw, in one day, our hopes and dreams for a democratic and free Haiti crushed. We feel we no longer have a hope that there will be a change in the country.

Another told me over the telephone the same day, "Kè-m grenn" (My heart is broken).

Namphy promised new elections under the protection of the army. With widespread irregularities reported and few of the eligible voters turning out, elections were, indeed, held on January 17 for president, members of the National Assembly, and mayors. My informants in Port-au-Prince and Cap-Haitien reported to me that most people stayed away from the polls. They also said that those involved in the polling knew of wholesale fraud. Those who walked by the polls during the twelve hours they were open told me that the polling stations were usually deserted. Their estimates of voter turnout varied from 1 to 20 percent.

It was announced that Leslie Manigat, originally a minor candidate but now a favorite of the military, had won the presidency, and on February 7, 1988, two years after the ouster of Jean-Claude Duvalier, Manigat was installed as the forty-fifth head of state of Haiti. In the early 1960s Manigat, a political science professor, had prophetically written, "The support of the police-army is needed to overthrow a government, and police-army opposition makes the election of any candidate insecure. It makes and un-makes chiefs of state."[120]

About four months later, from June 14 to June 19, Manigat was involved in an attempt to play off one segment of the army against another. Instead, the army remained united, and on June 20 Namphy took over the reins of government as Manigat fled into exile to the Dominican Republic. In rapid succession Namphy dissolved the parliament, established a government composed entirely of the military, suspended the constitution, and ruled out the possibility of any elections in the near future.

The violence in Haiti then escalated dramatically with the public perceiving a return to power of the tonton-makout. On Sunday, September 12, 1988, men armed with guns and machetes burst into the church of Aristide and killed at least three parishioners, wounded sixty others, and burned down the building. Gangs of men thought to be tonton-makout roamed the streets the rest of the day stoning the offices of groups opposed to the military regime of Namphy.

On June 19 in a ten-hour coup that began on the afternoon of Saturday, September 17, 1988, Namphy was forced out of the National Palace apparently by noncommissioned officers of the Presidential Guard fearful of the public reaction against the army and perhaps dissatisfied themselves with the level of violence in Haiti. Leadership was quickly handed over to Lt. Gen. Prosper Avril on Sunday morning. Namphy fled into exile in the Dominican Republic. In the week thereafter soldiers forcibly removed their commanding officers. The purging of the upper ranks of the Haitian Armed Forces continued throughout the following week with at least ten senior officers in the capital and one in Cap-Haitien being sacked. Less than two years later, on March 10, 1990, Avril resigned and his military successor, Maj. Gen. Hérard Abraham, turned over the government three days later to a civilian administration headed by former Supreme Court Justice Ertha Pascal-Trouillot. In August of that year American Vice President Dan Quayle threatened to cut off the approximately sixty million dollars in American aid if Haiti did not carry out free elections within the year. Scheduled once for November 4 and then postponed to December 16, the elections were monitored by more than four hundred international observers, including former American president Carter. Aristide won these elections in a landslide approaching 70 percent of the estimated 75 percent of the two million registered voters who cast ballots, and his election raised expectations to a high degree both in Haiti and elsewhere in the Caribbean, as is evidenced by the remark of Jamaica's prime minister, Michael Manley, who said at Aristide's inauguration that he sensed "a very great moment in Caribbean history after all the generations of struggle and tyranny."[121]

The press of North America, nevertheless, concentrated on two not entirely relevant aspects of the Aristide presidency. First of all, there was an enormous amount of whispering and speculation by anonymous sources both within the American government and from rightwing think tanks in North America concerning Aristide's political philosophy, a philosophy that is obviously more populist and perhaps socialist than capitalist in its approach to government. In some circles this philosophy was labeled communism, and when these views of Aristide were translated into journalistic terms, they come out as unenlightening phrases. The more respected newspapers reporting on Haiti, such as the *Christian Science Monitor, Miami Herald, New York Times,* and *Washington Post,* consistently used the words "leftist priest" in describing Aristide.[122] A rare example of a laudatory article on Aristide, somewhat idealistic but giving a much-needed insight into the high esteem in which he was held by Haitians, did appear in the *Los Angeles Times.*[123]

The other characterization of the Aristide administration was that it was composed of friends of Aristide who are inexperienced in government. This was a particularly strange criticism in view of the fact that any Haitian who had direct experience in government almost had to have been in the Duvalier regimes, and one of the major points of the election of Aristide was to root out all influence of the Duvalier years. In addition, the members of Aristide's cabinet and his advisers were almost always identified by the North American press by some previous occupation even though they may have been active for years in some human rights movement or even though they may have particular expertise in areas essential to government. For example, Aristide's prime minister, René Préval, was inevitably identified as a baker or perhaps "a bakery owner"[124] even though he was also a Belgian-trained agronomist. After he was in office for six months, the *New York Times* did editorially acknowledge that "President Aristide is clearly off to a smart start."[125]

These post-Duvalier political events have been rather well reported; however, the press rarely commented on the economic and ecological roots of Haiti's problems. Instead, as one journalist pointed out, "Haiti is perceived as an incompetent, downtrodden parody of a country that alternates between buffoonery and savagery."[126] One reason for this biased coverage seems to be that the basic problems of Haiti are very old and not "news." Soil erosion, for example, was a serious problem two centuries ago.[127] Another reason seems to be the consensus that the problems are beyond the reach of any mortals currently on the scene. If, however, the Haitian situation is carefully examined from an analytic perspective, solutions become clearer even though the problems may not become any less serious.

Haiti must, for example, avoid the deleterious grasp of North American capitalists seeking cheap labor. Haiti must obtain energy from sources other than its already denuded countryside. Haiti must turn in on its own resources and once again become self-sufficient in food production, and it must join in a collaboration with the rest of the Third World in resisting the monetary entanglements with First World financial institutions. Politically, Haiti must find a way to abolish its army. Never in modern history has the Haitian military been used for any purpose except to play deleterious political games and to oppress its own citizens.

Such efforts obviously require the cooperation of the government and significant segments of the Haitian population, which is primarily peasant farmers. In the past, grassroots organizations in the countryside have sprung up in response to Haiti's problems. Peasant rebellions and peasant resistance to exploitation have been a prominent part of Haitian history. Rarely, however, have the urban elite and the national government combined in concerted effort with the peasants to develop a strongly united and widely supported national policy.

The military government, in fact, seemed dedicated to suppressing popular organizations. On November 1, 1989, three grassroots organization leaders were illegally arrested by soldiers from the Palace Guard, and on the following day they were displayed on government-run television with their faces swollen, heads bandaged, and clothes soaked with blood. On January 4, 1990, a delegation of the Boston-based Association of Physicians for Human Rights visited them in jail and later declared in a press conference in Port-au-Prince, "The prisoners continue to suffer due to the beatings they received at the time of their arrests." This incident was only one among many that can be found documented in various Haitian-oriented publications in the United States such as *The Haiti Beat*, published by the Washington Office on Haiti. Obviously, one of President Aristide's first tasks was to get the army under control. Although Ismael Diallo, spokesperson for the United Nations Election Verification Mission, stated that "the armed forces and the security forces have been very professional,"[128] Aristide was obviously unable to control the army even though he seemed to have the overwhelming support of the masses of people.

Aristide did try to begin that process of controlling the army at the very time of his inauguration, turning to Abraham, then commander of the armed forces, and telling him to retire six generals and the colonel who headed the Palace Guard. Abraham followed these instructions and was himself retired five months later and succeeded by Brig. Gen. Raoul Cedras, who was—ironically—regarded as a professional, nonpolitical officer of the type that would be needed to put down the inevitable coups against Aristide.[129] Seven months later, Cedras found himself heading a coup against Aristide started by soldiers largely fearful of losing their jobs.

A final coup before the installation of Aristide was carried out by Roger Lafontant, former head of the tonton-makout, who earlier had returned from exile in the Dominican Republic to run for president but was disqualified for his close association with the Duvalier regimes. Early on the morning of January 7, 1991, Lafontant seized the National Palace and held provisional President Pascal-Trouillot hostage. He announced that he had annulled the December 16 presidential election and was replacing Pascal-Trouillot. About ten hours later the army stormed the palace and freed Pascal-Trouillot.

In response mobs killed several dozen known members of the tonton-makout. The mobs also ransacked and burned the colonial cathedral, the vatican residence, and the residence of the Conference of Catholic Bishops since Monsignor Giuseppe Leanza, the papal nuncio, Archbishop François Wolff Ligondé, and other church leaders are known for their opposition to Aristide and their support of the Duvaliers. Aristide later condemned the attacks as a "hideous spectacle," calling for "vigilance without vengeance."[130] Most of my informants thought that this condemnation came much too late and that its tardiness underlined Aristide's propensity to condone violence against his political enemies.

On July 30, 1991, after a twenty-hour trial—carried live on state television and radio—a twelve-member jury found Lafontant guilty. He was sentenced to life in prison. Seventeen of his twenty-one accomplices were also sentenced to life in prison, and the other four to ten years in prison. Lafontant was killed just about the time of the September 29 coup, and some of my informants think that his murder was done on the orders of Aristide—perhaps Aristide's last order before being ousted. Such an ignoble act may, however, spell the absolute and final end to the tonton-makout.

Despite the high hopes for Aristide's administration and the various setbacks that occurred, the best hope for Haiti and the best way for it to counter its perennial bad press lies with the persistence of the common people shown in various peasant organizations. One of the best known of these organizations is the Tet Ansanm movement in the northwest. Various other movements, such as the Peasant Movement of Papaye, are quite widespread throughout the countryside. Some of these organizations are supported by various Roman Catholic priests following the dictates of their conscience or of liberation theology, others are supported by various nongovernmental groups, and all of them draw on the patience and goodwill of the Haitian people.

Most of these peasant organizations focus on some aspect of agricultural cooperation. Some of these organizations have had great success in raising the productivity of rural areas. Most of these organizations also engage in some sort of adult education. This education may range from adult literacy programs to revolutionary programs explaining the systems of exploitation and injustice prevalent in Haiti. Most of the education programs serve to give peasants a sense of their importance and power in this still largely agricultural country. The educational and agricultural programs cover everything from contour farming to dry wall soil conservation techniques to health practices.

A problem with the focus of the world press on Duvalier and the end of that dynasty has been the assumption that all of Haiti's problems were the result of a father-son monster. Now that Haiti is rid of the monster, the expectation springing from the folk model of the outside world is that things must automatically improve. Both Haitians and outsiders must realize that the problems stem from forces, both ecological and societal, that do not lend themselves to facile explanations and easy solutions.

Certainly Haitians have the individual strength to survive their difficulties now, much as they have survived many past crises. They must also find the intellectual and cultural resources and harness the potential of their national identity to work their way through history and forever still the publicity about Haiti as some sort of neurotic abnormality among modern nations.

A Chronology
of the History of Haiti

1492	December 5: Columbus lands in Haiti.
1502	First black slaves brought to Hispaniola by Governor Nicholas Ovando.
1505	Sugar introduced to Hispaniola from Canary Islands.
1659	France takes Tortue Island.
1665	February: Settlement at Port-de-Paix established.
1679	First slave insurrection.
1697	Treaty of Ryswick in which Spain recognizes France's claim to western part of Hispaniola.
1751	Macandal, a slave, leads insurrection against French.
1758	Macandal captured and executed.
1779	Haitian troops fight in Savannah in support of American Revolution.
1789	July 4: French National Assembly seats six delegates from Saint Domingue (colonial Haiti).
1791	May 15: French National Assembly declares all free-born men of color eligible to be seated.
	August 22: The free-born coloreds begin their revolt.
1793	August 29: Liberation of slaves declared in province of the North.
	October 31:Full abolition of slavery in the remaining two provinces of South and West.
1794	February: Racially mixed delegation from Saint Domingue seated at Paris National Convention.
1796	April: Ex-slave Toussaint Louverture declared lieutenant governor.
1801	January: Toussaint invades Santo Domingo (Spanish part of the island).
	July 8: New constitution promulgated, and Toussaint declared governor-general-for-life.
1802	February: Napoleon's army arrives to re-enslave Haiti.

1803	April 7: Toussaint dies in captivity in France.
	November 18: French evacuate their colonial capital.
1804	January 1: Haitian independence declared by Jean-Jacques Dessalines in Gonaives.
	March: Most of the remaining French massacred.
1805	May 20: Ratification of Haiti's first constitution as a free nation.
1806	October 17: Dessalines killed.
	December: Haiti declared a republic.
1807	February 17: Henri Christophe proclaimed president of newly created nation in the north.
	March 11: Alexandre Pétion elected president of the Republic of Haiti (in the south).
1811	June 2: Christophe crowned King Henri I.
1816	The French artist Barincourt founds an art school in Port-au-Prince.
	June 2: Pétion declared president-for-life.
1818	March 29: Death of Pétion.
1820	October 8: Christophe takes own life.
	October 26: Haiti reunited.
1822–1844	Haiti occupies Santo Domingo.
1824	Immigration of U.S. black freedmen to Haiti.
1838	June 9: France recognizes Haiti's total independence.
1842	May 7: Great earthquake destroys many towns in the north.
1847	March 1: Faustin Soulouque elected president.
1849	Soulouque invades Santo Domingo.
	August 20: Soulouque proclaimed Emperor Faustin I.
1850	Emperor Soulouque founds Imperial Academy of Drawing and Art in Port-au-Prince.
1859	January 15: Soulouque abdicates.
1860	March 28: Concordat with the Vatican signed.
1862	June 5: United States recognizes Haiti.
1902	May 12: President Simon Sam abdicates. Riots erupt in Port-au-Prince.
	July 26: Civil war erupts.
	December 17: Nord Alexis acclaimed president.
1912	August 7: National Palace blown up, and 300 soldiers killed.
1915	July 27: President Guillaume Sam orders slaughter of political prisoners and is killed by mob.

	July 28: U.S. Marines land in Port-au-Prince, and U.S. Occupation begins.
	August 21: United States takes charge of Haitian customs houses.
1918	November: Caco rebellion begins in the north.
1919	October: U.S. Marines put down rebellion in the north.
1920	May 19: End of rebellion in rest of Haiti. Jean Price-Mars begins work on *Ainsi parla l'Oncle*.
1929	October: Student strike followed by general strike.
	December 4: Martial law declared.
	December 5: Massacre at Cayes carried out by U.S. Marines.
1934	August 14: End of the American Occupation.
1937	October: Massacre of thousands of Haitians in Dominican Republic.
1938	Appearance of *Les Griots*.
1944	May 14: Centre d'Art opens in Port-au-Prince founded by the North American DeWitt Peters and various Haitians.
1946	January: After general strike army assumes power.
	August 16: Dumarsais Estimé elected president.
1949	Port-au-Prince International Exposition.
1950	May 10: Estimé deposed, and army takes over.
	December 6: Paul Eugène Magloire installed as president.
1952	First bilateral agreement between Haiti and Dominican Republic for use of Haitians in Dominican sugarcane fields.
1957	September 22: François Duvalier elected president.
	October 22:Duvalier inaugurated.
1958	July 28: Attempted invasion (the deputy sheriffs' coup) thwarted.
1959	August 13: Attempted invasion in the south fails.
1961	April 30: Duvalier maneuvers a six-year term.
1963	April: Insurrection begins led by Clément Barbot, chief of Duvalier's paramilitary militia, popularly known as the tonton-makout.
	September: Another invasion attempt.
1964	April 1: Duvalier declares himself president-for-life.
	August 5: Still another invasion fails.
1968	May 20: National Palace bombed but an invasion fails.
1971	January 22: Duvalier announces his teenaged son will succeed him.

	April 21: Death of Duvalier and succession of his son Jean-Claude.
1972	December: Beginning of the migration of boat people to Florida directly from Haiti.
1977	Sharp increase in the number of boat people arriving in Florida.
	September 22: Committee for the Defense of Human Rights in Haiti pickets Haitian Office for Tourism and Haitian Consulate on twentieth anniversary of Duvalier's regime.
1979	August: Anti-Slavery Society denounces treatment of Haitians in Dominican Republic.
1980	May 27: Jean-Claude Duvalier marries Michèle Bennett in an extravagant wedding.
	July 20: Landmark case of *Haitian Refugee Center v. Civiletti* asserts rights of Haitian refugees in the United States.
	November 29: Nearly two hundred people arrested in government crack down on opposition.
1981	September 3: About six hundred Haitians protest their detention at Camp Krome in Miami.
1982	May: Total pig eradication project begins after African swine fever discovered.
1983	June: Pig eradication project ends.
1984	AIDS scare destroys tourism industry.
	January: Referendum approves Jean-Claude.
	February 5: American administration certifies human rights record in Haiti.
	May: Rioting begins in provincial towns, including riots over pig feed in Cap-Haitien.
	August: Haiti declared free of African swine fever.
1985	April 8: Haitians removed from U.S. Center for Disease Control AIDS list.
	July 22: Another "referendum" gives Jean-Claude 99.98 percent of the vote.
	November 27–28: Outbreaks of unrest in Gonaives.
	December 5: Duvalier closes two church radios in Port-au-Prince.
1986	January 5: The United States cuts back aid as reports of human rights abuses grow.
	January 7–8: Renewed antigovernment demonstrations occur in at least seven cities.

January 8: Schools ordered not to reopen.

January 31: Duvalier's embattled government declares state of siege.

February 2: Six-hour curfew imposed in Cap-Haitien, Haiti's second largest city.

February 7: Duvalier flees to France on an American jet at 3:46 A.M. Five-member Conseil National du Gouvernement (National Council of Government or CNG) headed by Lt. Gen. Henri Namphy takes control.

February: People celebrate by destroying anything associated with the Duvaliers and by killing tonton-makout.

February 10: Volontaires de la Sécurité Nationale (official name of the tonton-makout) formally abolished.

February 26: United States releases $26 million in aid suspended in January.

March 5: Large numbers of prisoners released.

March 21: Namphy restructures CNG, strengthening army position and sparking violent protests.

March 24–25: Mobs in Port-au-Prince demand civilian government.

June 5: Weeks of anti-CNG protest prompt Namphy to declare Haiti on the edge of anarchy.

June 7: CNG finally announces elections for November 1987.

June 13: United States agrees to give a twenty million dollar cash advance.

July 31: Decree sets out conditions for recognition of political parties.

August 4: The United States government releases plan to strengthen Haiti's armed forces.

October 19: Election of forty-one members to Assemblée Nationale Constituante (National Constitutional Assembly or ANC) with only about 5 percent voter turnout.

November: Soldiers kill two during anti-CNG protests in Port-au-Prince.

November 11: Namphy meets with President Ronald Reagan and declares that government will be turned over to elected civilians in February 1988.

December 10: The sixty-one-member ANC begins drafting new constitution.

1987 February: Port-au-Prince shocked by reports of several rapes.

March 29: General referendum overwhelmingly approves new constitution.

May 5: Formal filing of candidates for the presidency begins.

June 29: CNG dissolves Conseil Election Provisoire (Provisional Electoral Council or CEP), an autonomous body created by the constitution, and seizes control of the electoral process, provoking widespread rioting.

June 30: Soldiers kill three in second day of general strike against the CNG election decree.

July 17: CNG returns control of upcoming elections to the independent CEP and pledges allegiance to new constitution.

November 3: CEP disqualifies twelve presidential candidates for ties to Duvalier, leaving twenty-two candidates.

November 21: Popular Radio Lumiere set afire by gunmen.

November 24: Arsonists screaming, "Long live the army!" destroy huge open-air market in Port-au-Prince.

November 26: Violence escalates as population organizes vigilante groups for protection against gunmen, mostly recognized as former tonton-makout.

November 29: First free election in thirty years cancelled after widespread massacres of unarmed voters by former tonton-makout. Haitian army aids and abets the attack in Port-au-Prince and blocks the delivery of ballots to the provinces. The independent CEP dissolved in a decree read by Namphy over television. The members go into hiding.

November 30: United States cuts off all non-humanitarian aid to Haiti.

December 1: Namphy renews promise of elections and a new president by February 1988, implying that the new election will be run by the military.

December 6: Thousands of Haitians in Miami protest against the CNG.

December 10: Three leading presidential candidates, Marc Bazin, Gerard Gourgue, and Louis Dejoie II (to be joined by Sylvio Claude), vow to boycott elections.

December 12: CNG handpicks nine members of a new CEP and sets elections for January 17.

December 18: The CNG hands down new election law that eliminates the right to vote in privacy, creates the potential for widespread fraud, and seems designed to keep the army in power.

1988   January 10: CNG-appointed CEP announces that eight candidates barred from the upcoming presidential elections because of ties with the Duvalier regime.

January 17: Elections held for president and National Assembly with widespread irregularities reported and few of the four million eligible voters turning out.

January 24: CNG-appointed CEP announces that Leslie Manigat won the presidency.

February 7: Fifty-seven-year-old Manigat installed as the forty-fifth head of state while a general strike is carried out in protest.

June 18: Manigat fires Namphy as chief of staff and places him under house arrest.

June 20: Namphy seizes power, declares himself president, says he will rule by decree, and exiles Manigat to the Dominican Republic.

September 11: Attacks on the streets increase, and gunmen invade services at the Roman Catholic church of Jean-Bertrand Aristide, who will be elected president in just a little over two years.

September 17: Lt. Gen. Prosper Avril takes office in a soldiers' revolt, and Namphy goes into exile in the Dominican Republic.

1989   April 2: Avril is rescued by loyal troops as he is being driven to the airport in handcuffs to be flown into exile.

October 24: A divorce is granted to Jean-Claude and Michèle in the Dominican Republic.

1990   January 20: The government of Lt. Gen. Avril declares a thirty-day state of seige after the slaying of an army colonel.

January 21: Wholesale arrests and deportations of prominent civic and opposition leaders begin. Promised elections for October 28 are in doubt.

March 6: Protests begin over the army's killing of an eleven-year-old girl.

March 10: Avril resigns during a popular uprising against his military regime and turns power over to Maj. Gen Hérard Abraham, who promises a civilian government within days.

March 13: Supreme Court Justice Ertha Pascal-Trouillot is sworn in as provisional president.

April 20: More than fifty thousand people in New York City demonstrate against an FDA recommendation against accepting blood donations from Haitians.

July: During this month several former Duvalier officials return, resulting in protest strikes in Port-au-Prince.

August 9: Vice President Dan Quayle visits Port-au-Prince and promises that the United States will cut off all aid if the November 4 elections are not free.

September 8: Marjorie Judith Vincent, the daughter of refugees who fled Haiti in 1963, is named Miss America1991.

December 5: Seven people killed at one rally, but campaigning continues for the elections, postponed to December 16.

December 16: About eight hundred observers, including former president Jimmy Carter, monitor the elections with about two million people voting.

December 23: Jean-Bertrand Aristide, who ran on a generally populist platform, is declared the winner in a landslide.

1991   January 7: A coup, led by Roger Lafontant, former head of the tonton-makout, is put down by the army.

January 20: Run-off results for legislators in the National Assembly indicate that a center-left parliamentary bloc will support Aristide.

February 7: Five years to the day after the end of the Duvalier dictatorship Jean-Bertrand Aristide is installed as Haiti's president.

July 30: Lafontant is sentenced to life in prison.

September 30: Aristide is ousted by the military. Brig. Gen. Raoul Cedras takes over.

October 1: The coup is widely condemned throughout the world. American president George Bush suspends economic and military aid. Aristide is in Venezuela.

October 3: The Organization of American States (OAS) confronts the military regime in the first of several meetings. Reports are that at least 150 were killed and three hundred wounded in week-long confrontations between the army and Aristide supporters.

October 4: Bush meets with Aristide in Washington, D.C.,

and pledges support. The OAS calls for all members to cut trade, financial, military, and diplomatic ties with Haiti.

October 8: After a day in which soldiers stormed the Legislative Palace and roughed up lawmakers, the National Assembly names a supreme court justice, Joseph Nerette, as interim president.

November 5: The American trade embargo takes effect with the only exceptions being food staples, cooking oil, essential medicines, and commercial flights.

November 15: The twentieth overloaded Haitian vessel is intercepted by the U.S. Coast Guard since the coup and contains 110 Haitians seeking refuge from continuing violence in which at least one thousand have been killed.

November 26: OAS-mediated talks break down.

December 30: Haiti's economy appears to grind to a halt as a result of the thirty-four-nation embargo.

*N*otes

Introduction

1. (1966:vi)
2. (Murray 1977:3)
3. (Goldberg 1981:129–131)
4. This distinction has been discussed under many different names by many social scientists, though the anthropologist Paul Bohannan first elaborated on the terms *folk* and *analytic* in an innovative textbook (i.e., 1963:12–14). I have expanded on this distinction in a 1979 textbook.
5. (1968:49–50)
6. (Lawless 1968:50)
7. (1986:33)
8. (1987:358)
9. (Bellegarde-Smith 1984:266)

Chapter 1

1. (Conway and Buchanan 1985:95)
2. (Staff 1986c:133, my translation) The fact that the modern media provides little intellectual leadership is a consequence of the interaction of folk and analytic models within the historical function of the western press, as I discussed in the introduction. It is a fact that requires more elaboration and a fact to which I will return.
3. (Heinl and Heinl 1978:665)
4. (Diederich and Burt 1969)
5. (Street 1971:599)
6. (McCoy 1988:A1)
7. (Herskovits 1937)
8. For a review, see (Lawless 1990).
9. (e.g., Bellegarde-Smith 1989; Brinkerhoff and Garcia-Zamor, eds., 1986; Dash 1988; Dupuy 1988; Fass 1988; Laguerre 1989; Trouillot 1990)
10. (e.g., DeWind and Kinley 1988; Ferguson, J. 1987; Plant 1987; Wilentz 1989)

11. (e.g., Buchanan 1980; Deckelbaum 1983; Dejean, P. 1980; Laguerre 1984; Lawless 1986; McCoy, ed., 1984; Miller 1984; Portes and Stepick 1987; Stepick 1984a, 1984b; Stepick and Portes 1986; Stepick and Stepick 1990; Woldemikael 1980)

12. (e.g., Allman 1986; Coreil 1987, 1988; Farmer 1988; Gustafson 1986; Kirkpatrick and Cobb 1990; Landry 1987; Mitacek, St. Vallieres, and Polednak 1986; Parker, Stansfield, Augustin, Boulos, and Newman 1988; Raccurt, Lowrie, Katz, and Duverseau 1988; Singer, Davidson, and Gerdes 1988; Webb and Hyatt 1988).

13. The Haitian scholar Michel Laguerre has published an extensive bibliography in two volumes (1982). A more general bibliography lists materials readily available in most good libraries (Chambers 1983). And one inclusive bibliography lists most of the items in English on Haiti (Lawless 1990).

14. (Staff 1980:19)

15. (Buchanan 1980:2)

16. (Anderson, J. 1975:50)

17. (Lawless 1986:29)

18. (1984:62)

19. (i.e., Banks 1985)

20. (Andersen 1985)

21. (Lawless 1986:29)

22. (Lawless 1986:41)

23. (Staff 1979a)

24. (see Stepick and Stepick 1990)

25. (Moody 1986:43)

26. (1984b:4; cf. Richman 1984:53)

27. (1984b:5)

28. (1984b:6)

29. (1984b:13)

30. (Stepick 1984b:passim; cf. Keely, Elwell, Fragomen, and Tomasi 1978:5)

31. (Flocks and Lawless 1988:531)

32. (Flocks and Lawless 1988:531-532)

33. (1984b:18)

34. (1984:passim; cf. Koeppel 1982)

35. (Richman 1984:53)

36. (Murray 1977:300)

37. (1984:18)

38. (Lanier 1984:120)
39. (Cerquone 1986:2)
40. (Lanier 1984:120)
41. (Farmer 1989:137)
42. (Gilman 1988:102)
43. (quoted in Lanier 1984:120)
44. (Staff 1985a:8A)
45. (Associated 1985b:10A)
46. (Associated 1985b:10A)
47. (Associated 1985a:6A)
48. (Clark, M. 1985:62)
49. (Staff 1983:10A)
50. (Cooley 1983:47)
51. (Woodford 1985:5C)
52. (Woodford 1985:5C)
53. (Cerquone 1986:2)
54. (Woodford 1985:5C)
55. (Staff 1985c)
56. (Raymond 1985:7)
57. (e.g., Laverdière et al. 1983; LeBlanc et al. 1983; Pitchenik et al. 1983; Vieira et al. 1983)
58. (Lanier 1984:126; cf. Greco 1983:516)
59. (Herskovits 1937:119)
60. (Vieira et al. 1983:125)
61. (LeBlanc et al. 1983:1205-1206)
62. (Pitchenik et al. 1983:283)
63. (Pitchenik et al. 1983:279)
64. (1984:17)
65. (Durand 1984:18)
66. (1984:17)
67. (Durand 1984:20)
68. (quoted in Cooley 1983:48)
69. (i.e., Pape et al. 1983)
70. (Seligmann, J. 1985:73)
71. (Altman 1985)
72. (i.e., Moore and Le Baron 1986)
73. (Moore and LeBaron 1986:81)
74. (Lanier 1984:126; cf. Greco 1983:516)
75. (quoted in Lanier 1984:126)

76. (de Cock 1984:308)
77. (Farmer 1990b:440)
78. (Pape et al. 1983:949)
79. (Farmer 1990b:419)
80. (Pape et al. 1983:948)
81. (Siegal and Siegal 1983:83)
82. (Clark, M. 1987:62)
83. (Morris, E. 1987:A1)
84. (Lorch 1990)
85. (1990c; see also 1989; 1990a)
86. (1990c:23)
87. (1990c:21)
88. (Farmer 1990c:21)
89. (Farmer 1990c:22)
90. (Paquin 1983:246)
91. (Tivnan 1979:188)
92. (1979:188-189)
93. (Wallis 1983:60)
94. (1991)
95. (1991)
96. (1991)
97. (1991)
98. (i.e., 1929)
99. (1942:281)
100. (1937:139)
101. (Abbott 1988:7)
102. (Gold 1988:27A)
103. (Bastien 1966:47)
104. (e.g., Yasumoto and Kao 1986)
105. (1985:193-196)
106. (Davis, E. 1985:203-206)
107. (Davis, E. 1985:206-211)
108. (i.e., 1938) Although Davis only hinted that a large number of maroons existed (1988: 219), some who posited the importance of the maroons claimed that thirty to fifty thousand existed in the mountains of Haiti at the time of the French Revolution. The source for these figures is usually the inflated number given in Jean Fouchard's work. Davis himself stated, "The single most valuable source for my work was Fouchard"(1989: 281). The historian David Geggus has

demonstrated, "The number of slaves who absconded for a few days each year was doubtless extremely large. Those who lived permanently in organized bands was extremely small."

Geggus has pointed out the inaccuracies in Fouchard's data and the faulty methods used (1986: 114–17). One careful study by Geggus illustrated that the percentage of slaves listed as missing on the plantations averaged only around 1 percent (1982b:308–311). The few famous bands in the 1780s numbered under two hundred members.

Actually, the notion of large numbers of maroons probably plays into the common folk model by suggesting that slaves and ex-slaves could not mount a revolution and that the French were defeated by "wild" blacks coming down from the mountains. The final word is not yet in, but it is doubtful that the maroons played an important role in the Haitian Revolution. It is less doubtful that they had any singular importance in post-revolutionary society, contrary to Davis's notions.

109. (1988:3)
110. (1988:1) I have elsewhere reviewed in detail the faults of both these books (Lawless 1989).
111. (Davis, E. 1985:233)
112. (1985:224–232)
113. Such as have already been described in the literature on Haiti (i.e., Hall, R. B. 1929; Métraux, R. 1952).
114. (October 17, 1983, p. 60)
115. (February 24, 1986, p. 64)
116. (1988:3)
117. (1985:158)
118. (e.g., Chester 1908; Anon. 1920)

Chapter 2

1. In 1883 Boas lived with the Eskimos at Baffin Island in northeast Canada north of the Hudson Strait. In 1888 he started a lifetime study of the Northwestern Indian tribes, the Tlingit and Kwakiutl, in British Columbia. Malinowski began his fieldwork in the Trobriand Islands in 1915, now part of Papua New Guinea.
2. Verlinden 1970:35–38)
3. (Jordan 1968:7)

4. (cf. Jordan 1968:6)
5. (Marshall and Williams 1982:34–37)
6. (Cole, R. 1972:60)
7. (Cole, R. 1972:64)
8. (Marshall and Williams 1982:239)
9. (quoted in Marshall and Williams 1982:238)
10. (Curtin 1964:30)
11. (1734)
12. (Wood 1974:3)
13. (Anon. 1792:16)
14. (Anon. 1792:16)
15. (Parkhill 1861:xiii)
16. (St. John 1884:vii)
17. (Lyle 1906:7152)
18. (Ober 1908:258)
19. (Ober 1908:269)
20. (Anon. 1920:497)
21. (i.e., Chester 1908)
22. (1920:150)
23. (1920:120)
24. (1920:109)
25. (1920:111)
26. (Loederer 1935:102)
27. (1970:xii-xiii)
28. (1774:353)
29. (Moreau 1985[1797–1798]:42)
30. (Moreau 1985[1797–1798]:39)
31. (Moreau 1985[1797–1798]:13)
32. (Verrill 1914:310)
33. (Lyle 1906:7152)
34. (Craige 1933:3)
35. (Craige 1933:1)
36. (Craige 1933:310)
37. (Seabrook 1929:45)
38. (Loederer 1935:22)
39. (Davis, E. 1985:65)
40. (Ferguson J. 1987:14)
41. (Franck 1920:106)
42. (Ober 1908:259)

43. (Ullman 1970:168)
44. (Ober 1908:128)
45. (Lyle 1906:7154)
46. (Velie 1962:124)
47. (Anon. 1920:497)
48. (Taft 1938:69)
49. (1873:323)
50. (1985:305)
51. (Banks 1985:309–310; cf. Davis, E. 1985:passim)
52. (Fermor 1950:247)
53. (Verrill 1914:310–311)
54. (Gobineau 1967[1915]:48)
55. (Fermor 1950:246)
56. (Verrill 1914:309)
57. (Verrill 1914:358)
58. (1973:x)
59. (Léger 1970[1907]:300)
60. (Loederer 1935:2)
61. (MacKenzie 1971[1830]:8; Ober 1908:158; Verrill 1914:320)
62. (e.g., Moran 1951)
63. (Daley 1979)
64. (e.g., Laleau 1953)
65. (e.g., Bellegarde 1953)
66. (e.g., Cole, H. 1967; Heatter 1972)
67. (e.g., Dubroca 1802)
68. (Beard 1971[1863])
69. (1949)
70. (e.g., Mossell 1896)
71. (Parkinson 1978)
72. (Waxman 1931)
73. (e.g., Stephen 1814)
74. (e.g., Jerome 1978)
75. (e.g., Tyson, ed., 1973)
76..(e.g., James 1963)
77. (e.g., Korngold 1944)
78. (Griffiths 1970)
79. (Syme 1971)
80. (1854:69)
81. (Anon. 1792:5)

82. (Anon. 1792:14)
83. (Anon. 1792:5,7)
84. (Jordan 1968:380–384)
85. (Jordan 1968:380)
86. (Stoddard 1914:viii; cf. Hassal 1808; Chazotte 1840)
87. (e.g., Rainsford 1805)
88. (1971[1818]:164)
89. (Barskett 1971[1818]:164–172)
90. (Clark, G. 1980:356)
91. (Nicholls 1979:1)
92. (Weinstein and Segal 1984:109)
93. (Nicholls 1979:30)
94. (1973:177–178)
95. (Ott 1973:178)
96 (1973:190)
97. (1973:190)
98. (Baur 1970:409; cf. Geggus 1982:125)
99. (Geggus 1982:127)
100. (Jordan 1968:380)
101. (Baur 1970:413)
102 (1971[1828]:409)
103. (1971[1827])
104. (Parkhill 1861:xiv)
105. (Redpath 1970a[1861]:9)
106. (1971[1869]:xxvii)
107. (St. John 1884:131)
108. (Lyle 1906:7155)
109. (Barskett 1971[1818]:176)
110. (1970a[1861]:9)
111. (DuBois 1970[1861]:99)
112. (1970:417)
113. (1970:417–418; cf. Fordham 1975)
114. (Baur 1970:403)
115. (Chester 1908:216)
116. (Buell 1929:328)
117. (Bellegarde-Smith 1984:266)
118. (Bellegarde-Smith 1984:267)

Chapter 3

1. (e.g., Beard 1971[1863])
2. (e.g., Bird 1971[1869]; Hanna 1836)
3. (1971[1827])
4. (1971[1830])
5. (i.e., Franklin 1971[1828])
6. (e.g., Barskett 1971[1818]; Candler 1842)
7. (1884:v–xiv)
8. (Pritchard 1910)
9. (1972[1837])
10. (e.g., Craige 1933, 1934)
11. (e.g., Fermor 1950; Franck 1920)
12. (e.g., Loederer 1935; Seabrook 1929)
13. (e.g., Léger 1970[1907])
14. (e.g., Davis, H. P. 1936)
15. (1937)
16. (1959)
17. (e.g., Métraux, A. 1960; Nemours 1975; Zéndegui 1972)
18. (1966) Much of the writing on Haitian politics combines an uncritical acceptance of the prevailing folk model of politics of the Haitian elite with an often unconscious extension of the racist arguments of earlier white commentators. In the hands of a skilled historian such writing may prove profitable (e.g., Nicholls 1979), but in the hands of even very skilled journalists it becomes quite simplistic with one, for example, making the startling statement that "between 1806 and 1820, Haiti was divided into two mutually hostile states—a black monarchy and a mulatto republic" (Ferguson, J. 1987:13).
19. (Paquin 1983)
20. (1972[1837])
21. (1971[1863])
22. (1971[1863])
23. (1964:33)
24. (Trouillot 1990:9)
25. (e.g., Franklin 1971[1828]; MacKenzie 1971[1830]; St. John1884)
26. (Loederer 1935:2)
27. This section gives only a quick overview of the Duvalier dynasty,

concentrating on the father François. The importance of understanding the Duvaliers to understanding Haiti and also Haiti's bad press cannot be overemphasized. In chapter 6 I will discuss the son Jean-Claude.

28. (Wingfield and Parenton 1965:339)
29. (e.g., Diederich and Burt 1969)
30. (Weinstein and Segal 1984:45)
31. (Weinstein and Segal 1984:43)
32. (e.g., Hooper 1984:284)
33. (1984)
34. (1984)
35. (Preeg 1984:142)
36. Apparently impressed with Dessalines' antipathy toward whites, Duvalier came to see himself facing the hostility of United States policy, especially as exemplified by John F. Kennedy, in the same way that Dessalines guided Haiti through the uncertainties of French foreign policy. Duvalier's isolationism, then, was in the tradition of Dessalines and, in a sense, historically correct.
37. One difficulty that writers on Haiti face in discussing the Duvaliers is that social scientists have not yet offered an effective analytic model of the Duvalier regimes. There is not any good comprehensive model of the social structure of Haitian society. There are new, suggestive writings, including some by Haitian scholars, such as Patrick Bellegarde-Smith (e.g., 1980) and the anthropologist Michael-Rolph Trouillot (e.g., 1990), North American anthropologists who have worked in Haiti, such as Glenn Smucker (e.g., 1982) and others who have worked among Haitians in North America, such as Susan Buchanan (e.g., 1983) and a few other scattered works (e.g., Casimir-Liautaud 1975, 1982; Dupuy 1982; Fleurant 1973; Paul 1982).
38. (Farrell 1963:29)
39. (Dower 1986)
40. (1985:288)
41. In saying this the Jamaican unknowingly echoed the words of the nineteenth century English racist St. John, who wrote page after page about how ugly the people of Haiti are (e.g., 1884:168–169). Also, W. B. Seabrook's notorious *Magic Island* (1929) has grotesque drawings by Alexander King that exaggerate negroid features.
42. (1884:vii)
43. (1884:132)
44. (1884:viii)

45. (1933:129)
46. (1933:241)
47. (1933:241)
48. (1933:28)
49. (1933:18)
50. (1942:272–273)
51. (Angell 1922; Barau 1969; Gindine 1974; Gwoup 1984a, 1984b; Healy 1976; Hughes 1932; Miyè 1984; Montague 1940; Paquin 1983; Paterson 1980; Plummer 1981)
52. (e.g., Lyle 1906)
53. (Nicholls 1979:6)
54. (1933; 1934)
55. (i.e., Burke 1962:26–46; McCrocklin 1956; Thomas 1933:181–242; Wirkus and Dudley 1931; Wise 1929)
56. (Paterson 1980:45)
57. (1920:117)
58. (1920:160)
59. (1920:161)
60. (Taft 1938:15)
61. (Gilmore 1946:59–60)
62. (Staff 1986b:17)
63. (1952:86)
64. (1947:73)
65. (1935:2)
66. (Fermor 1950:279)
67. (Cooley 1984:16)
68. (1935:187–188)
69. (1935:38)
70. (1935:passim)
71. (Moreau 1985[1797–1798]:42)
72. (1884:x)
73. (Anon. 1827:xvii)
74. (Barham 1823:15)
75. (Franklin 1971[1828]:408–409)
76. (Lyle 1906:7151)
77. (Léger 1970[1907]:287)
78. (Ober 1908:263)
79. (Millspaugh 1929:560)
80. (Austin 1912:176)

81. (Franck 1920:153)
82. (Alatas 1977)
83. It is a sad fact of history that the pioneering British anthropologists lent their expertise to these exploitative colonial plantations. In a 1929 article the famous anthropologist Bronislaw Malinowski wrote, "The simplest experience teaches that to everybody work is...unpleasant, but a study of primitive conditions shows that very efficient work can be obtained, and the Natives can be made to work with some degree of real satisfaction if propitious conditions are created for them.... In Melanesia I have seen this applied on some plantations. Use was made of such stimuli as competitive displays of the results, or special marks of distinction for industry, or again of rhythm and working songs.... In every community I maintain there are such indigenous means of achieving more intensive labour and greater output, and it is only necessary to study the facts in order to be able to apply efficient incentives"(1929:35–36). In following the folk model of his time Malinowski seemed to accept the notion that the indigenes were naturally lazy but that they could be made to work.
84. (Goldberg, A. 1981:134)
85. (Millspaugh 1929:560)
86. (Leyburn 1966:5)
87. (Clark, S. 1972:120)
88. (Lundahl 1979:5)
89. (e.g., Verdet 1976; Seligman 1977; Goldberg, A. 1981:134; Koeppel 1982; Chierici 1987:111)
90. (1984:52)
91. (1984:60)
92. (Teepen 1986:12A)
93. (Davis, H. G. 1986:10A)
94. (Lowenthal 1978:393; cf. Herskovits 1937:139; Smucker 1984:56)
95. (1985[1797-1798]:1)
96. (Smucker 1984:56)
97. (1959:15)
98. (1937:139)
99. Since these pioneering works were first published, anthropologists and others investigating religion in Haiti have added considerably to the understanding of Voodoo, though a complete analytic model of Voodoo does not yet exist. Such a model could adapt the exemplary work of the anthropologist Anthony F. C. Wallace in his *Religion: An*

Anthropological View (1966) by setting up behavioral, organizational, and cognitive categories for a full discussion of Voodoo. Wallace's behavioral categories, for example, include prayer, music, physiological manipulation, exhortation, cosmology, pantheon, myth, moral imperatives, simulation, feasts, sacrifice, congregation, inspiration, and symbolism. I do not here have the space or the data to do this sort of justice to Voodoo, but such a study is necessary and can be done since Voodoo is—just as is the language of Haiti—an independent and legitimate religion.

100. (1984:39)
101. (1984:39)
102. (1984:41)
103. (1944:351-372)
104. (Smucker 1984:43)
105. (Smucker 1984:43)
106. (1959:39)
107. (e.g., 1970, 1976)
108. (1978)
109. (1984:43)
110. (1977)
111. (e.g., 1980)
112. (1985[1797-1798]:3–4)
113. (1985[1797-1798]:6)
114. (1985[1797-1798]:6)
115. (1985[1797-1798]:5–7)
116. (e.g., Davis, E. 1985)
117. (1884:182-228)
118. (see Métraux, A. 1959:16)
119. (1873)
120. (Anderson, M. 1979:11–12)
121. (Chester 1908:215)
122. (Chester 1908:214)
123. (Ober 1908:268)
124. (Anon. 1920:500)
125. (Austin 1912:177)
126. (Austin 1912:170)
127. (Morris, J. 1951:175)
128. (Verrill 1914:352)
129. (1959:55)

130. (Lawrence, comp. 1976:1282)
131. (Gindine 1974:48)
132. (1929:42)
133. (Loederer 1932)
134. (Loederer 1935)
135. (see, e.g., Herskovits 1935:308; Davis, H. P. 1935:10)
136. (quoted in Staff 1935:610)
137. (i.e., Allen, E. 1935)
138. (1935:308)
139. (1926)
140. (1935:6)
141. (Herskovits 1935:308)
142. (Pattee 1935:1561)
143. (Pattee 1935:1561)
144. (1938) The British version is titled *Voodoo Gods*.
145. (1952)
146. Bach mentioned only the accounts of St. John (1884), Seabrook
     (1929), Loederer (1935), and Wirkus (1933–1934) but never the
     available accounts of Voodoo by anthropologists such as Herskovits
     (1937), George Simpson (1940a, 1940b, 1942, 1945, 1946, 1948), and
     Métraux (1946).
147. (R.H. 1953:42)
148. (Opie 1952:5)
149. (Scofield 1961:227)
150. (Hannau 1962:87)
151. (Farrell 1963:29)
152. (Stowe 1963:222)
153. (Stowe 1963:223)
154. (Stowe 1963:224)
155. (Patterson 1976:78)
156. (Patterson 1976:78)
157. (ONTRP c.1984:3)
158. (Smucker 1984:55)
159. (1984:28)
160. (Balaguer 1949:110, repeated in 1984:83)
161. (see, e.g., Lawless 1988a)
162. A by-product of these folk notions of unknowability is the use of
     intermediaries by writers on Haiti. These intermediaries are almost
     never Haitians—not even western-educated Haitians—but are in-

stead the renegade, expatriate white person who has lived in Haiti for years and has allegedly, like Loederer's Herr Henckel, "delved deeper into the negro mentality than any other white man before him"(1935:255). For example, just after the turn of the century a writer in a popular magazine article on the worship of snakes in Haiti talked about "those few white men who have gained admittance in disguise to the Voodoo rites [which occur in an] inaccessible place on a mountain side or in a jungle"(Austin 1912:176). For anyone to imagine that any white man could disguise himself and travel undiscovered in rural Haiti stretches the gullibility of even the most naive reader.

Franck apparently obtained much of his "information" from conversations with "courageous" white Americans and the French priests from Brittany (1920:172–173). Loederer acknowledged "a host of friends in Haiti who generously opened to the author doors to the vast storehouse of story and legend ordinarily hidden behind Haitian reticence" (1935:iii). Expanding on this alleged reticence, he noted, "I never imagined for a moment that it would be possible to visit one of those negro festivals" (1935:266). Actually Haitians are quite open about their religion except during times of active government suppression of Voodoo. So open are the Haitians that anthropologists who specialize in West Africa have been known to come to Haiti to study various ceremonies that they could not observe in Africa, such as female initiation rites.

163. (1935:19)
164. (e.g., Oakley 1941:130–131; Scofield 1961:256–259; Rodman 1961:65)
165. (1952:12)
166. (1959:17)
167. (1970:13)
168. (Devillers 1985:402)
169. (1985:44, 50, passim)
170. (Drake 1977:1)
171. (Newman 1974:4)
172. (Moreau 1985[1797–1798]:44)
173. (Redpath 1970b[1861]:132)
174. (Foster 1980:10)
175. (Staff 1979b:817)
176. (Manigat 1964:7)

177. (Goldberg, J. 1988:44)
178. The language situation in Haiti is often categorized as diglossic—
even by linguists (e.g., Racine 1970:35-37), though it is clearly not
one of diglossia, as defined in the classic study of Charles Ferguson,
which discussed diglossia as occurring in social situations that used
"two or more varieties of the same language"(1959:325).
179. The concept of diglossia does, indeed, come from Ferguson's article,
but the application of diglossia to Haiti is based on a misunderstanding
of Ferguson's. The four examples that Ferguson used to illustrate
diglossia were Swiss German and standard German, vernacular Greek
and standard Greek, Arabic and standard Arabic, and Haitian Creole
and French. The Haitian example, however, is not comparable with
the other three. Ferguson cites and was apparently mislead by the
linguist Robert Hall's erroneous assessment of Creole as "classed
among the Romance languages"(1953:12).
180. (1961:33)
181. (Williams 1972:21)
182. (Morris 1951:175)
183. (1884:299)
184. (Thoby-Marcelin and Marcelin 1944:xxv)
185. (Scofield 1961:230)
186. (Colbert 1980:236)
187. (Richardson 1985:10G)
188. (Winn 1987:244)
189. (Associated 1986:8A)
190. (Whitehall 1979:vii) Modern journalism is not much of an improvement over the popular writers in the early part of this century who
simply claimed that Creole was not a language but instead "a degen-
erate West Indian *patois*."(Taft 1938:213)
191. (Franck 1920:107)
192. (Fermor 1950:245)
193. (Bims 1973:77)
194. (Franck 1920:115)
195. (Anon. 1811:3 my translation)
196. (Steif 1979:38)
197. (DiPerna 1985:10)
198. (Simons 1986:17)
199. (Keoun 1975:67)
200. One of the first linguists to emphasize the African component of

Creole was Suzanne Comhaire-Sylvain (1936). A decade later other linguists supported a similar position (e.g., Pressoir 1947). Still other linguists have followed alternative components of the folk model and have claimed that creoles are mixed languages (e.g., Taylor, D. 1956). Some have been specific in saying that creoles have vocabularies from European languages and grammars from African languages (e.g., Weinreich 1958). Such a position does, of course, ignore the creoles developed by Asian peoples. A well-known hypothesis that answered the difficulty about Asian creoles is that all creoles developed from a Portuguese pidgin (e.g., Whinnom 1956; Thompson 1961).

201. (1988b:477)
202. (1936:117–118)
203. (1981)
204. (cf. Taylor, D. 1963:800)

Chapter 4

1. (Parkhill 1861:vii)
2. (Moran 1951:9)
3. (Scofield 1961:227)
4. (quoted in Bellegarde-Smith 1985:51)
5. (i.e., Césaire 1955; Fanon 1963; Mannoni 1956; Memmi 1965)
6. (Krajick 1979:19)
7. (1986:6G)
8. (quoted in Weinstein and Segal 1984:69)
9. (Winn 1987:244, my emphasis)
10. (Paquin 1983:245; cf. English 1984:10)
11. (Paquin 1983:245)
12. (Cook 1946:411)
13. (quoted in Bellegarde-Smith 1985:123)
14. (Bellegarde-Smith 1985:164)
15. (Bellegarde-Smith 1985:123)
16. (Manigat 1964:3)
17. (Landesman 1983:29; also Landesman, Frank, and Vieira 1984:301)
18. (1982:28)
19. (Buchanan 1979:301)
20 (Monaghan 1986:1)
21. (Buchanan 1980:163–164; cf. Hoffmann 1984:69)
22. (e.g., Valdman 1984)

23. (Joseph, C. 1984:354)
24. (Woldemikael 1980:163)
25. (Leonidas 1982)
26. (1982:26)
27. (1982:27)
28. (1982:27)
29. (1982:27)
30. (cf. Buchanan 1980:139)
31. (1982:27)
32. (cf. Dougé 1982:28)
33. (Williams 1972:21)
34. (Ferguson, J. 1987:8)
35. (Weinstein and Segal 1984:70)
36. (Johnson, H. 1970:16)
37. (cf. Chardy 1986a, 1986b)
38. (Benjamin 1986:5, my translation)
39. (e.g., Cooper 1986) For some on-the-scene details about these attacks on Voodoo priests, see (Danner 1989b:104–110).
40. (Nicholls 1985:26)
41. (Maass 1990:vi)
42. (Maass 1990:179)

Chapter 5

1. (e.g., Montague 1940; Plummer 1981)
2. (Ober 1908:43)
3. (Lyle 1906:7152)
4. (Lyle 1906)
5. (Pamphile 1986; Plummer 1982)
6. (i.e., Seligmann, H. 1920)
7. (i.e., Gruening 1934)
8. (i.e., 1920a, 1920b, 1920c, 1920d, 1920e)
9. (e.g., Knight 1926; Fuller 1930)
10. (e.g., Buell 1929)
11. (i.e., Anon. 1920)
12. (i.e., Mead 1927)
13. (quoted in Allen, J. 1930:325)
14. (i.e., U.S. 1921–1922, 1922) However, an interpretation of even this cleansed report could be highly favorable to the complaints of Haitians (e.g., Bausman et al. 1922).

15. (quoted in Schmidt 1987:76)
16. (quoted in Ferguson, J. 1987:27)
17. (Coulthard 1962; Filostrat 1978)
18. (Antoine 1981; Damas 1967)
19. (Cobb 1978; Lubin 1987)
20. (e.g., Wise 1929)
21. (e.g., Wirkus and Dudley 1931)
22. (e.g., Craige 1933, 1934)
23. (e.g., Bedford-Jones 1932; Chamberlain 1927; Davis, B. 1925; Franklyn 1931; Holt 1932; Roscoe 1935; Taylor, J. 1932)
24. (Pressoir 1945:83)
25. (Johnson, H. 1970:ix)
26. (Weinstein and Segal 1984:73)
27. (Smucker 1984:36)
28. (Johnson, H. 1970:19)
29. (Johnson, H. 1970:19)
30. (Johnson, H. 1970:51–52)
31. (Johnson, H. 1970:37)
32. (cf. Bourguignon 1951:180)
33. (Burdick 1970:n.p.)
34. (e.g., Anderson, M. 1979:11–12)
35. (Comaroff and Comaroff 1986:2)
36. (Majeke 1953:3)
37. (cf. Conway 1980:24–25)
38. (Johnson, H. 1970:19)
39. (e.g., Crummey 1972; Etherington 1978; Lawless 1985a; Oliver 1952; Rigby 1981)
40. (quoted in Dachs 1972:468)
41. (Ekechi 1972:xiii)
42. (1937:xvii)
43. (Latourette 1937–1945)
44. (1937:7)
45. (1979:349–352)
46. (1979:352)
47. (Kraft 1979:352)
48. (Robinson 1981:41)
49. (English 1984:44)
50. (English 1984:23)
51. (Latortue, P. 1983:155)

52. (Maguire 1981:14)
53. (1984:2)
54. (A.I.D. 1982)
55. (A.I.D. 1982:ii)
56. (1982:iii, my emphasis; cf. English 1984:22)
57. (Harrison 1987:8A)
58. (Preeg 1984:1)
59. (i.e., Dewind and Kinley 1988)
60. (DeWind and Kinley 1988:83; cf. Honorat 1982:19)
61. (1982:9)
62. (Bartelt 1983)
63. (Diederich 1985:16)
64. (Staff 1986a:3)
65. (e.g., Krajick 1979; Walsh 1980:420; Schey 1981:7; Miller 1984:79;
    Mohl 1985:64; Nicholls 1985:194)
66. (1982:187)
67. (quoted in Kurzban 1980:1)
68. (Loescher and Scanlan 1984:314)
69. (e.g., Gollobin 1979:40; Wortham 1980; Weinstein and Segal 1984:109;
    Miller 1984:98–99)
70. (Kurzban 1980:1; cf. Schey 1981)
71. (quoted in Kurzban 1980:1)
72. (Lehman 1983:9)
73. (Commission 1980:33)
74. (Walsh 1980)
75. (Boswell 1982:20)
76. (Walsh 1979:43)
77. (cf. Flocks and Lawless 1988:529)
78. (1982:178–179)
79. (Lawless 1986:42)
80. (1984:92)
81. (1984:93)
82. (1984:104)
83. (Miller 1984:109)
84. (quoted in Miller 1984:112)
85. (quoted in Kurzban 1980:1)
86. (Miller 1984:123)
87. (Lawless 1986:54)
88. (1982:195; cf. Ryan 1982)
89. (Samuels 1991)

90. (Flocks and Lawless 1988:528)
91. (quoted in Cerquone 1986:3)
92. (1984:108)
93. (Lawless 1986:35; cf. Buchanan 1980:341–342, 346)
94. (Lawless 1985b:1)
95. (1982:x)
96. (Staff 1987:9A)
97. (Associated 1988)
98. (Staff 1989)
99. (Staff 1990:8A)
100. (Alvarez 1991)
101. (e.g., Allman and May 1979:506)
102. (Allman and May 1979:509)
103. (Richman 1984:61)
104. (Keely, Elwell, Fragomen, and Tomasi 1978:5)
105. (Flocks and Lawless 1988:532)
106. (Hall, A. 1987:1B)
107. (Flocks and Lawless 1988:532)
108. (Lane 1991:40)

Chapter 6

1. (quoted in Danner 1987:57)
2. (Serrill 1986:37)
3. (Bellegarde-Smith 1980:116)
4. (e.g., Alcántara 1984)
5. (1974)
6. (1974)
7. (Despradel 1974:85, my translation)
8. (Despradel 1974:94–97; cf. Murphy 1986)
9. (Despradel 1974:86; cf. Murphy 1986)
10. (Despradel 1974:94, my translation)
11. (Hoetink 1982:192)
12. (Despradel 1974:87, my translation)
13. (Despradel 1974:97, my translation)
14. (Despradel 1974:98)
15. (1986:14–17)
16. (Despradel 1974:106)
17. (e.g., Deive 1979; López 1980)
18. (see Moya Pons 1972)

19. (García 1906:144, my translation)
20. (quoted in Despradel 1974:102)
21. (Balaguer 1984:63)
22. (Murphy 1986:4, my translation)
23. (Murphy 1986:4, my translation)
24. (quoted in Murphy 1986:5, my translation)
25. (i.e., Cornielle 1980:235–268)
26. (Despradel 1974:106, my translation)
27. (Alcántara 1984)
28. (1985:21)
29. (1949:25, repeated in 1984:37)
30. (1949:122, repeated in 1984:52)
31. (1949:23, repeated in 1984:35)
32. (1949:12)
33. (French 1991a)
34. (French 1991a:15)
35. (Plant 1987:136)
36. (cf. Valdman 1984:77; Winford 1985:349–350)
37. (see Lawless 1977)
38. This widespread use of Creole and the simplicity of the language situation in Haiti allows an adequate analytic model to build on only two aspects that W. H. Whiteley proposed in his paper on national language policy in Tanzania, that is, the ideological and the technical. "The ideological aspect," Whiteley explained, "is concerned with mobilizing the nation's sentiments and with ensuring that the image of the language is polished on every suitable occasion; the technical aspect deals with the practical problems of implementing such an ideology" (1968:340).
39. (Bien–Aime 1986:17, my translation)
40. (Bien-Aime 1986:19, my translation)
41. (Clark, V. 1983:479)
42. (Weinstein and Segal 1984:68)
43. (e.g., 1978b, 1984)
44. (1978)
45. (1975)
46. See Dominique Batravil (1978), Georges Castera (1974), Pauris Jean-Baptiste (1975a), Paul Laraque (1974), Jan Mapou (1981), Morisseau-Leroy (1981, 1982a, 1982b, 1983), Pierre-Richard Narcisse (1979), Madlèn Payè (c.1978), and Emile Roumer (1964)
47. (1975)

48. (1975)
49. (1979a)
50. (1979b)
51. (1970)
52. (1982)
53. (e.g., Audain 1877; Bigelow 1877; Bowman and Antoine, eds., 1938; Comhaire-Sylvain 1937–1938; Courlander 1960; Fayo c.1980; Jean-Baptiste 1975b, 1985; Jeanty and Brown 1976; Parsons 1933, 1936, 1943)
54. (Anon. 1811) Even before the eighteen hundreds a report by Justin Girod-Chantrans titled *Voyage d'un Suisse dans différentes colonies d'Amérique* contained a number of letters from the New World to an imaginary correspondent, and one, dated 1782 from Saint Domingue, was in a "mixture of French and Creole, a conversation in which a woman explains to her lover why she has been unfaithful to him" (Williams 1972:20). A Haitian scholar of the literature identifies the first written Creole as the work of a colonist dated in 1749 (Laroche 1987:308). By the time of the slave uprising the "widespread use of Creole was sufficiently recognized to make it necessary or desirable to publish in Creole some official documents of the colonial period. The first official texts in Haitian Creole, five of which are extant, are official proclamations issued by representatives of the French government between 1793 and 1802" (Williams 1972:22; found in Denis, ed. 1935). After independence Haitians were occupied with other matters. The new elite began aping the French model, and very few examples of writings in Creole can be found until almost a century later when the Haiti novelist Justin Lhérisson wrote *La famille des Pitite-Caille* in 1897 [i.e., 1982{1897}], which had some conversation in Creole and creolized French"(Williams 1972:223). In 1906 he came out with *Zoune chez sa ninnaine* (1953[1906]), a novel that used a lot of Creole in its conversations between characters.
55. (e.g., Dougé 1982)
56. (Hoffmann 1984:69)
57. This discussion is in the terms of Whiteley's criteria.
58. (e.g., Staff 1953; Clotaire 1955)
59. (e.g., Staff 1959–1960)
60. (e.g., Direksyon 1985a, 1985b, 1986)
61. (e.g., Déroche c.1968, 1981; Komite 1984)
62. (e.g., Joseph, F. 1981a, 1981b, 1982)
63. (Désir 1980)

64. (e.g., Trouillot 1977)
65. (e.g., Dejean and Ogis 1981a, 1981b, 1981c, 1981d, 1981e, 1981f, 1981g, 1981h)
66. (quoted in Anon. 1979)
67. (1976)
68. (e.g., Dutcher 1982)
69. (cf. Regt 1984:132)
70. (i.e., Valdman 1981)
71. (Dejean, Y. 1980a, 1980b)
72. (Smat 1980)
73. (Valdman 1984:90) Georges Sylvain's early translation into Creole of the fables of La Fontaine (1929) well illustrates the difficulties in reading and writing Creole with Frenchified spellings.
74. (quoted in Valdman 1984)
75. (Asanble 1987:2, my translation)
76. (Regt 1984:119)
77. (Landry 1988:10)
78. (Landry 1988:10)
79. (Regt 1984:122)
80. (Regt 1984:123)
81. (Regt 1984:131)
82. (Dejean, P. 1980:25)
83. (Regt 1984:124)
84. (Dejean, P. 1980:102)
85. (Hurbon 1979:72–73)
86. (Hoffmann 1984:75)
87. (1984:95)
88. (Slavin 1991a)
89. (Clark, V. 1983:266)
90. (Buchanan 1980)
91. (Buchanan 1980:130–131)
92. (Lawless 1986:36)
93. (Buchanan 1980:131)
94. (Smucker 1984:37)
95. (Latortue, R. 1982)
96. (Thoby-Marcelin and Marcelin 1970)
97. (Simpson 1980:188)
98. (Herskovits 1937:153)
99. (Rotberg 1976:344)

100. (Jahn 1961:54)
101. (Smucker 1984:41)
102. (Paquin 1983:246)
103. (Devillers 1985:395)
104. (Smucker 1984:38)
105. (Rotberg 1976:342; cf. Byers 1970:308)
106. (Bourguignon 1959:36)
107. (Cooper 1986:43)
108. (Asanble 1987:4, my translation)
109. (Asanble 1987:4, my translation)
110. (1970[1907]:309–332)
111. (Sagan 1988:5–6)
112. (Staff c.1985d)
113. (e.g., Gold 1965)
114. (e.g., Gold 1972)
115. (i.e., Laraque, F. 1979)
116. Although I've talked with people who were classmates of Jean-Claude during the years that he went to school in Port-au-Prince and others in the government who had direct dealings with him, I've never found anyone who claimed to have had a real conversation with him. It seems that Jean-Claude never had any clear idea of what to do as President-for-Life of Haiti. He occasionally put competent people into positions of power, but, then, fired them after protests from those whose corruption would be exposed.
117. (Billard 1987:16)
118. (i.e., Assemblée 1987)
119. (i.e., Asanble 1987)
120. (1964:28)
121. (quoted in Hayward 1991:5A)
122. (e.g., French 1991b; Germani 1991; Hockstader 1991; Marquis 1991)
123. (Stumbo 1991)
124. (Staff 1991a)
125. (Staff 1991b)
126. (Power 1988:6A)
127. (see Moreau 1985[1797–1798]:167–174)
128. (quoted in Glass 1990:6A)
129. (Slavin 1991b)
130. (Emerson 1991:41)

*B*ibliography

Abbott, Elizabeth. 1988. *Haiti: The Duvaliers and Their Legacy.* McGraw-Hill.

A.I.D. 1982. Country Development Strategy Statement FY 1984. Washington, D.C.: Agency for International Development, Department of State.

Alatas, Syed Hussein. 1977. *The Myth of the Lazy Native: A Study of the Image of the Malays, Filipinos and Javanese from the 16th to the 20th Centuries and Its Function in the Ideology of Colonial Capitalism.* London: Cass.

Alcántara Almánzar, José. 1984. "Black Images in Dominican Literature." Paper read at the 26th Annual Conference on Popular Culture, National Identity, and Migration in the Caribbean. Gainesville: Center for Latin American Studies, University of Florida.

Alexis, Stéphen. 1949. *Black Liberator: The Life of Toussaint Louverture.* New York: Macmillan.

Allen, Edward Frank. 1935. "Haiti Interpreted by the Flaring Light of Voodooism." *New York Times Book Review* (July 28):3.

Allen, John H. 1930. "An Inside View of Revolutions in Haiti." *Current History* 32:325–329.

Allman, James, and John May. 1979. "Fertility, Mortality, Migration and Family Planning in Haiti." *Population Studies* 33:505–521.

Allman, Suzanne. 1986. "Childbearing and the Training of Traditional Birth Attendants in Rural Haiti." *Medical Anthropology Quarterly* 17:40–43.

Altman, Lawrence K. 1985. "AIDS in Africa: A Pattern of Mystery." *New York Times* (November 8):1, 8.

Alvarez, Lizette. 1991. "Record Number of Haitians Allowed Back to Miami to Pursue Asylum." *Miami Herald* (April 3):4B.

Andersen, Kurt. 1985. "New York: 'Final Destination.'" *Time* (July 8):46–49.

Anderson, Jervis. 1975. "The Haitians of New York." *New Yorker* (March 31):50, 52–54, 58–60, 62–75.

Anderson, Mildred. 1979. *Beyond all This: Thirty Years with the Mountain Peasants of Haiti*. Grand Rapids, Michigan: Baptist Haiti Mission.

Angell, Katharine Sargeant. 1922. "A Great Ditch in Haiti." *New Republic* 30:107–109.

Anon. 1792. *A Particular Account of the Commencement and Progress of the Insurrection of the Negroes in St. Domingo*, 2nd ed. London: Sewell.

————. 1811. *Idylles et chansons, ou essais de poësie créole*. Philadelphia: Edwards.

————. 1827. "Prefatory Letter to The Right Hon. The Earl Bathurst, K.G." In *The Rural Code of Haiti in French and English*. Pp. iii–xviii. London: Ridgway.

————. 1920. "Haiti and Its Regeneration by the United States." *National Geographic* 38:497–512.
————. 1979. *Notes on a Conference About Haitian Creole*. Port-au-Prince: Institut Pédagogique National.

Antoine, Jacques Carmeleau. 1981. *Jean Price-Mars and Haiti*. Washington, D.C.: Three Continents.

Asanble Konstitiyant la. 1987. *Konstitisyon Repiblik Ayiti*. [Port-au-Prince]: Ministè Enfòmasyon ak Kowòdinasyon.

Assemblée Nationale Constituante. 1987. *Constitution de la Republique d'Haiti*. Port-au-Prince: Scolha.

Associated Press. 1985a. "Ferraro: Action for AIDS Urgent." *Gainesville Sun* (March 18):6A.

―――. 1985b. "300,000 Said to Be Infected by AIDS." *Gainesville Sun* (February 2):10A.

―――. 1986. "In the Eyes of Haitian Exiles, Jean-Juste Is Their Born Leader." *Gainesville Sun* (February 10):8A.

―――. 1988. "Coast Guard Intercepts Boats Carrying Haitians." *Gainesville Sun* (December 26):2B.

Audain, J. J. 1877. *Recueil de proverbes créoles*, 2nd ed. Port-au-Prince: Audain.

Austin, Henry. 1912. "The Worship of the Snake: Voodooism in Haiti To-Day." *New England Magazine* 47(June):170–182.

Bach, Marcus. 1952. *Strange Altars*. Indianapolis: Bobbs-Merrill.

Balaguer, Joaquín. 1949. *Dominican Reality: Biographical Sketch of a Country and a Regime*. Mexico.

―――. 1984. *La Isla al Revés: Haití y el Destino Dominicano*. Santo Domingo: Libereria Dominicana.

Banks, Russell. 1985. *Continental Drift*. New York: Harper and Row.

Barau, Jean L. 1969. "Hayti under the Yankee Heel." In *Negro: Anthology 1931–1933*. Nancy Cunard, ed. Pp. 465–467. New York: Negro Universities Press (first published 1934).

Barham, J. F. 1823. *Considerations on the Abolition of Negro Slavery and the Means of Practically Effecting It*. London: Ridgway.

Bartelt, Leland E. 1983. "A Report on the African Swine Fever Eradication Program in Haiti." *Journal of the American Veterinary Medical Association* 183:352–353.

Barskett, James. 1971. *History of the Island of St. Domingo: From Its First Discovery by Columbus to the Present Period.* Westport, Connecticut: Negro Universities Press (first published 1818).

Bastien, Rémy. 1966. "Vodoun and Politics in Haiti." In *Religion and Politics in Haiti.* Harold Courlander and Rémy Bastien. Pp. 39–68. Washington, D.C.: Institute for Cross-Cultural Research.

Batravil, Dominique. 1978. *Boulpik (poèmes).* Port-au-Prince: Choucoune.

Baur, John E. 1970. "International Repercussions of the Haitian Revolution." *Americas* 26:394–418.

Bausman, Frederic, et al. 1922. *The Seizure of Haiti by the United States.* New York: Foreign Policy Association.

Beard, John R. 1971. *Toussaint L'Ouverture: A Biography and Autobiography.* Westport, Connecticut: Negro Universities Press (first published 1863).

Bedford-Jones, H. 1932. *Drums of Dumbala.* New York: Covic-Friede.

Bellegarde, Dantès. 1953. "Alexandre Pétion: The Founder of Rural Democracy in Haiti." *Caribbean Quarterly* 3:167–173.

Bellegarde-Smith, Patrick D. 1980. "Haitian Social Thought in the Nineteenth Century: Class Formation and Westernization." *Caribbean Studies* 20(1):5–33.

———. 1984. "Overview of Haitian Foreign Policy and Relations: A Schematic Analysis." In *Haiti—Today and Tomorrow: An Interdisciplinary Study.* Charles R. Foster and Albert Valdman, eds. Pp. 265–281. Lanham, Maryland: University Press of America.

———. 1985. *In the Shadow of Powers: Dantès Bellegarde in Haitian Social Thought.* Atlantic Highlands, New Jersey: Humanities.

———. 1989. *Haiti: The Breached Citadel.* Boulder, Colorado: Westview.

Benjamin, Marcel. 1986. "Une lettre au conseil nationale de gouvernement." *Le Nouvelliste* (February 17):5.

Bickerton, Derek. 1981. *Roots of Language.* Ann Arbor: Karoma.

Bien-Aime, Gabriel. 1986. *Sistem politik ak lafwa kretyen an Ayiti.* Haiti: n.p.

Bigelow, John. 1877. *The Wit and Wisdom of the Haytians.* New York: Scribner and Armstrong.

Billard, Annick. 1987. "Haiti: Hope, Return, Disillusion." *Refugees* (39):15–18.

Bims, Hamilton. 1973. "Haiti: New Stirrings of Hope." *Ebony* 28(3):70–72, 74–79.

Bird, M. B. 1971. *The Black Man: Or Haytian Independence Deduced from Historical Notes.* Freeport, New York: Books for Libraries (first published 1869).

Bohannan, Paul. 1963. *Social Anthropology.* New York: Holt, Rinehart and Winston.

Boswell, Thomas D. 1982. "The New Haitian Diaspora: Florida's Most Recent Residents." *Caribbean Review* 11(1):18–21.

Bourguignon, Erika Eichhorn. 1951. Syncretism and Ambivalence in Haiti: An Ethnohistorical Study. Ph.D. dissertation, Northwestern University.

———. 1959. "The Persistence of Folk Belief: Some Notes on Cannibalism and Zombis in Haiti." *Journal of American Folklore* 72:36–46.

———. 1970. "Ritual Dissociation and Possession Belief in Caribbean Negro Religion." In *Afro-American Anthropology: Contemporary Perspectives.* Norman E. Whitten, Jr., and John F. Szwed, eds. Pp. 87–100. New York: Free.

———. 1976. *Possession.* San Francisco: Chandler and Sharp.

———. 1978. "Spirit Possession and Altered States of Consciousness: The Evolution of an Inquiry." In *The Making of Psychological Anthropology.* George D. Spindler, ed. Pp. 479–515. Berkeley: University of California Press.

Bowman, Laura, and LeRoy Antoine, eds. 1938. *The Voice of Haiti.* New York: Williams.

Brathwaite, Edward. 1970. Introduction. In *Life in a Haitian Valley.* Melville J. Herskovits. New York: Knopf.

Brinkerhoff, Derick W., and Jean-Claude Garcia-Zamor, eds. 1986. *Politics, Projects, and People: Institutional Development in Haiti.* New York: Praeger.

Brown, Jonathan. 1972. *The History and Present Condition of St. Domingo.* 2 vols. London: Cass (first published 1837).

Buchanan, Susan Huelsebusch. 1979. "Language and Identity: Haitians in New York City." *International Migration Review* 13:298–313.

———. 1980. Scattered Seeds: The Meaning of the Migration for Haitians in New York City. Ph.D. dissertation, New York University.

———. 1983. "The Cultural Meaning of Social Class for Haitians in New York City." *Ethnic Groups* 5:7–30.

Buell, Raymond Leslie. 1929. *The American Occupation of Haiti.* Foreign Policy Association Information Service 5:327–392.

Burdick, Sandra L. 1970. Preface. In *God Is No Stranger.* Sandra L. Burdick, comp. Grand Rapids, Michigan: Baker.

Burke, E. Davis. 1962. *Marine! The Life of Lt. Gen. Lewis B. (Chesty) Puller, USMC(Ret.).* Boston: Little, Brown.

Byers, James F. 1970. "Voodoo: Tropical Pharmacology or Psychosomatic Psychology?" *New York Folklore Quarterly* 26:305–312.

Candler, John. 1842. *Brief Notices of Hayti: With Its Conditions, Resources, and Prospects.* London: Ward.

Casimir-Liautaud, Jean. 1975. "Haitian Social Structure in the Nineteenth Century." In *Working Papers in Haitian Society and Culture.* Sidney W. Mintz, ed. Pp. 35–49. New Haven, Connecticut: Antilles Research Program, Yale University.

————. 1982. "Two Classes and Two Cultures in Contemporary Haiti." In *Contemporary Caribbean: A Sociological Reader,* Vol. 2. Susan Craig, ed. Pp. 181–210. Maracas, Trinidad and Tobago: College Press.

Castera, Georges. 1974. *Konbèlann: 1958–1974.* Montréal: Nouvelle Optique.

Célestin-Mégie, Emile. 1975. *Lanmou pa gin baryè,* 1st part. Port-au-Prince: Fardin.

Cerquone, Joseph. 1986. "Continuing Unfairness Marks Haitians' Lives in the United States, Advocates Say." *Refugee Reports* 7(9):1–2.

Césaire, Aimé. 1955. *Discours sur le colonialisme,* 2nd ed. Paris: Presence Africaine.

Chamberlain, George Agnew. 1927. *The Silver Cord.* New York: Putnam's.

Chambers, Frances. 1983. *Haiti.* World Bibliographic Series. Santa Barbara, California: CLIO.

Chardy, Alfonso. 1986a. "The Church Tests Its Power." *Miami Herald* (February 17):1A,6A.

————. 1986b. "Youths: We Were Seed of Haitian Revolt." *Miami Herald* (February 15):1A,13A.

Chazotte, Peter S. 1840. *Historical Sketches of the Revolutions, and the Foreign and Civil Wars in the Island of St. Domingo.* New York: Applegate.

Chester, Colby M. 1908. "Haiti: A Degenerating Island." *National Geographic* 19:200–217.

Chierici, Rose-Marie. 1987. "Making It to the Center: Migration and Adaptation among Haitian Boat People." *New York Folklore* 13(1/2):107–116.

Clark, George P. 1980. "The Role of the Haitian Volunteers at Savannah in 1779: An Attempt at an Objective View." *Phylon* 41:356–366.

Clark, Matt. 1985. "AIDS: The Blood-Bank Scare." *Newsweek* (January 28):62.

————. 1987. "A New Clue in the AIDS Mystery." *Newsweek* (November 9):62.

Clark, Sydney. 1972. *All the Best in the Caribbean: Including Puerto Rico and the Virgin Islands.* New York: Mead.

Clotaire, Max. 1955. *Liv.* Port-au-Prince: Seksion de l'Edukasion dè Zadult, Direksion Jénéral de l'Edukasion Nasional.

Cobb, Martha K. 1978. *Harlem, Haiti, and Havana: A Comparative Critical Study of Langston Hughes, Jacques Roumain, and Nicolás Guillén.* Washington, D.C.: Three Continents.

Colbert, Lois. 1980. "Haitian Aliens—A People in Limbo." *Crisis* 87:235–238.

Cole, Hubert. 1967. *Christophe: King of Haiti.* New York: Viking.

Cole, Richard G. 1972. "Sixteenth-Century Travel Books as a Source of European Attitudes Toward Non-White and Non-Western Culture." *Proceedings of the American Philosophical Society* 116:59–67.

Comaroff, Jean, and John Comaroff. 1986. "Christianity and Colo- nialism in South Africa." *American Ethnologist* 13:1–22.

Comhaire-Sylvain, Suzanne. 1936. *Le créole haïtien, morphologie et syntaxe.* Weteren, Belgium: Meester.

————. 1937–1938. "Creole Tales from Haiti." *Journal of American Folklore* 50:207–295 and 51:219–346.

Commission on Civil Rights. 1980. The Tarnished Golden Door. Washington, D.C.: Government Printing Office.

Conway, Frederick J. 1980. "Pentecostalism in Haiti: Healing and Hierarchy." In *Perspectives on Pentecostalism: Case Studies from the Caribbean and Latin America*. Stephen D. Glazier, ed. Pp. 7–26. Washington, D.C.: University Press of America.

Conway, Frederick J., and Susan Huelsebusch Buchanan. 1985. "Haitians." In *Refugees in the United States: A Reference Handbook*. David W. Haines, ed. Pp. 95–109. Westport, Connecticut: Greenwood.

Cook, Mercer. 1946. The Haitian Novel. French Review 19:406–412.

Cooley, Martha. 1983. Haiti: The AIDS Stigma. NACLA 17(5):47–48.

————. 1984. Suspicion. Tropic: Magazine of the Miami Herald (November 25):10–11,16–17.

Cooper, Nancy. 1986. Haiti's Voodoo Witch Hunt. Newsweek (May 26):43.

Coreil, Jeannine. 1987. Maternal-Child Supplementary Feeding Programmes in Haiti. Journal of Tropical Pediatrics 33:203–207.

————. 1988. Innovation Among Haitian Healers: The Adoption of Oral Rehydration Therapy. Human Organization 47:48–57.

Cornielle Segura, Carlos. 1980. Proceso Histórico Dominico-Haitiano: Una Advertencia a la Juventud Dominicana. Santo Domingo: Publicaciones América.

Coulthard, G. R. 1962. Race and Colour in Caribbean Literature. London: Oxford University Press.

Courlander, Harold. 1944. Gods of the Haitian Mountains. Journal of Negro History 29:339–372.

————. 1960. The Drum and the Hoe: Life and Lore of the Haitian People. Berkeley: University of California Press.

Coxe, Arthur C. 1873. Visitation of the Mission in Haiti. Spirit of Missions 38:320–326.

Craige, John Houston. 1933. Black Bagdad. New York: Minton, Balch.

————. 1934. Cannibal Cousins. New York: Minton, Balch.

Crummey, Donald. 1972. Priests and Politicians: Protestant and Catholic Missions in Orthodox Ethiopia 1830–1868. Oxford: Clarendon.

Curtin, Philip D. 1964. The Image of Africa: British Ideas and Action, 1780–1850. Madison: University of Wisconsin Press.

Dachs, Anthony J. 1972. Missionary Imperialism—The Case of Bechuanaland. Journal of African History 13:647–658.

D'Alaux, Gustave. 1861. Soulouque and His Empire. Richmond, Virginia: Randolph (first published 1856).

Daley, Guilbert A. 1979. A Trilogy of the Haitian Revolutionary Triumvirate. Plays. Ph.D. dissertation, Southern Illinois University.

Dalzel, Archibald. 1793. The History of Dahomey: An Island Kingdom of Africa. London: Spilsbury.

Damas, Léon G. 1967. Price-Mars: The Father of Haitianism. Negritude: Essays and Studies. Albert H. Berrian and Richard A. Long, eds. Pp. 24–38. Hampton, Virginia: Hampton Institute Press.

Danner, Mark D. 1987. The Struggle for a Democratic Haiti. New York Times Magazine (June 21):38–42,49,57,59,61–62.

————. 1989a. A Reporter at Large: Beyond the Mountains—I. New Yorker (November 27):55–56, 58, 60, 62, 64–70, 75–100.

————. 1989b. "A Reporter at Large: Beyond the Mountains—III." New Yorker (December 11):100–102, 104–114, 116–124, 126, 129–131.

Dash, J. Michael. 1988. *Haiti and the United States: National Stereotypes and the Literary Imagination.* New York: St. Martin's.

Davis, Beale. 1925. *The Goat Without Horns.* New York: Brentano's.

Davis, E. Wade. 1983. "The Ethnobiology of the Haitian Zombi." *Journal of Ethnopharmacology* 9:85–104.

———. 1985. *The Serpent and the Rainbow.* New York: Simon and Schuster.

———. 1988. *Passage of Darkness: The Ethnobiology of the Haitian Zombie.* Chapel Hill: University of North Carolina Press.

Davis, H. P. 1935. "Smoke Rises from the Voodoo Fires." *Saturday Review of Literature* 12(13):10.

———. 1936. *Black Democracy: The Story of Haiti,* rev. ed. New York: Biblo and Tannen.

Davis, Horance G. 1986. "Just One of Reagan's Faults." *Gainesville Sun* (June 19):10A.

Deckelbaum, Yetta. 1983. Little Haiti: The Evolution of a Community. M.A. thesis, Florida Atlantic University.

de Cock, Kevin M. 1984. "AIDS: An Old Disease from Africa." *British Medical Journal* 289:306–308.

Deive, Carlos Esteban. 1979. *Vodú y Magia en Santo Domingo.* Santo Domingo: Museo del Hombre Dominicano.

Dejean, Paul. 1980. *The Haitians in Quebec.* Ottawa: Tecumseh.

Dejean, Yves. 1980a. "Ann kase koub otograf la." *Sèl* (48/49):4–5.

———. 1980b. "Ap reponn keksyon *Sèl* sou nouvo otograf kreyòl la." *Sèl* (48/49):25–33.

Dejean, Yves, and Michayél Ogis. 1981a. *Bòs tayé.* Cambridge, Massachusetts: Evaluation, Dissemination, and Assessment Center, Lesley College.

———. 1981b. *Fèbyin*. Cambridge, Massachusetts: Evaluation, Dissemination, and Assessment Center, Lesley College.

———. 1981c. *Kondision jamè faché*. Cambridge, Massachusetts: Evaluation, Dissemination, and Assessment Center, Lesley College.

———. 1981d. *Mari-Roz*. Cambridge, Massachusetts: Evaluation, Dissemination, and Assessment Center, Lesley College.

———. 1981e. *Plat manjé Bouki*. Cambridge, Massachusetts: Evaluation, Dissemination, and Assessment Center, Lesley College.

———. 1981f. *Sòmadélèn*. Cambridge, Massachusetts: Evaluation, Dissemination, and Assessment Center, Lesley College.

———. 1981g. *Ti baton gran papa*. Cambridge, Massachusetts: Evaluation, Dissemination, and Assessment Center, Lesley College.

———. 1981h. *Ti fi ki réspékté vié grann*. Cambridge, Massachusetts: Evaluation, Dissemination, and Assessment Center, Lesley College.

Denis, Serge, ed. 1935. *Nos Antilles*. Orléans: Luzeray.

Deren, Maya. 1970. *Divine Horsemen: The Voodoo Gods of Haiti*. New York: Chelsea (first published 1952).

Déroche, F. Louis. c.1968. *Abréjé istoua Daiti, 1492–1945*. Port-au-Prince: Comité Protestant d'Alphabétisation.

———. 1981. *Kout flach sou istwa peyi Ayiti: depi nan tan lontan rive jouk 1804, primye pati*. [Port-au-Prince]: Komite Liv CPAL la.

Désir, Roger. 1980. "Lékòl Radio Soléy." In *Créole et Enseignement Primaire en Haiti*. Albert Valdman, ed. Pp. 107–125. Bloomington: Indiana University.

Despradel, Lil. 1974. "Las Etapas del Antihaitianismo en la República Dominicana: El Paper de los Historiadores." In *Política y Sociología en*

Haití y la República Dominicana. Pp. 84–108. México: Universidad Nacional Autónoma de México.

Devillers, Carole. 1985. "Haiti's Voodoo Pilgrimages of Spirits and Saints." *National Geographic* 167:394–408.

DeWind, Josh, and David H. Kinley III. 1988. *Aiding Migration: The Impact of International Development Assistance on Haiti.* Boulder, Colorado: Westview.

Diederich, Bernard. 1985. "Swine Fever Ironies: The Slaughter of the Haitian Black Pig." *Caribbean Review* 14(1):16–17, 41.

Diederich, Bernard, and Al Burt. 1969. *Papa Doc: The Truth about Haiti Today.* New York: McGraw-Hill.

DiPerna, Paula. 1985. "Haiti." *Calypso Log.* 12(3):8–10.

Direksyon Edikasyon Sanite. 1985a. *An nou fè lijyèn pou proteje sante nou.* [Port-au-Prince]: Depatman Sante Piblik ak Popilasyon.

―――. 1985b. *Gid pou moun kap bay metòd planin.* [Port-au-Prince]: Ministè Sante Piblik ak Popilasyon.

―――. 1986. *An nou aprann byen manje pou nou an sante.* [Port-au-Prince]: Ministè Sante Piblik ak Popilasyon.

Dougé, Daniel. 1982. *Caribbean Pilgrims: The Plight of the Haitian Refugees.* Smithtown, New York: Exposition.

Dower, John W. 1986. *War Without Mercy: Race and Power in the Pacific War.* New York: Pantheon.

Drake, Glendon F. 1977. *The Role of Prescriptivism in American Linguistics, 1820–1970.* Amsterdam: Benjamins.

DuBois, F. E. 1970. "Call for Immigration." In *A Guide to Hayti.* James Redpath, ed. Pp. 97–99. Westport, Connecticut: Negro Universities Press (first published 1861).

Dubroca, Louis. 1802. *The Life of Toussaint Louverture*. London: Symonds.

Duffus, R. L. 1929. "Review of *Magic Island*." *New York Times* (January 6):6.

Dupuy, Alex. 1982. "Class Formation and Underdevelopment in Nineteenth-Century Haiti." *Race and Class* 24:17–31.

————. 1988. *Haiti in the World Economy: Class, Race, and Underdevelopment Since 1700*. Boulder, Colorado: Westview.

Durand, Guy. 1984. "AIDS—The Fallacy of a Haitian Connexion." *Bulletin de l'Association des Médecins Haitiens à l'Etranger* 19(9):17–20.

Dutcher, Nadine. 1982. *The Use of First and Second Languages in Primary Education: Selected Case Studies*. World Bank Staff Working Papers, No. 504. Washington, D.C.: World Bank.

Ekechi, F. K. 1972. *Missionary Enterprise and Rivalry in Igboland 1857–1914*. London: Cass.

Ellison, Ralph. 1952. *Invisible Man*. New York: Random.

Emerson, Tony. 1991. "Haiti: The Scourge of Violence." *Newsweek* (January 21):41.

English, E. Philip. 1984. *Canadian Development Assistance to Haiti*. Ottawa: North-South Institute.

Etherington, Norman. 1978. *Preachers, Peasants and Politics in Southeast Africa, 1835–1880: African Christian Communities in Natal, Pondoland and Zululand*. London: Royal Historical Society.

Fanon, Frantz. 1963. *The Wretched of the Earth*. New York: Grove.

Farmer, Paul. 1988. "Bad Blood, Spoiled Milk: Bodily Fluids as Moral Barometers in Rural Haiti." *American Ethnologist* 15:62–83.

————. 1989. "AIDS as Human Suffering." *Daedalus* 118(2):135–160.

————. 1990a. "AIDS and Accusation: Haiti, Haitians, and the Geography of Blame." In *Culture and AIDS*. Douglas A. Feldman, ed. New York: Praeger.

————. 1990b. "The Exotic and the Mundane: Human Immunodeficiency Virus in Haiti." *Human Nature* 1:415–445.

————. 1990c. "Sending Sickness: Sorcery, Politics, and Changing Concepts of AIDS in Rural Haiti." *Medical Anthropology Quarterly* 4:6–27.

Farrell, Barry. 1963. "It's Hell to Live in Haiti with Papa Doc." *Life* 54(10):28–35.

Fass, Simon M. 1988. *Political Economy in Haiti: The Drama of Survival*. New Brunswick, New Jersey: Transaction.

Fayo (Raphaël G. Urciolo). c.1980. *3333 Proverbs in Haitian Creole*. Port-au-Prince: Fardin.

Ferguson, Charles A. 1959. "Diglossia." *Word* 15:325–340.

Ferguson, James. 1987. *Papa Doc, Baby Doc: Haiti and the Duvaliers*. Oxford, England: Basil Blackwell.

Fermor, Patrick Leigh. 1950. *The Traveller's Tree: A Journey Through the Caribbean Islands*. London: Murray.

Filostrat, Christian. 1978. The Search for an African Identity in the Caribbean: Genesis and Rise of Haitianism and Negritude. Ph.D. dissertation, Howard University.

Fleurant, Gerdes. 1973. "Caste, Class Conflict, and Status Quo in Haiti." In *Ethnic Conflicts and Power: A Cross-National Perspective*. Donald E. Gelfaud and Russell D. Lee, eds. Pp. 178–193. New York: Wiley.

Flocks, Joan, and Robert Lawless. 1988. "Haitian Exodus: Refugees in Southern Florida." *World & I* (July):525–533.

Fordham, Monroe. 1975. "Nineteenth-Century Black Thought in the United

States: Some Influences of the Santo Domingo Revolution." *Journal of Black Studies* 6:115–126.

Foster, Charles R. 1980. "Creole in Conflict." *Migration Today* 8(5):8–13.

Foster, Charles R., and Albert Valdman, eds. 1984. *Haiti—Today and Tomorrow: An Interdisciplinary Study.* Lanham, Maryland: University Press of America.

Fouchard, Jean. 1981. *The Haitian Maroons: Liberty or Death.* New York: Blyden (first published 1972).

Franck, Harry A. 1920. *Roaming Through the West Indies.* New York: Century.

Frankétienne. 1975. *Dézafi.* Port-au-Prince: Fardin.

————. 1978a. *Pèlin-tèt (pyès téyet).* Port-au-Prince: Port-au-Princiennes.

————. 1978b. *Troufoban (pyès téyet).* Port-au-Prince: Port-au-Princiennes.

————. 1984. *Bobomasouri (pyèsteyat).* NP: Koleksyon Espizal.

Franklin, James. 1971. *The Present State of Hayti (Santo Domingo): With Remarks on Its Agriculture, Commerce, Laws, Religion, Finances, and Population.* London: Cass (first published 1828).

Franklyn, Irwin R. 1931. *Knights of the Cockpit: A Romantic Epic of the Flying Marines in Haiti.* New York: Dial.

French, Howard W. 1991a. "Haitians Expelled by Santo Domingo." *New York Times* (August 11):15.

————. 1991b. "Haiti's Victors Working to Soothe Fears." *New York Times* (January 11):C1.

Fuller, R. Nelson. 1930. "American Achievements in Haiti." *Current History* 32:86–90.

García Gabriel, José. 1906. *Historia Moderna de la República Dominicana.* Santo Domingo: ¡Ahora!

Gedeon, Michaele. 1988. *Oral Rehydration Therapy: A Successful Child Health Technology at Reducing Childhood Mortality.* Cajanus 21:177–182.

Geggus, David Patrick. 1982a. "British Opinion and the Emergence of Haiti, 1791–1805." In *Slavery and British Society, 1776–1846.* James Walvin, ed. Pp. 123–149. Baton Rouge: Louisiana State University.

————. 1982b. *Slavery, War, and Revolution: The British Occupation of Saint Domingue, 1793–1798.* Oxford: Clarendon.

————. 1986. "On the Eve of the Haitian Revolution: Slave Runaways in Saint Domingue in the Year 1790." In *Out of the House of Bondage: Runaways, Resistance and Maroonage in Africa and the New World.* Gad Heuman, ed. Pp. 112–128. London: Cass.

————. 1988. Personal communication dated March 11.

Germani, Clara. 1991. "Failed Coup Clears Air for New Haitian Leader." *Christian Science Monitor* (January 9):1B.

Gilliam, E. W. 1972. *1791: A Tale of San Domingo.* Freeport, New York: Books for Libraries (first published 1890).

Gilman, Sander. 1988. "AIDS and Syphilis: The Iconography of Disease." In *AIDS: Culture Analysis/Cultural Activism.* Douglas Crimp, ed. Pp. 87–107. Cambridge, Massachusetts: MIT Press.

Gilmore, Cecile. 1946. *Inherited Husband.* New York: Curl.

Gindine, Yvette. 1974. "Images of the American in Haitian Literature During the Occupation, 1915–1934." *Caribbean Studies* 14(3):37–52.

Glass, Robert. 1990. "Observers: Leftist Tops Haitian Vote." *Gainesville Sun* (December 17):6A.

Glick, Nina Barnett. 1975. The Formation of a Haitian Ethnic Group. Ph.D. dissertation, Columbia University.

Gobineau, Arthur de. 1967. *The Inequality of Human Races.* New York: Fertig (first published 1915).

Gold, Herbert. 1965. "Haiti: Hatred Without Hope." *Saturday Evening Post* 238(8):74–76, 79–81.

———. 1972. "Progress in Haiti—Leopards in Sneakers Instead of Tonton Macoutes." *New York Times Magazine* (March 12):34–35, 50, 52, 54, 56, 58, 60.

———. 1988. "Haiti: Voting by Gunfire." *Miami Herald* (September 22):27A.

Goldberg, Alan. 1981. Commercial Folklore and Voodoo in Haiti: International Tourism and the Sale of Culture. Ph.D. dissertation, Indiana University.

Goldberg, Jeff. 1988. "Omni's Five Star Travelogue." *Omni* (March):42–44.

Gollobin, Ira. 1979. "Haitian 'Boat People' and Equal Justice Under Law: Background and Perspective." *Migration Today* 7(4):40–41.

Greco, Ralph S. 1983. "Haiti and the Stigma of AIDS." *Lancet* (8348):515–516.

Greene, Graham. 1966. *The Comedians.* New York: Viking.

Griffiths, Ann. 1970. *Black Patriot and Martyr: Toussaint of Haiti.* New York: Messner.

Gruening, Earnest H. 1934. "At Last We're Getting Out of Haiti." *Nation* 138:700–701.

Gustafson, Marilyne Backlund. 1986. "Visual Communication with Haitian Women: A Look at Pictorial Literacy." *Hygie* 5(2):9–13.

Yon Gwoup Ayisyen. 1984a. "Diskisyon sou okipasyon ameriken." *Sèl* (59/60):20–42.

———. 1984b. "Diskisyon sou okipasyon ameriken (dezyèm pati)." *Sèl* (61/62):36–54.

Hall, Al. 1987. "Haitian Crack Dealer Is Convicted." *Gainesville Sun* (May 20):1B.

Hall, Robert A., Jr. 1953. *Haitian Creole: Grammar, Texts, Vocabulary.* Philadelphia: Memoirs of the American Folklore Society, Vol. 43.

Hall, Robert Burnett. 1929. "The Société Congo of the Ile à Gonave." *American Anthropologist* 31:685–700.

Hanna, Stewart William. 1836. *Notes on a Visit to Some Parts of Haiti.* London: Seeley, Ditton, and Surrey.

Hannau, Hans W. 1962. *Islands of the Caribbean.* Munich: Andermann.

Harrison, Lawrence E. 1987. "Haiti's Desperate Heritage." *Washington Post* (November 29):8A.

Harvey, W. W. 1971. *Sketches of Hayti: From the Expulsion of the French to the Death of Christophe.* London: Cass (first published 1827).

Hassal, Mary. 1808. *Secret History: Or the Horrors of St. Domingo.* Philadelphia: Bradford and Inskeep.

Hayward, Susana. 1991. "Priest Becomes Haiti's First Freely Elected President." *Gainesville Sun* (February 8):5A.

Healy, David. 1976. *Gunboat Diplomacy in the Wilson Era: The U.S. Navy in Haiti, 1915–1916.* Madison: University of Wisconsin Press.

Heatter, Basil. 1972. *A King in Haiti: The Story of Henri Christophe.* New York: Farrar, Straus and Giroux.

Heinl, Robert Debs, Jr., and Nancy Gordon Heinl. 1978. *Written in Blood: The Story of the Haitian People, 1492–1971.* Boston: Houghton Mifflin.

Herskovits, Melville J. 1935. "Voodoo Nonsense." *Nation* 141:308.

————. 1937. *Life in a Haitian Valley.* New York: Knopf.

Herskovits, Melville J., and Frances S. Herskovits. 1936. *Surinam Folk-Lore.* New York: Columbia University Press.

Hockstader, Lee. 1991. "Haiti to Inaugurate Leftist Priest Today." *Washington Post* (February 7):5.

Hoetink, H. 1982. *The Dominican People, 1850–1900: Notes for a Historical Sociology.* Baltimore: Johns Hopkins University Press.

Hoffmann, Léon-François. 1984. "Francophilia and Cultural Nationalism in Haiti." In *Haiti—Today and Tomorrow: An Interdisciplinary Study.* Charles R. Foster and Albert Valdman, eds. Pp. 57–76. Lanham, Maryland: University Press of America.

Holt, Gavin. 1932. *Drums Beat at Night.* New York: Hodder and Stoughton.

Honorat, Jean-Jacques. 1982. The African Swine Fever in Haiti: From Epizootic Control to Elite Reinforcement and Accrued National Dependency. Typescript in University of Florida Latin American Collection.

Hooper, Michael S. 1984. "The Politicization of Human Rights in Haiti." In *Haiti—Today and Tomorrow: An Interdisciplinary Study.* Charles R. Foster and Albert Valdman, eds. Pp. 283–302. Lanham, Maryland: University Press of America.

Hudicourt, Pierre L. 1985. "Prejudice and Paranoia." *Caribbean Review* 14(4):21.

Hughes, Langston. 1932. "White Shadows in a Black Land." *Crisis* 41:157–158.

Hurbon, Laënnec. 1979. *Culture et dictature en Haïti: l'Imaginaire sous contrôle.* Paris: Harmattan.

Hurston, Zora Neale. 1938. *Tell My Horse.* Philadelphia: Lippincott.

Jahn, Janheinz. 1961. *Muntu: An Outline of the New African Culture.* New York: Grove.

James, C. L. R. 1963. *The Black Jacobins: Toussaint L'Ouverture and the San Domingo Revolution,* 2nd ed. New York: Vintage.

Jean-Baptiste, Pauris. 1975a. *Chouichoui gran chimin.* Port-au-Prince: Bon Nouvèl.

———. 1975b. *Dézièm kout flach sou 300 provèb Dayiti.* Port-au-Prince: Bon Nouvèl.

———. 1979a. *Peyi zoulout.* Port-au-Prince: Fardin.

———. 1979b. *Sogo nan kwazman granchimin.* Port-au-Prince: Bon Nouvèl.

———. 1985. *Kout flach sou 250 pwoveb Dayiti.* Port-au-Prince: Phalange.

Jeanty, Edner A., and O. Carl Brown. 1976. *Paròl Granmoun: Haitian Popular Wisdom.* Port-au-Prince: Learning Center.

Jerome, Yves J. 1978. *Toussaint L'Ouverture.* New York: Vantage.

Johnson, Harmon A. 1970. *The Growing Church in Haiti.* Coral Gables, Florida: West Indies Mission.

Johnson, James Weldon. 1920a. "The Truth About Haiti." *Crisis* 10:217–224.
———. 1920b. "Self-Determining Haiti: I. The American Occupation." *Nation* 111:236–238.

———. 1920c. "Self-Determining Haiti: II. What the United States Has Accomplished." *Nation* 111:265–267.

————. 1920d. "Self-Determining Haiti: III. Government of, by, and for the National City Bank." *Nation* 111:295–297.

————. 1920e. "Self-Determining Haiti: IV. The Haitian People." *Nation* 111:345–347.

Jordan, Winthrop D. 1968. *White Over Black: American Attitudes Toward the Negro, 1550–1812*. Chapel Hill: University of North Carolina.

Joseph, Carole Berotte. 1984. "The Child, the Family, and the School in English-Haitian Education." In *Haiti—Today and Tomorrow: An Interdisciplinary Study*. Charles R. Foster and Albert Valdman, eds. Pp. 351–358. Lanham, Maryland: University Press of America.

Joseph, François Jn. 1981a. *Méyè gad kò sé véyé kò*. Port-au-Prince: Lékòl Radio Solèy.

————. 1981b. *Vitès nan fanmi*. Port-au-Prince: Lékòl Radio Solèy.

————. 1982. *Groupman kominotè: manm yo*. Port-au-Prince: Lékòl Radio Solèy.

Keely, Charles B., Patricia J. Elwell, Austin T. Fragomen, Jr., and Silvano M. Tomasi. 1978. *Profiles of Undocumented Aliens in New York City: Haitians and Dominicans*. Occasional Paper No. 5. Staten Island, New York: Center for Migration Studies.

Keoun, Ian. 1975. *Lovers' Guide to the Caribbean and Mexico*. New York: Macmillan.

Kirkpatrick, Sharon Minton, and Ann Kuckelmen Cobb. 1990. "Health Beliefs Related to Diarrhea in Haitian Children: Building Transcultural Nursing Knowledge." *Journal of Transcultural Nursing* 1(2):2–12.

Koeppel, Barbara. 1982. "Haitians: Latest in an Old American Tradition: The Migrants Stoop, the Growers Conquer." *Progressive* 46(3):42–44.

Komite Liv CPAL la. 1984. *Kout flach sou jewografi Dayiti*. [Port-au-Prince]: Boukan.

Korngold, Ralph. 1944. *Citizen Toussaint.* Boston: Little, Brown.

Knight, Melvin M. 1926. "Haiti's Progress under American Protectorate." *Current History* 24:351–358.

Kraft, Charles H. 1979. *Christianity in Culture: A Study in Dynamic Biblical Theologizing in Cross-Cultural Perspective.* Maryknoll, New York: Orbis.

Krajick, Kevin. 1979. "Refugees Adrift: Barred from America's Shores." *Saturday Review* 6(21):17–20.

Kurzban, Ira. 1980. "Haitian Refugees: A Flight from Persecution." *Rights* 26(3–4):1,13–15.

Laguerre, Michel S. 1982. *Urban Life in the Caribbean: A Study of a Haitian Urban Community.* Cambridge, Massachusetts: Schenkman.

———. 1984. *American Odyssey: Haitians in New York City.* Ithaca, New York: Cornell University Press.

———. 1989. *Voodoo and Politics in Haiti.* New York: St. Martin's.

Laleau, Léon. 1953. "Makers of a Nation." *Américas* 5(11): 8–9, 27–28.

Landesman, Sheldon H. 1983. "The Haitian Connection." In *The AIDS Epidemic.* Kevin M. Cahill, ed. Pp. 28–37. New York: St. Martin's.

Landesman, Sheldon H., Elliot Frank, and Jeffrey Vieira. 1984. "AIDS in Haitian-Americans." In *AIDS: The Epidemic of Kaposi's Sarcoma and Opportunistic Infections.* Alvin E. Friedman-Kein and Linda J. Laubenstein, eds. Pp. 301–304. New York: Masson.

Landry, Robert. 1987. "Healers New and Old: Medical Care in Haiti." *IDRC Reports* 16(3):22.

———. 1988. "Education: Haiti's Elusive Dream." *IDRC Reports* 17(1):10.

Lane, Charles. 1991. "Rejecting the Refugees." *Newsweek* (December 1):40.

Lanier, Alfredo S. 1984. "AIDS: The Haitian Factor." *Chicago Magazine* (August):120–122, 126.

Laraque, Franck. 1979. "Haitian Emigration to New York." *Migration Today* 7(4):23–31.

Laraque, Paul. 1974. *Fistibal.* Montréal: Nouvelle Optique.

Laroche, Maximilien. 1987. "Haiti." In *Handbook of Latin American Literature.* David William Foster, ed. Pp. 307–320. New York: Garland.

Latortue, Paul R. 1983. "The External Debt Situation of Haiti." In *Foreign Debt and Latin American Economic Development.* Antonio Jorge, Jorge Salazar-Carillo, and Rene P. Higonnet, eds. Pp. 155–161. New York: Pergamon.

Latortue, Régine. 1982. The Woman in the Haitian Novel. Ph.D. dissertation, Yale University.

Latourette, Kenneth Scott. 1937. *A History of the Expansion of Christianity, Vol. 1: The First Five Centuries.* New York: Harper and Brothers.

———. 1937–1945. *A History of the Expansion of Christianity,* 7 vols. New York: Harper and Brothers.

Laverdière, Michel, Jacques Tremblay, René Lavallée, Yvette Bonny, Michel Lacombe, Jacques Boileau, Jacques Lachapelle, and Christian Lamoureux. 1983. "AIDS in Haitian Immigrants and in a Caucasian Woman Closely Associated with Haitians." *Canadian Medical Association Journal* 129:1209–1212.

Lawless, Robert. 1968. "Anthropology and Journalism." *General Education Journal* (14):48–53.

———. 1977. "The National Language Question in the Philippines: A Survey and a Proposal." *Florida Journal of Anthropology* 2(2):17–32.

———. 1979. *The Concept of Culture.* Minneapolis: Burgess.

————. 1985a. *An Ethnoethnography of Missionaries in Kalingaland.* Studies in Third World Societies 26:1–18.

————. 1985b. Introduction. In *Bibliography on Haiti: English and Creole Items.* Robert Lawless, comp. Occasional Papers No. 6. Pp. 1–3. Gainesville: Center for Latin American Studies, University of Florida.

————. 1986. "Haitian Migrants and Haitian-Americans: From Invisibility into the Spotlight." *Journal of Ethnic Studies* 14(2):29–70.

————. 1988a. "The Cognition of Intersections: An Analysis of Kalinga, American, and Haitian Folk Models." *Florida Anthropologist* 41(2):5–19.

————. 1988b. "Creole Speaks, Creole Understands." *World & I* (January):474–483.

————. 1989. "Review of *The Serpent and the Rainbow,* Davis; and *Passage of Darkness,* Davis." *Latin American Anthropology Review* 1(1):5–6.

————. 1990. *Haiti: A Research Handbook.* New York: Garland.

Lawless, Robert, and Paul Monaghan. 1991. Personal communication to Bill O'Reilly dated February 22.

Lawrence, Alberta, comp. 1976. *Who Was Who Among North American Authors, 1921–1939,* 2 vols. Detroit: Gale (first published 1921–1939).

LeBlanc, Robert P., Marie Simard, Kenneth M. Flegel, and Norbert J. Gilmore. 1983. "Opportunistic Infections and Acquired Cellular Immune Deficiency Among Haitian Immigrants in Montreal." *Canadian Medical Association Journal* 129:1205–1209.

Léger, J. N. 1970. *Haiti: Her History and Her Detractors.* Westport, Connecticut: Negro Universities Press (first published 1907).

Lehman, Mel. 1983. "The Journey for Haitians Is Not Over Yet." *Refugees and Human Rights Newsletter* (Summer):9–10.

Leonidas, Jean-Robert. 1982. "Depression a la Haitian: A Linguistic Misinterpretation." *New York State Journal of Medicine* 82:754–755.

Lett, James W., Jr. 1986. "Anthropology and Journalism." *Communicator* 40(5):33–35.

———. 1987. "An Anthropological View of Television Journalism." *Human Organization* 46:356–359.

Leyburn, James G. 1966. *The Haitian People*, rev. ed. New Haven, Connecticut: Yale University Press.

Lhérisson, Justin. 1953. *Zoune chez sa Ninnaine*, 2nd ed. Port-au-Prince: n.p. (first published 1906).

———. 1982. *La famille des Pitite-Caille: les fortunes de chez nous.* Port-au-Prince: Fardin (first published 1897).

Loederer, Richard A. 1932. *Wudu-Feuer auf Haiti.* Wien: Wolf.

———. 1935. *Voodoo Fire in Haiti.* New York: Literary Guild.

Loescher, Gilburt, and John Scanlan. 1984. "Human Rights, U.S. Foreign Policy, and Haitian Refugees." *Journal of Interamerican Studies and World Affairs* 26:313–356.

Long, Edward. 1774. *The History of Jamaica.* London: Lowndes.

López, José Gabriel. 1980. Dominican Vodú: Historical and Contemporary Perspectives. M.A. thesis, University of Florida.

Lorch, Donatella. 1990. "Demonstrators Protest F.D.A. Policy Against Haitian Blood Donors." *New York Times* (April 21):10.

Lowenthal, Ira P. 1978. "Ritual Performance and Religious Experience: A Service for the Gods in Southern Haiti." *Journal of Anthropological Research* 34:392–414.

Lubin, Maurice A. 1987. "Langston Hughes and Haiti." *Langston Hughes Review* 6:4–7.

Lundahl, Mats. 1979. *Peasants and Poverty: A Study of Haiti.* New York: St. Martin's.

Lyle, Eugene P., Jr. 1906. "What Shall Haiti's Future Be?" *World's Work* 11:7151–7162.

Maass, Harold William. 1990. Catholic Development Strategies in Rural Haiti. M.A. thesis, University of Florida.

McCoy, Charles. 1988. "Black Magic Casts a Deepening Spell Over Troubled Haiti." *Wall Street Journal* (October 20):A1,A10.

McCoy, Terry L., ed. 1984. *Haitian Migration and the Haitian Economy.* Occasional Papers No. 3. Gainesville: Center for Latin American Studies, University of Florida.

McCrocklin, James H. 1956. *Garde d'Haiti: Twenty Years of Organization and Training by the United States Marine Corps.* Annapolis, Maryland: Naval Institute.

MacKenzie, Charles. 1971. *Notes on Haiti: Made During a Residence in That Republic,* 2 vols. London: Cass (first published 1830).

Maguire, Robert. 1981. *Bottom-Up Development in Haiti,* 2nd ed. Rosslyn, Virginia: Inter-American Foundation.

Majeke, Nosipho. 1953. *The Role of the Missionaries in Conquest.* Johannesburg: Society of Young Africa.

Malinowski, Bronislaw. 1929. "Practical Anthropology." *Africa* 2:22–38.

Manigat, Leslie F. 1964. *Haiti of the Sixties: Object of International Concern.* Washington, D.C.: Washington Center of Foreign Policy Research.

Mannoni, Octave. 1956. *Prospero and Caliban: The Psychology of Colonization.* New York: Praeger.

Mapou, Jan. 1981. *Pwezigram.* New York: Sosyete-Koukouy.

Marquis, Christopher. 1991. "U.S. to Give New Haiti Regime 'Helpful' Boost with More Aid." *Miami Herald* (February 12):6B.

Marshall, P. J., and Glyndwr Williams. 1982. *The Great Map of Mankind: Perceptions of New Worlds in the Age of Enlightenment.* Cambridge, Massachusetts: Harvard University Press.

Mead, Elwood. 1927. "The New Haiti." *Review of Reviews* 75:175–180.

Memmi, Albert. 1965. *The Colonizer and the Colonized.* New York: Orion.

Métraux, Alfred. 1946. "The Concept of Soul in Haitian Vodu." *Southwestern Journal of Anthropology* 2:84–92.

————. 1959. *Voodoo in Haiti.* New York: Oxford University Press.

————. 1960. *Haiti: Black Peasants and Voodoo.* New York: Universe.

Métraux, Rhoda. 1952. "Affiliations Through Work in Marbial, Haiti." *Primitive Man* 25:1–22.

Miller, Jake C. 1984. *The Plight of Haitian Refugees.* New York: Praeger.

Millspaugh, Arthur C. 1929. "Our Haitian Problem." *Foreign Affairs* 7:556–570.

Mintz, Sidney W. 1966. Introduction to the Second Edition. In *The Haitian People,* rev. ed. James G. Leyburn. Pp. v–xlvi. New Haven, Connecticut: Yale University Press.

Mitacek, E. J., D. St. Vallieres, and A. P. Polednak. 1986. "Cancer in Haiti 1979–84: Distribution of Various Forms of Cancer According to Geographical Area and Sex." *International Journal of Cancer* 38:9–16.

Miyè, Ketli. 1984. "Okipasyon ameriken ak abitan ayisyen." *Sèl* (59/60):14–19.

Mohl, Raymond A. 1985. "An Ethnic 'Boiling Pot': Cubans and Haitians in Miami." *Journal of Ethnic Studies* 13(2):51–74.

Monaghan, Paul. 1986. Monthly Report for September. Typescript. Gainesville: Center for Latin American Studies, University of Florida.

Montague, Ludwell Lee. 1940. *Haiti and the United States, 1714–1938.* Durham, North Carolina: Duke University Press.

Moody, John. 1986. "Elusive Dreams in Exile." *Time* (February 17):43.

Moore, Alexander, and Ronald D. Le Baron. 1986. "The Case for a Haitian Origin of the AIDS Epidemic." In *The Social Dimensions of AIDS: Method and Theory.* Douglas A. Feldman and Thomas M. Johnson, eds. Pp. 77–93. New York: Praeger.

Moran, Charles. 1951. *Black Triumvirate: A Study of Louverture, Dessalines, Christophe—The Men Who Made Haiti.* New York: Exposition.

Moreau de Saint-Méry, Médéric-Louis-Elie. 1985. *A Civilization That Perished: The Last Years of White Colonial Rule in Haiti.* Lanham, Maryland: University Press of America (first published 1797–1798).

Morisseau-Leroy, Félix. c.1953. *Antigone en créole.* Petionville, Haiti: Culture (first produced 1953).

———. 1978. *Roua kréon ak pep-la..* Dakar: Jadinkréyol.

———. 1981. *Ten Selected Poems.* Miami: Jadinkréyòl.

———. 1982a. *Ravinodyab: la ravine aux diables: contes haitiens.* Paris: Harmattan.

———. 1982b. *Vilbone: kont chante.* Miami: Jadenkreyòl.

———. 1983. *Dyakout 1, 2, 3 ak twa lòt poèm.* Miami: Jaden Kreyòl.

Morris, Eugene. 1987. "UF May Hand Out Condoms to Help Combat AIDS." *Gainesville Sun* (February 21):1A,11A.

Morris, Joe Alex. 1951. "Cruel Beauty of the Caribbean." *Saturday Evening Post* 224(20):38–39, 173, 175–176, 178–180.

Mossell, C. W. 1896. *Toussaint L'Ouverture: The Hero of Saint Domingo, Soldier, Statesman, Martyr.* Lockport, New York: Ward and Cobb.

Moya Pons, Frank. 1972. *La Dominación Haitiana, 1822–1844*. Santiago, Dominican Republic: Universidad Católica Madre y Maestra.

Murphy, Martin F. 1986. Preguicio Anti-Haitiano y la Formación de la Identidad Nacional Dominicana. Unpublished manuscript.

Murray, Gerald F. 1977. The Evolution of Haitian Peasant Land Tenure: A Case Study in Agricultural Adaptation to Population Growth. Ph.D. dissertation, Columbia University.

————. 1980. "Population Pressure, Land Tenure, and Voodoo: The Economics of Haitian Peasant Ritual." In *Beyond the Myths of Culture: Essays in Cultural Materialism*. Eric B. Ross, ed. Pp. 295–321. New York: Academic.

Narcisse, Pierre-Richard. 1979. *Dèy ak lespoua*. Port-au-Prince: Choucoune.

Nemours, Aurélie. 1975. *Haiti ô Erzulie*. Faverolles: Editions de la Tour.

Newman, Edwin. 1974. *Strictly Speaking: Will America Be the Death of English?* Indianapolis: Bobbs–Merrill.

Nicholls, David. 1977. "Poorest Nation of the Western World." *Geographical Magazine* 50:47–54.

————. 1979. *From Dessalines to Duvalier: Race, Colour and National Independence in Haiti*. Cambridge, England: Cambridge University Press.

————. 1984. "Past and Present in Haitian Politics." In *Haiti—Today and Tomorrow: An Interdisciplinary Study*. Charles R. Foster and Albert Valdman, eds. Pp. 253–264. Lanham, Maryland: University Press of America.

————. 1985. *Haiti in Caribbean Context: Ethnicity, Economy and Revolt*. New York: St. Martin's.

Niles, Blair. 1926. *Black Haiti: A Biography of Africa's Eldest Daughter*. New York: Putnam's.

————. 1935. "Review of *Voodoo Fire in Haiti*, Loederer." *Books* (August 4):6.

Numa, Nono. 1975. *Jénéral Rodrig*. Port-au-Prince: Bon Nouvèl.

Oakley, Amy. 1941. *Behold the West Indies*. New York: Appleton-Century.

Ober, Frederick A. 1908. *A Guide to the West Indies and Bermudas*. New York: Dodd, Mead.

Oliver, Roland. 1952. *The Missionary Factor in East Africa*. London: Longmans, Green.

ONTRP. 1977. *Données statistiques de l'année 1976 et analyse comparative des années 1973–1974–1975–1976*. Port-au-Prince: Office National de Tourisme et des Relations Publiques.

————. c.1984. *Haiti: It's Spellbinding*. Port-au-Prince: Office National de Tourisme et des Relations Publiques.

Opie, T. F. 1952. "Review of *Strange Alters*, Bach." *Chicago Sunday Tribune* (October 26):5.

O'Reilly, Bill. 1991. Personal communication to Robert Lawless and Paul Monaghan dated February 27.

Ott, Thomas O. 1973. *The Haitian Revolution, 1789–1804*. Knoxville: University of Tennessee Press.

Pamphile, Léon D. 1986. "The NAACP and the American Occupation of Haiti." *Phylon* 47:91–100.

Pape, Jean W., Bernard Liautaud, Franck Thomas, Jean-Robert Mathurin, Marie-Myrtha A. St. Amand, Madeleine Boncy, Vergniaud Péan, Molière Pamphile, A. Claude Laroche, and Warren D. Johnson, Jr. 1983. "Characteristics of the Acquired Immunodeficiency Syndrome (AIDS) in Haiti." *New England Journal of Medicine* 309:945–950.

Paquin, Lyonel. 1983. *The Haitians: Class and Color Politics*. Brooklyn: Multi-Type.

Parker, Barnett R., Sally K. Stansfield, Antoine Augustin, Reginald Boulos, and Jeanne S. Newman. 1988. "Optimization of Task Allocation for Community Health Workers in Haiti." *Socio-Economic Planning Sciences* 22:3–14.

Parkhill, John H. 1861. Introduction. In *Soulouque and His Empire*. Gustave D'Alaux. Pp. v–xv. Richmond, Virginia: Randolph.

Parkinson, Wenda. 1978. *"This Gilded African": Toussaint L'Ouverture*. London: Quartet.

Parsons, Elsie Clews. 1933,1936,1943. "Folklore of the Antilles, French and English." *Memoirs of the American Folklore Society*, Vol. 26, Pts. 1,2,3.

Paterson, Thomas G. 1980. "The Marine Occupation of Black Haiti." *Negro History Bulletin* 43:45, 50.

Pattee, Richard. 1935. "Stranger Than the Truth." *Christian Century* 52:1561–1562.

Patterson, Carolyn Bennett. 1976. "Haiti: Beyond Mountains, More Mountains." *National Geographic* 149:70–97.

Paul, Max. 1982. "Racial Ideology and Political Development: The Cases of Haiti and Bermuda." *Sociologus* 32:64–80.

Paultre, Carrié. 1970. *Ti Jak*. Port-au-Prince: Comité Protestant d'Alphabétisation et de Littérature (first published 1965).

———. 1982. *Tonton Libin*. Port-au-Prince: Editions Boukan (first published 1976).

Payè, Madlèn. c.1978. *Insèbadjo: kont chanté*. Potoprins: La Phalange.

Pitchenik, Arthur E., Margaret A. Fischl, Gordon M. Dickinson, Daniel M.

Becker, Arthur M. Fournier, Mark T. O'Connell, Robert M. Colton, and Thomas J. Spira. 1983. "Opportunistic Infections and Kaposi's Sarcoma Among Haitians: Evidence of a New Acquired Immunodeficiency State." *Annals of Internal Medicine* 98:277–284.

Plant, Roger. 1987. *Sugar and Modern Slavery: A Tale of Two Countries.* Atlantic Highlands, New Jersey: Zed.

Plummer, Brenda Gayle. 1981. Black and White in the Caribbean: Haitian-American Relations, 1902–1934. Ph.D. dissertation, Cornell University.

———. 1982. "The Afro-American Response to the Occupation of Haiti, 1915–1934." *Phylon* 43:125–143.

Porter, Darwin. 1992. *Caribbean '92.* Englewood Cliffs, New Jersey: Prentice-Hall.

Portes, Alejandro, and Alex Stepick. 1987. *Haitian Refugees in South Florida, 1983–1986.* Dialogue No. 77. Miami: Latin American and Caribbean Center, Florida International University.

Power, Jonathan. 1988. "What Haiti Wants." *Baltimore Sun* (January 10):6A.

Preeg, Ernest. 1984. Introduction. In *Haiti—Today and Tomorrow: An Interdisciplinary Study.* Charles R. Foster and Albert Valdman, eds. Pp. 1–14. Lanham, Maryland: University Press of America.

Pressoir, Charles Fernand. 1945. *Le Protestantisme haitien.* Port-au-Prince: Societe Biblique et des Livre Religieux d'Haiti.

———. 1947. *Débate sur le créole et le folklore.* Port-au-Prince: Imprimerie de l'Etat.

Price-Mars, Jean. 1976. *La vocation de l'elite.* Port-au-Prince: Fardin (first published 1919).

Pritchard, H. Hesketh. 1910. *Where Black Rules White: A Journey Across and About Hayti,* new and revised ed. London: Nelson.

R.H. 1953. "The Hispanic American Bookshelf." *Hispanic American Report* 6(5):41–43.

Raccurt, Christian P., Robert C. Lowrie, Jr., Stephen P. Katz, and Yarseth T. Duverseau. 1988. "Epidemiology of *Wuchereria bancrofti* in Leogane, Haiti." *Transactions of the Royal Society of Tropical Medicine and Hygiene* 82:721–725.

Racine, Marie Marcelle Buteau. 1970. French and Creole Lexico-Semantic Conflicts: A Contribution to the Study of Languages in Contact in the Haitian Diglossic Situation. Ph.D. dissertation, Georgetown University.

Rainsford, Marcus. 1805. *An Historical Account of the Black Empire of Hayti.* London: Cundee.

Raymond, Adrien. 1985. "The Incidence of AIDS in Haiti." *Newsweek* (September 16):7.

Redpath, James. 1970a. Introduction. In *A Guide to Hayti.* James Redpath, ed. Pp. 9–11. Westport, Connecticut: Negro Universities Press (first published 1861).

―――. 1970b. "The People of Hayti." In *A Guide to Hayti.* James Redpath, ed. Pp. 129–137. Westport, Connecticut: Negro Universities Press (first published 1861).

Regt, Jacomina P. de. 1984. "Basic Education in Haiti." In *Haiti—Today and Tomorrow: An Interdisciplinary Study.* Charles R. Foster and Albert Valdman, eds. Pp. 119–139. Lanham, Maryland: University Press of America.

Richardson, Mary. 1985. "Haiti: An Island of Contrasts." *Gainesville Sun* (August 4):1G, 10G.

Richman, Karen E. 1984. "From Peasant to Migratory Farmworker: Haitian Migrants in U.S. Agriculture." In *Haitian Migration and the Haitian Economy.* Occasional Papers No. 3. Terry L. McCoy, ed. Pp. 52–65. Gainesville: Center for Latin American Studies, University of Florida.

Rigby, Peter. 1981. "Pastors and Pastoralists: The Differential Penetration of Christianity among East African Cattle Herders." *Comparative Studies in Society and History* 23:96–129.

Roberts, Kenneth. 1947. *Lydia Bailey*. New York: Doubleday.

Robinson, Scott S. 1981. "Fulfilling the Mission: North American Evangelism in Ecuador." In *Is God an American? An Anthropological Perspective on the Missionary Work of the Summer Institute of Linguistics*. Søren Hvalkof and Peter Aaby, eds. Pp. 41–49. Copenhagen: International Work Group for Indigenous Affairs and Survival International.

Rodman, Selden. 1961. *Haiti: The Black Republic*, new rev. ed. New York: Devin-Adair.

Roscoe, Theodore. 1935. *Murder on the Way!*. New York: Dodge.

Rotberg, Robert I. 1976. "Vodun and the Politics of Haiti." In *The African Diaspora: Interpretive Essays*. Martin L. Kilson and Robert I. Rotberg, eds. Pp. 342–365. Cambridge, Massachusetts: Harvard University Press.

Roumer, Emile. 1964. *Rosaire: couronne sonnets*. Port-au-Prince: Panorama.

Ryan, Michael C. P. 1982. "Political Asylum for the Haitians?" *Case Western Reserve Journal of International Law* 14:155–176.

Sagan, Carl. 1988. "The Common Enemy." *Parade* (February 7):4–7.

St. John, Spenser. 1884. *Hayti: Or the Black Republic*. London: Smith, Elder.

Samuels, Christina A. 1991. "Haitian Advocates Push for Policy Changes." *Gainesville Sun* (August 11):2B.

Schey, Peter A. 1981. "The Black Boat People: Founder on the Shoals of U.S. Policy." *Migration Today* 9(4/5):7–10.

Schmidt, Hans. 1987. *Maverick Marine: General Smedley D. Butler and the Contradictions of American Military History.* Lexington: University of Kentucky Press.

Scofield, John. 1961. "Haiti—West Africa in the West Indies." *National Geographic* 119:226–269.

Seabrook, William B. 1929. *The Magic Island.* New York: Harcourt, Brace and World.

———. 1942. *No Hiding Place.* Philadelphia: Lippincott

Seligman, Linda. 1977. "Haitians: A Neglected Minority." *Personnel and Guidance Journal* 55:409–411.

Seligmann, Herbert J. 1920. "The Conquest of Haiti." *Nation* 111:35–36.

Seligmann, Jean. 1985. "A Nasty New Epidemic." *Newsweek* (February 4):72–73.

Serrill, Michael S. 1986. "Small Stirrings of Change." *Time* (January 13):37.

Siegal, Frederick P., and Marta Siegal. 1983. *AIDS: The Medical Mystery.* New York: Grove.

Simons, Marlise. 1986. "Church in Haiti Launches Literacy Drive." *New York Times* (March 11):17.

Simpson, George Eaton. 1940a. "Haitian Magic." *Social Forces* 19:95–100.

———. 1940b. "The Vodun Service in Northern Haiti." *American Anthropologist* 42:236–254.

———. 1942. "Loup Garou and Loa Folktales from Northern Haiti." *Journal of American Folklore* 55:219–227.

———. 1945. "The Belief System of Haitian Vodun." *American Anthropologist* 47:35–59.

———. 1946. "Four Vodun Ceremonies." *Journal of American Folklore* 59:154–167.

———. 1948. "Two Vodun-Related Ceremonies." *Journal of American Folklore* 61:49–52.

———. 1980. "Ideas about Ultimate Reality and Meaning in Haitian Vodun." *Ultimate Reality and Meaning* 3:187–199.

Singer, Merrill, Lani Davidson, and Gina Gerdes. 1988. "Culture, Critical Theory, and Reproductive Illness Behavior in Haiti." *Medical Anthropology Quarterly* 2:370–385.

Slavin, J. P. 1991a. "New Literacy Program is on Haiti's Front Burner." *National Catholic Reporter* (May 17):10.

———. 1991b. "Purge of Army Continues in Haiti." *Miami Herald* (July 4):12A.

Smat, Wilyam. 1980. "You moso nan istwa lang kreyòl an Ayiti." *Sèl* (48/49):17–20.

Smucker, Glenn R. 1982. Peasants and Development Politics: A Study in Haitian Class and Culture. Ph.D. dissertation, New School for Social Research.

———. 1984. "The Social Character of Religion in Rural Haiti." In *Haiti—Today and Tomorrow: An Interdisciplinary Study*. Charles R. Foster and Albert Valdman, eds. Pp. 35–56. Lanham, Maryland: University Press of America.

Snelgrave, William. 1734. *A New Account of Some Parts of Guinea: And the Slave Trade*. London: Knapton.

Sokol, Mariene. 1985. "U.S. Companies Readily Admit Exploitation." *Florida Times-Union* (February 12):A–1, A–6.

Staff. 1935. *Book Review Digest*. New York: Wilson.

————. 1953. *M-ap aprann li*. Port-au-Prince: Section de l'Education des Adultes, Direction Générale de l'Education Nationale.

————. 1959–1960. *Kréòl*, 3 vols. Port-au-Prince: Division du Développement Rural.

————. 1979a. "Update—Haiti." *NACLA Report on the Americas* 13(6):49–51.

————. 1979b. *Webster's New Universal Unabridged Dictionary*. New York: Simon and Schuster.

————. 1980. "New York's New Immigrants: What and Where They Are." *New York University Education Quarterly* 11(4):19.

————. 1983. "Researcher Links AIDS, Swine Fever." *Boston Globe* (April 29):10A.

————. 1985a. "Haitian Coalition Lauds Decision." *Miami Herald* (April 10):8A.

————. 1985b. *Information Please Almanac*. Boston: Houghton Mifflin.

————. 1985c. "The New Victims." *Life* (July):12–19.

————. c.1985d. "U.S. and Haiti: Alliance Against a People." *Haiti Beat* 1(1):1.

————. 1986a. "Haiti After Duvalier." *TransAfrica Forum Issue Brief* 5(2):1–3.

————. 1986b. "Perspectives." *Newsweek* (June 2):17.

————. 1986c. "Vudú: Magia, Miedo y Muertos Vivientes en la Isla de Haití." *Cambio16* (April 7):133.

————. 1987. "Haitian Refugees Intercepted, Sent Home." *Gainesville Sun* (January 5):9A.

————. 1989a. *Fodor's 90 Caribbean*. New York: Fodor's Travel Publications.

————. 1989b. "Haitians Drain Time from Patrols." *Gainesville Sun* (March 31):4B.

————. 1990. "Haitian Migrants Caught, Returned." *Gainesville Sun* (October 16):8A.

————. 1991a. "Aristide Names 12 to Cabinet." *Miami Herald* (February 21):6B.

————. 1991b. "A Smart Start in Haiti." *New York Times* (August 19):A14.

Steif, William. 1979. "Hopeless in Haiti." *Progressive* 43(10):39–40.

Stephen, James. 1814. *The History of Toussaint Louverture,* new ed. London: n.p.

Stepick, Alex. 1982. "Haitian Boat People: A Study in the Conflicting Forces Shaping U.S. Refugee Policy." *Law and Contemporary Problems* 45:163–196.

————. 1984a. *The Business Community of Little Haiti.* Occasional Papers Series, Dialogue No. 32. Miami: Latin American and Caribbean Center, Florida International University.

————. 1984b. *Haitians Released from Krome: Their Prospects for Adaptation and Integration in South Florida.* Occasional Papers Series, Dialogue No. 24. Miami: Latin American and Caribbean Center, Florida International University.

Stepick, Alex, and Alejandro Portes. 1986. "Flight into Despair: A Profile of Recent Haitian Refugees in South Florida." *International Migration Review* 20:329–350.

Stepick, Alex, and Carol Dutton Stepick. 1990. "People in the Shadows: Survey Research among Haitians in Miami." *Human Organization* 49:64–77.

Stoddard, T. Lothrop. 1914. *The French Revolution in San Domingo.* Boston: Houghton Mifflin.

Stowe, Leland. 1963. "Haiti's Voodoo Tyrant." *Reader's Digest* 83(499):222–226, 228.

Street, John M. 1971. "Problems of Health and Nutrition in Haiti." *Geographical Review* 61:599–600.

Stumbo, Bella. 1991. "From Horror to Hope." *Los Angeles Times* (April 21):1B–5B.

Sylvain, Georges. 1929. *Cric? Crac!* Port-au-Prince: Bibliothèque Haïtienne (first published 1901).

———. 1971. *Toussaint L'Ouverture: A Biography and Autobiography.* Freeport, New York: Books for Libraries (first published 1863).

Syme, Ronald. 1971. *Toussaint: The Black Liberator.* New York: Morrow.

Taft, Edna. 1938. *A Puritan in Voodoo-Land.* Philadelphia: Penn.

Taylor, Douglas R. 1956. "Language Contacts in the West Indies." *Word* 12:399–414.

Taylor, J. Gibson, Jr. 1932. *Dark Dawn.* New York: Mohawk.

———. 1963. "The Origin of West Indian Creole Languages: Evidence from Grammatical Categories." *American Anthropologist* 65:800–814.

Teepen, Tom. 1986. "'Family' Report is Voodoo Sociology." *Gainesville Sun* (November 22):12A.

Thoby-Marcelin, Philippe, and Pierre Marcelin. 1944. *Canapé-Vert.* New York: Farrar and Rinehart.
———. 1970. *All Men Are Mad.* New York: Farrar, Straus and Giroux.

Thomas, Lowell. 1933. *Old Gimlet Eye: The Adventures of Smedley D. Butler.* New York: Farrar and Rinehart.

Thompson, Robert W. 1961. "A Note on Some Possible Affinities Between the Creole Dialects of the Old World and Those of the New." In *Creole*

Language Studies, Vol. 2. R. B. Le Page, ed. Pp. 107–113. London: Macmillan.

Tivnan, Edward. 1979. "The Voodoo That New Yorkers Do." *New York Times Magazine* (December 2):182, 184, 186, 187–189, 191.

Trouillot, Michel-Rolph. 1977. *Ti difé boulé sou istoua Ayiti.* New York: Koleksion Lakansiel.

———. 1990. *Haiti: State Against Nation: The Origins and Legacy of Duvalierism.* New York: Monthly Review Press.

Tyson, George F., Jr., ed. 1973. *Toussaint L' Ouverture.* Englewood Cliffs: Prentice-Hall.

Ullman, James Ramsey. 1970. *Caribbean: Here & Now,* revised and enlarged. New York: Macmillan.

U.S. Congress. 1921–1922. Inquiry into Occupation and Administration of Haiti and Santo Domingo. Hearings of the Select Committee on Haiti and the Dominican Republic, 67th Congress, 1st and 2nd Sessions.

———. 1922. Inquiry into Occupation and Administration of Haiti and the Dominican Republic. Report of the Select Committee on Haiti and the Dominican Republic. 67th Congress, 2nd Session, Report No. 794.

Valdman, Albert. 1981. *Haitian-Creole-English-French Dictionary,* 2 vols. Bloomington: Creole Institute, Indiana University.

———. 1984. "The Linguistic Situation of Haiti." In *Haiti—Today and Tomorrow: An Interdisciplinary Study.* Charles R. Foster and Albert Valdman, eds. Pp. 77–99. Lanham, Maryland: University Press of America.

Velie, Lester. 1962. "The Case of Our Vanishing Dollars in Haiti." *Reader's Digest* 80(479):122–126.

Verdet, Paule. 1976. "Trying Times: Haitian Youth in an Inner-City High School." *Social Problems* 24:228–233.

Verlinden, Charles. 1970. *The Beginnings of Modern Colonization*. Ithaca, New York: Cornell University Press.

Verrill, A. Hyatt. 1914. *Porto Rico: Past and Present and San Domingo of Today*. New York: Dodd, Mead.

Vieira, Jeffrey, Elliot Frank, Thomas J. Spira, and Sheldon H. Landesman. 1983. "Acquired Immune Deficiency in Haitians: Opportunistic Infections in Previously Healthy Haitian Immigrants." *New England Journal of Medicine* 308:125–129.

Wallace, Anthony F. C. 1966. *Religion: An Anthropological View*. New York: Random.

Wallerstein, Immanuel. 1974. *The Modern World-System: Capitalist Agriculture and the Origins of the European World-Economy in the Sixteenth Century*. New York: Academic.

Wallis, Claudia. 1983. "Zombies: Do They Exist?" *Time* (October 17):60.

Walsh, Bryan O. 1979. "Haitians in Miami." *Migration Today* 7(4):42–44.

———. 1980. "The Boat People of South Florida." *America* 142:420–421.

Walters, Barbara. 1986. "Interviewing the Duvaliers." *Miami Herald* (July 13):5G–6G.

Waxman, Percy. 1931. *The Black Napoleon: The Story of Toussaint Louverture*. New York: Harcourt, Brace.

Webb, Ryland E., and Susan A. Hyatt. 1988. "Haitian Street Foods and Their Nutritional Contribution to Dietary Intake." *Ecology of Food and Nutrition* 21:199–209.

Weinreich, Uriel. 1958. "On the Compatibility of Genetic Relationship and Convergent Development." *Word* 14:374–379.

Weinstein, Brian, and Aaron Segal. 1984. *Haiti: Political Failures, Cultural Successes*. New York: Praeger.

Whinnom, Keith. 1956. *Spanish Contact Vernaculars in the Philippine Islands*. Hong Kong: University Press.

Whitehall, Harold. 1979. "Outline History of the English Language." In *Webster's New Universal Unabridged Dictionary*. Pp. vii–xi. New York: Simon and Schuster.

Whiteley, W. H. 1968. "Ideal and Reality in National Language Policy: A Case Study from Tanzania." In *Language Problems of Developing Nations*. Joshua A. Fishman, Charles A. Ferguson, and Jyotirindra Das Gupta, eds. Pp. 339–350. New York: Wiley

Wilentz, Amy. 1989. *The Rainy Season: Haiti Since Duvalier*. New York: Simon and Schuster.

Williams, Perry Arthur. 1972. La Fontaine in Haitian Creole: A Study of *Cric? Crac!* By Georges Sylvain. Ph.D. dissertation, Fordham University.

Winford, Donald. 1985. "The Concept of 'Diglossia' in Caribbean Creole Situations." *Language in Society* 14:345–356.

Wingfield, Roland, and Vernon J. Parenton. 1965. "Class Structure and Class Conflict in Haitian Society." *Social Forces* 43:338–347.

Winn, Peter. 987. "Haiti." In *1988 Year Book*. Pp. 244–245. New York: Macmillan.

Wirkus, Faustin E. 1933–34. "The Black Pope of Voodoo." *Harper's* 168:38–49, 189–198.

Wirkus, Faustin E., and Taney Dudley. 1931. *The White King of La Gonave*. Garden City, New York: Doubleday, Doran.

Wise, Frederic May. 1929. *A Marine Tells It to You*. New York: Sears.

Woldemikael, Taklemariam. 1980. Maintenance and Change of Status in a Migrant Community: Haitians in Evanston, Illinois. Ph.D. dissertation, Northwestern University.

Wood, Peter H. 1974. *Black Majority: Negroes in Colonial South Carolina from 1670 Through the Stone Rebellion*. New York: Knopf.

Woodford, Carol. 1985. "Haitian Immigrants No Longer Listed as High-Risk Group for Contracting AIDS." *Gainesville Sun* (April 10):5C.

Wordsworth, William. 1854. *The Poetical Works of William Wordsworth*, Vol. III. Boston: Houghton, Mifflin.

Wortham, Jacob. 1980. "The Black Boat People." *Black Enterprise* (April):32, 34–35.

Yasumoto, Takeshi, and C. Y. Kao. 1986. "Tetrodotoxin and the Haitian Zombie." *Toxicon* 24:747–749.

Zellers, Margaret, ed. 1978. *Fodor's Caribbean, Bahamas, and Bermuda 1978*. New York: McKay.

Zéndegui, Guillermo de. 1972. "Image of Haiti." *Américas* 24(3[supplement]):1–24.

*I*ndex

Abolitionist movement, 44, 45, 51-52

See also Slavery, abolition of

Africa

claims about black life in, 32, 33

early European perceptions of, 31-32

folk models of, 29, 33-34

See also Haiti, and links with Africa

African swine fever, 12, 118-119, 120-121, 176

and pig eradication project, 118-123, 176

Agriculture and farming, xxii, 63, 118, 172

and pig eradication project, 118-123

and role of pigs, in Haiti, 119-120

Aid, to Haiti. *See* Foreign aid; United States, aid to Haiti

A.I.D., *See* U.S. Agency for International Development

AIDS, 16

and American homosexuals visiting Haiti, 15-16

folk model explanation of, in Haiti, 18

and homosexual practices, 13-15

inclusion of Haitians in high risk category, 11, 12, 14, 16, 176

and perception of Haitians as carriers, 1, 10-18

and tourism in Haiti, xxiii, 176

American Occupation of Haiti, xx, 45, 48, 53, 64, 65-66, 107-109, 109-110, 175

Analytic models. *See* Folk models, and analytic models

Anthropologists, xiii

and analytic models, xvi-xvii

beliefs of, xiv-xiv, xvii

and cultural perspectives, xiii-xiv

and fieldwork, xvii, 30

and folk models, xv, xvi, xvii, xviii

and informants, 84

and transcultural experiences, xvii, 82-83, 84

Anthropology, xiv, 30

contribution to knowledge about AIDS, 18

and models, xv, xvi, xvii, xviii

vs. journalism, xviii

and studies of Haiti, 3-4

Aristide, Jean-Bertrand, xxi, 59, 141, 152, 158-159, 168-169, 170-171, 179, 180

Asylum. *See* Political asylum

Avril, Lt. Gen. Prosper, 167, 168, 179

Balaguer, Joaquín, 140, 141

Biases, against Haiti and Haitians

current, 1-27

development of, 51-92

in Dominican Republic, 137-141

origins of, 29-48

See also Haitians, as depicted in

Biographical Note

Robert Lawless received his Ph.D. in anthropology from the New School for Social Research in New York and is currently a professor at Wichita State University. He is well versed in Haitian politics and history and his studies include fieldwork in Haiti as well as among Haitian immigrants in the U.S. He has been a reliable resource for several Florida newspapers for up-to-date information on Haiti and Haitian-Americans.

The photographers, Paul Monaghan and Joan Flocks, are both former students of Robert Lawless at the University of Florida. They have worked in several Haitian development projects since 1983. Mr. Monaghan is an anthropologist currently researching frontier expansion in the Mexican rainforests and Ms. Flocks is an attorney in Tampa, Florida.